Taking Charge

Taking Charge

Leading with Passion and Purpose in the Principalship

Paul L. Shaw

Foreword by Michael Fullan
Afterword by Andy Hargreaves

Teachers College, Columbia University
New York and London

Published by Teachers College Press, 1234 Amsterdam Avenue, New York, NY 10027

Library of Congress Cataloging-in-Publication Data

Shaw, Paul L.
   Taking charge : leading with passion and purpose in the principalship / Paul L. Shaw
    ; foreword by Michael Fullan ; afterword by Andy Hargreaves.
      p. cm.
   Includes bibliographical references and index.
   ISBN 978-0-8077-5290-6 (pbk. : alk. paper)
   ISBN 978-0-8077-5291-3 (hardcover : alk. paper)
    1. School principals—United States. 2. School management and organization—United States. 3. Educational leadership—United States. I. Title.
   LB2831.92.S533 2012
   371.2'012--dc23   2011041064

ISBN 978-0-8077-5290-6 (paper)
ISBN 978-0-8077-5291-3 (hardcover)

Printed on acid-free paper
Manufactured in the United States of America

19 18 17 16 15 14 13 12   8 7 6 5 4 3 2 1

This book is for Deanna,
whose love, support, intellect, and grace
I deeply cherish.

Contents

Foreword

Early in my career as an educational researcher, in 1986, one of the teachers' unions in Ontario asked me to write a book geared toward principals. They gave me three criteria and a title. The criteria were (i) write something that is deeply insightful; (ii) make it action oriented and practical; and (iii) be brief. Normally from an academic you can get two out of three but not all three. The title they gave me was *What's Worth Fighting for in the Principalship?*

I knew some of the theory at the time but not enough to be practically inspiring and helpful. I turned to the principal I knew who seemed to combine passion and a penchant for action. In fact he was feisty enough to just touch the border of being eccentric—at least I imagined so in the eyes of his bosses, and very likely his peers. I presented ten guidelines for action, and I am quite sure that Guideline 5 was modeled upon this principal: Practice Fearlessness and Other Forms of Risk-Taking.

The principal in question was none other than Paul Shaw. I love *Taking Charge* because it combines passion with hard-nosed action. Shaw argues for perpetual learning both personal and collective; the wise use of evidence without being a slave to data; capacity-building clearly operationalized as six core competencies; orchestrating learning how to work together; and, above all, taking charge of the learning agenda.

Paul has modeled and led the learning agenda himself in diverse settings—a small rural school that badly needed a wake-up call; a large urban school in a rough neighborhood that had a hard time attracting teachers; and a highly diverse school in which he helped develop a collaborative staff skilled at tackling the intricacies of language and literacy among new immigrant non-English-speaking students.

He then spent another 20 years learning to understand leadership and helping to develop it on a large scale as a statewide project coordinator, consultant, researcher, and university professor. He has experienced compelling challenges of almost every kind. He has honed his work around the twin platforms of moral purpose and participatory cultures.

Now, in *Taking Charge*, we get the benefit of this wisdom in clear, crisp prose. He integrates this wisdom in four interrelated pillars: knowing pupils well, developing intellectual capital through continuous personal and collective professional learning, building deep professional relationships, and cultivating pedagogical responsiveness and coherence.

He rightly concludes that there is no other job as fulfilling as being a principal who helps to lead the transformation of a school. Shaw knows enough to warn the reader that every context is different, and leaders will have to figure out their own course of action. But *Taking Charge* gives plenty of reassurance and guidance. Delve into this book and be rewarded. It will help you think more deeply and act more confidently as a principal. It will lead you to action that positively impacts the lives of all students in your school, your teachers and staff, and your parents and community. Become a participative learning leader. Paul Shaw has been there.

—Michael Fullan

Introduction: Leadership and Student Achievement

Schooling is about improving the *life chances* of each student. This view of education presents a powerful way of examining, reflecting on, and defining a school's goals. Life chances represent all those elements that enable youngsters to succeed in life, relationships, the community, and the workplace. In schools, this idea broadens the scope of our purpose and our definition of what counts as progress. It pushes our thinking and goals beyond that which is simply measurable toward more important dimensions of our practice, including attitudes, values, independence, interdependence, and initiative. It is about the students' lived experience in school and how and to what degree this experience approximates lifelong learning behaviors. It challenges us to bring to the fore learning that promotes creativity, ingenuity, novelty, and perseverance. It informs the purposes we embrace and the pedagogical practices we engage in. Improving life chances frames the work of this book.

Founded on the simple idea that the future of the young people for whom we are responsible is not preordained, this book argues for strong, purposeful, and participative (sometimes called shared or distributive) leadership that transcends constraints and seizes opportunities to improve the life opportunities for all. This kind of leadership focuses the work of the school on morally compelling purposes and requires many skills. But the preeminent qualities of a participative leader are courage and the willingness to *take charge* in what, for some, are often less than conducive contexts. "Courage," said Winston Churchill, "is rightly esteemed the first of human qualities because it is the quality which guarantees all others."[1]

In a recent macro-review of the relationship between leadership and pupil achievement, Leithwood et al. found that there were two key factors related to student achievement: (1) the quality and responsiveness of teaching and learning across the organization and (2) school leadership.[2] Leadership isn't just one aspect of achievement: it is second only to quality teaching among school-related factors in its impact on student learning. However,

1

what we know is that for leadership to make a significant improvement in the learning of all, it must dramatically increase the skills and knowledge of principals and teachers. This calls for a radical departure from the role leaders typically play, demanding very different skills and abilities and a remarkable change in the nature of the work and capacity of schools.

Furthering our knowledge of the impact of different types of leadership on a range of valued student outcomes, Viviane Robinson derived five types, or dimensions, of leadership from a meta-analysis of 11 studies that measured the relationship between leadership types and student outcomes.[3] Figure I.1 summarizes her findings.

Figure I.1. Leadership and Student Outcomes

Leadership Dimension	Meaning of Dimension	Effect SizeEstimate
1. Establishing Goals and Expectations	Includes the setting, communicating, and monitoring of learning goals, standards, and expectations; and the involvement of staff and others in the process so there is clarity and consensus about goals.	Average ES = 0.35 (*See Chapter 1*)
2. Strategic Resourcing	Involves aligning resource selection and allocation to priority teaching goals. Includes provision of appropriate expertise through staff recruitment.	Average ES = 0.34 (*See Chapter 6*)
3. Planning, Coordinating, and Evaluating Teaching and the Curriculum	Direct involvement in the support and evaluation of teaching through regular classroom visits and the provision of formative and summative feedback to teachers. Direct oversight of curriculum through schoolwide coordination across classes and year levels and alignment to school goals.	Average ES = 0.42 (*See Chapters 2 and 3*)
4. Promoting and Participating in Teaching, Learning, and Development	Leadership that not only promotes but directly participates with teachers in formal or informal professional learning.	Average ES = 0.84 (*See Chapters 4 and 5*)
5. Ensuring an Orderly and Supportive Environment	Protecting time for teaching and learning by reducing external pressures and interruptions and establishing an orderly and supportive environment both inside and outside classrooms.	Average ES = 0.27 (*See Chapters 6 and 7*)

Although my book is not organized around Robinson's five dimensions, there is a rough correspondence. As noted by the references in the table, many of my chapters illustrate how school leaders can develop the objectives she names. What is compelling about her findings is the very large effect of Dimension Four (0.84), which surely supports this book's focus on capacity-building and the extraordinarily influential role leaders can play in this regard.

KNOWING STUDENTS WELL AND DEVELOPING INTELLECTUAL CAPITAL

Improving the life chances of all begins with knowing the individual student extraordinarily well. This demands that teachers spend significant time with their students, closely and frequently engrossed in activities that address their individual interests, learning needs and styles, specific intellectual abilities, and social, emotional, and physical development. Teachers must constantly use data gathered collaboratively with their students to deeply inform teaching and learning. Knowing students well is about uncovering their intentions and relating them to those of the teacher and the curriculum. The implications for how schools are structured, how classes are constituted, and how timetables are organized are predicated on intimate and lasting relationships between teacher and pupil.

Improving schools and life chances of pupils is also about broadly enabling the learning experiences of the adults who work in and around classrooms. This is sometimes thought of as developing intellectual capital. Historically, schools have more or less always been focused on the learning of their pupils but have failed to recognize the importance of adult learning. It is only through continuous capacity-building and increased capability across the organization that teaching and learning are improved. Schools and districts simply cannot afford to finance the amount and quality of learning necessary for all teachers to diversify their instruction and enact the responsive teaching necessary to meet the needs of all students. This can only be achieved when learning and capacity-building (intellectual capital) become part of the day-to-day activity of educational professionals in their workplace; teachers' work leads to teachers' learning! Synonymous with this is ensuring that every practitioner, from the initial teaching years forward, is continuously developing as a leader—and that, as a result, we are building "leaderful schools." This book explores what it takes to rethink and redesign the work of the school so that teachers who see themselves as leaders can engage in continuous learning and review to build capacity and respond to pupil need.

Continuous learning, in part, centers around the facility to question, gather, organize, and dialogue about what constitutes the learning experience and accomplishments of our pupils. It is not enough that some educators are skillful at data collection and analysis; it is, if anything, more important that educators collectively share their data and examine the assumptions underpinning what they observe. It is only through examining underlying assumptions forming our behavior that we can deepen our understanding and move to new and improved practice. It is this continuous review of learning and teaching that not only builds capacity but also addresses the big issues of assessment and internal accountability, enabling school staff to become experts in evaluating the quality of teaching and the learning accomplishments of pupils. Powerful internal accountability counters the pernicious effects of high-stakes testing by giving principals and teachers greater access to more persuasive data, making them confident and articulate in speaking to the needs of students.

Schools can only truly change and improve the life chances of all pupils when teachers work together, learn together, and make the important decisions collaboratively. Although much has been written about the need for collaborative schools instead of professionally private workplace cultures, the harsh reality is that the former remain a rarity. The norms of teacher, principal, and district isolation are unfortunately alive and well. Although every chapter of the book addresses this topic, I devote Chapter 7 specifically to learning to work together. There, I uncover some of the practicalities of this compelling yet difficult leadership work.

STRUCTURE OF THIS BOOK

In this book, I have attempted to harness the narrative possibilities of school leadership, to begin to tell stories of practice, in order to examine underlying assumptions about teaching, learning, and leadership. The book begins with two chapters that set the groundwork for the remaining text; they are, by necessity, more conceptual than the chapters that follow. Chapter 1 examines the practicalities of "morally compelling purpose" as the very foundation that underpins school leadership. It is the key to building commitment, excitement, energy, and coherence around the work of improving the life chances of all pupils. In this chapter, I draw on stories of my own experience and the experience of others in an attempt to make sense of this much-talked-about and little-understood driving force behind good leadership.

Chapter 2 addresses the principal and the curriculum. Moral purpose includes working with the curriculum, standards, and the associated (often imposed) measures of assessment and accountability. For many principals, the curriculum is a given—something never to be questioned, just accepted, "covered," and implemented. Curriculum is nothing so benign! Raising questions that I believe all pedagogical leaders need to ask about teaching responsively to student needs, I posit very practical answers and describe a constructive way forward.

In Chapter 3, I show how evidence-gathering and sharing can engage colleagues in an ongoing inquiry into and dialogue about students' experiences with the curriculum. Providing a powerful alternative for those who feel constrained by rigid testing regimes, this chapter identifies the kinds of information that are most useful and suggests how to engage and transform these data into action to improve the learning of all. To that end, I conceptualize and illustrate four practical strategies. Finally, the chapter uses the example of teachers and parents sharing responsibility to raise issues of accountability.

Chapter 4 describes the learning school and portrays examples of personal, collective, and organizational capacity-building. Educators everywhere need to be lifelong learners themselves if they are to develop the personal, collective, and organizational capacity necessary to improve the life chances of all pupils. Attitudes, values, and pervasive productive habits begin with the leader's own learning.

Chapter 5 explores the potential of professional learning communities and the notion of the learning school. Bringing together the lessons of earlier chapters, we now examine the practicalities of whole-school approaches to learning and improving. I share a case study from my own work as principal at Southern Cross Public School to illustrate how capacity-building principles and real-world strategies come together as a cohesive whole in a high-performing learning community.

Chapter 6 presents four case studies that illustrate how to design and implement strategic directions and actions that will embody the moral purposes of the school. Each case presents the strategic actions of a principal in the first 15 months at a school. The actions flow from purposes agreed to by all stakeholders, but moving from direction to specific action is always the challenge. Throughout the chapter, I demonstrate the importance of taking action quickly.

Chapter 7 explores some of the practicalities of orchestrating the collective work of the school to make learning paramount. Here we visit three schools whose practices raise key ideas about building a participatory community. Paramount to this discussion are issues such as working with and valuing colleagues who hold diverse worldviews, building commitment and trust, finding consensus, and moving to action fast.

In the final chapter, Chapter 8, I define the nature of the work and leadership traits required to *take charge* and provide the purpose and capacity to improve the life chances of all. Pulling together the major themes of the book, I identify four basic pillars of improvement and two important foundations upon which they rest. The two foundations are morally compelling purpose and the enactment of a participatory workplace culture. The four pillars are:

1. Knowing the student well
2. Strong, inclusive professional relationships
3. Continuous development of intellectual capital
4. Powerful and cohesive pedagogical responsiveness in teaching across all classrooms

When professional relationships and intellectual capacity run deep, we attain the collective wisdom needed to take the action that improves teaching and the life chances of all.

CHAPTER 1

Purpose and Passion
in Leadership

Understanding and using the concept of compelling moral purpose prioritizes the work of the school leader and is key to unleashing the commitment and engagement of teaching colleagues. In this chapter you will learn

- what "moral purpose" means;
- the importance of using moral purpose to build commitment and guide actions and work—and the consequences of not doing so;
- practical strategies for involving stakeholders, identifying the needs of students, and using wide-ranging information to inform consensus-building around purpose; and
- how continuous learning, informed by concepts of lifelong learning and related values, refines common purpose and builds capacity in the organization called school.

It was my second year as principal of Cloverdale Public School, a large multi-ethnic, multilingual, urban elementary school. My work was becoming increasingly stressful due to a continual overload of demands for which there wasn't enough time in the day to resolve. More than 70 educators, each acting individually according to his or her own values, needs, assumptions, and beliefs, created the feeling of a chaotic organization without purpose or coherence. Instead of creating a beautiful fireworks display that was coordinated, where colors and sounds added value and coherence to the experience, it was as if someone had thrown a match into the storeroom and we had rockets, sparklers, and firecrackers going off in all directions. Because the school was larger than any I'd previously led, I found I was working harder and longer to stay ahead of the greater demands on my time. Our discreet custodian Roberto, who was always at school first in the morning, had become accustomed to occasionally finding me asleep on the couch in the teachers' lounge and knew to wake me and direct me to the showers before anyone else arrived.

I had tried to become the "super principal." If a teacher had a difficult student, I could deal with the student for him or her. If a teacher was worried about a parent interview, I could handle that. If more resources were required, then I could find them. If a teacher needed to take his or her own child to the doctor, I could teach the class. These scenarios and many more like them, multiplied by the many adults in the building, meant that I didn't have enough waking hours in a day to fulfill so many needs and demands. I was constantly "putting out fires" rather than building the capabilities of my teacher colleagues to *take charge* and fulfill the purposes of the school. Consequently, I ran out of energy. My weary body said, "Enough," and I took to my bed to recoup.

After taking a few days to mull over the purposes of the school and the effectiveness of my now beleaguered role, I finally concluded that the problem was a misunderstanding, on my part and others', of the true purpose of the school and my own role in helping to achieve it. Had I asked myself earlier what I could do to improve the life chances of all the pupils in my school, my role would have become clearer. In the long term, my present behavior would help neither all pupils nor my teacher colleagues. In reflecting, I reached a few conclusions:

1. I personally could do little for the 980+ students in my school. What I could do was focus on building the capacity of and bringing coherence to the work of its 70 teachers. With increased capacity and purpose, they could improve the life chances of all our pupils.
2. My main role was to improve the quality of teaching and learning across the school by embracing professional and organizational learning.
3. I could not do anything about the first two unless I changed my behavior and priorities. Instead of needing me to be the resident problem-solver, my teaching colleagues needed opportunities to develop their capacity and responsibility in order to extend their commitment and leadership.

I came up with a somewhat crass but workable credo: "I will not deprive my colleagues of the opportunity to show leadership and responsibility and will use every chance to enable them to improve their skills." Moreover, I resolved, "I will not do anything for another who, with support, is capable of doing it for themselves."

On my first day back at school after spending the previous 5 in bed, I was determined to try out my new credo. Michelle, a grade 2 teacher, was having difficulties with one of her boys again and wanted to know if I could handle it. "Well, no, Michelle," I said. "Let's both sit down with your boy at break time and see if I can help *you* resolve the discipline problem." Later that morning, I was walking down the hall and Catherine asked if she could take her class to the park. "Well, I don't know," I answered.

"*Can* you take your class to the park?" I am sure she thought I was being a smart aleck, but at least I was turning responsibility back to where it belonged. It was a start.

I decided that if I was truly serious about changing the life chances of all pupils through improved teaching and learning, I would need to devote at least 50% of my time to my new role. Yet, how could I do this given the tremendous demands of my schedule? As Michael Fullan explains,

> On the one hand, educators are constantly faced with multiple innovations and policies that must be contended with simultaneously. . . . On the other hand, a host of unplanned changes and problems, including technological developments, multi-ethnic demographic factors, family and community complexities, economic and political pressures, and more compounds overload. Fragmentation occurs when pressures and even opportunities for reform appear disjointed, work at cross-purposes, and appear incoherent. Overload and fragmentation reduce motivation for working on reform as the situation lacks meaning or seems hopeless.[1]

It seemed to me that the secret to addressing overload and fragmentation was to uncover moral purpose and invest in the capacity of, relationships with, and leadership of my colleagues. I was not merely to be the instructional leader, but rather the leader of instructional leaders. I was to develop what Margaret Wheatley calls the Leaderful Organization, in which every teacher contributes to the leadership and improvement of the school.[2]

MOVING TO PURPOSE AND COHERENCE

Having defined the problem of role and purpose in school leadership, I jump forward in time from Cloverdale Public School to my work several years later with a group of principals in order to show how these leaders experienced and approached these same issues. As director of a university–school district partnership, I met regularly with 20 smart and talented elementary and secondary school principals. We learned a lot together as we struggled to make sense of pervasive, sweeping educational reform. Schools were expected to implement new curriculum in every subject and use new assessment, evaluation, and reporting procedures. The concurrent loss of resources had led to less time for teachers to prepare their lessons and a reduction in staff for special education, English as a second language, guidance, and library services. Changes in roles and relationships had occurred, as principals, against their wishes, were legislated out of the teacher union and had to form a professional association of their own. At the same time as the pressure to perform mounted, teachers' unions were fighting the reduction in resources by working to rule and appointing shop stewards in each school. Principals with reduced resources and increased pressures suffered great overload and struggled to find purpose, coherence, and satisfaction in their work.

Within our group of principals, even those who were renowned for the quality of their schools' teaching and student learning found it almost impossible to continue their efforts to improve student achievement. Rather than attending to the paramount work of building capacity and focusing on teaching and learning, more and more of their time had to be used to address administrative policy and accountability tasks. More and more, these school leaders were required to prove they were following policy that at times was at odds with their everyday reality—demonstrating, for instance, how more students were receiving second language learning support while at the same time the number of teachers responsible for this was being cut by half.

I have represented this phenomenon in Figure 1.1 with two continuums, each with two extremes. One continuum runs from *operational*, which may be thought of as administrative and includes reporting, recording, and controlling policy and the behavior of others, to *teaching and learning*, which represents extensive participation in planning, coordinating, and supporting classroom practice. On the second continuum, *compliance* is about checking, enforcing, and supervising teachers with a view to ensuring they are "covering" the mandated curriculum. In contrast, at the other end of the continuum, *capacity-building* can be defined as improving the capabilities and learning of all teachers to respond effectively to student need.

The intersection of the continuums produces four categories—or quadrants—to describe the work of principals and schools. Quadrant one is seen as growth-inhibiting, where the principal acts out a managerial role. The externally dictated purposes that drive this kind of school result in little ownership. Likewise, the curriculum is mandated, rigid, and expected to be "covered" in its entirety. School organization and structures are predefined and the complexities and overload almost paralytic in nature. Teachers essentially do their own thing and work in isolation.

In quadrant two, the ideological school is seen as growth-misleading and is characterized by efforts to train teachers to follow specific approaches and policies. Policy and procedure are the name of the game, and leading without risk preoccupies leaders of these schools. Training tends to be expert driven from outside sources and often can be ideologically driven. Covering the curriculum is more important than helping individuals learn.

The prescriptive school in quadrant three is viewed as a growth-controlled school, which takes an approach in which teaching and learning are an important focus. Here we often hear about the "teacher-proof curriculum." Although support and training are minimal, the intent is to get all teachers to follow the prescribed program. Textbooks, worksheets, quick tests, and quizzes are commonplace, as is regular monitoring of classrooms to ensure that teachers comply with the prescribed program.

In quadrant four, the learning school is viewed as growth-provoking, inspired by intensive, internally driven professional learning and development. The entire focus of the school is on improved teaching and student learning. The collective documentation of pupils' learning experience underpins the ongoing professional dialogue that is the mainstay of professional learning and development.

The four quadrants portray differing images of teachers and teaching. From a culture of professional privacy and isolation in quadrant one, we move to images of external control and manipulation in quadrants two and three. Quadrant two, being more ideologically driven, is concerned with policy, whereas quadrant three, while attentive to classroom programming

Figure 1.1. Schools' Potential Response to Overload and External Pressures to Reform

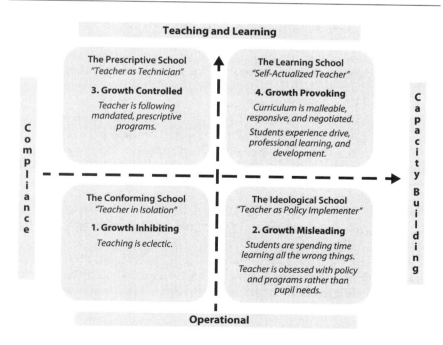

and teaching, relies on external mandates and the conformity of teachers. Finally, in quadrant four, we capture the image of the teacher as a professional. Deeply informed, working collaboratively with others on the crucial issues of teacher development and student learning, the teacher exercises professional judgment in negotiating the curriculum according to student need, passion, and intentions.

Within our group of principals, as the quantity and complexity of new policy and the pressure to comply increased while resources decreased, school leaders found that they were being forced toward quadrant one as they struggled to conform with a flurry of mandates. Morally unacceptable to this group of talented leaders, this phenomenon was hugely stressful. In every successful school I know, principals spend the bulk of their time in quadrant four. When policymakers try to micromanage schools and their districts, principals find that they have to spend more time at the compliance game and less in building capacity, the critical work of the pedagogical leader.

What I have learned about being a principal from my own experience and from working with this group of 20 school leaders is that the intrinsic rewards, the fun and passion for the job, lie in learning to live and play in quadrant four. This represents my view of effective schools and school leadership. Leadership in schools is about mobilizing the capabilities and unleashing the passions of colleagues in order to better fulfill the purposes of the organization. Effective schools are those that deliberately improve the life chances of all students. For instance, in schools with significant numbers of new immigrant pupils, morally compelling purposes relate to ensuring the success of those who are disadvantaged by the demands of a curriculum designed for students who have a different first language and have grown up in a different culture.

The school's responsiveness to the diverse needs of individuals is a true measure of its effectiveness. How responsive the school is has to do with the capacity and coherence of the organization and the principal's ability to build these values with colleagues. It begins with uncovering moral purposes.

UNCOVERING MORALLY COMPELLING PURPOSE

Educating other people's children is a deeply moral and ethical task. It involves making choices that ensure no child is harmed and that all (regardless of their abilities and experience as learners and their social, racial, linguistic, and cultural heritage) have the opportunity to succeed. It means making decisions that are consistently and coherently grounded in the purposes of the school (that is, leading with integrity) and not being swayed or distracted by the immediacy of personal needs, tradition, external pressures, conflicting policies, or constraints. In effective schools, educators are focused and bring coherence to their work. They have *taken charge* of the learning agenda.

Coherence emerges from purposes that principals, teachers, pupils, and parents find compelling and that guide and focus the attention of school personnel and the decisions they make. This view of the work of schools raises a number of questions:

- What are the purposes of a school?
- Who decides what they are?
- Do they guide decision-making and behavior, or are they merely wishy-washy generic statements?
- Do they evoke ownership, passion, and commitment?
- How and to what extent do they relate to the real learning needs of all pupils?
- Are they realistic and achievable?
- Do the assessment and evaluation procedures truly reflect and inform the purposes?
- Do assessment procedures promote and provide information about pupils' genuine learning experience as they encounter the meanings embedded in the natural, social, and cultural worlds they inhabit?
- How and to what extent do all stakeholders perceive the purposes of the school as morally compelling?
- How and to what extent do the purposes bring meaning to the lives of the people who work and learn at school?

As many of the predictable underpinnings of education (family, community, expectations, politics, and technology) change rapidly, effective teachers and principals have found gratification, meaning, and purpose in *taking charge* of change in their workplace. *Taking charge* usually begins with uncovering that which is enduringly purposeful, in terms of teaching and learning—by identifying, usually through a process of inquiry, the core purposes that are morally compelling to teachers, pupils, and parents alike. Fullan tells us that finding moral purpose in education is necessary for making a difference in the life chances of students.[3] Identifying and acting on the core purposes of the school also allows educators to gain control over their work.

Sirotnik, more than a decade ago, stated some abiding principles and raised questions about moral purpose. He said that

> the implications of moral commitments to inquiry, knowledge, competence, caring and social justice go farther than curriculum and classroom experiences. They go to the very moral ecology of the organization itself. This can be readily seen in the extent to which these commitments are reflected in the work environment of educators outside the school per se. To what extent does the organizational culture encourage and support educators as inquirers into what they do and how they might do it better? To what extent do educators consume, critique, and produce knowledge? To what extent do they competently engage in discourse and action to improve the conditions, activities and outcomes, of schooling? To what extent do educators care about themselves and each other in the same way they care (or ought to care) about students?[4]

Further, what is morally compelling is in many ways made so by the way in which it is uncovered and the assumptions participants in the process hold. The ideal process involves all stakeholders and provides sufficient time for informed dialogue and thinking.

For example, the teachers at Thornwood Public School, in defining moral purpose, used a process of facilitated and informed consensus-building (see Chapter 7) to determine what was important and necessary to improve the life opportunities of their pupils.[5] The work began with a focus question: What do teachers at Thornwood have to do to improve the life chances of all our students? The process involved collecting and discussing data about student needs and then identifying key elements in response to the focus question. They decided that they wanted to make a difference in the literacy learning of all pupils and collectively developed a set of principles to guide their actions. Specifically, they would

- *establish* an inclusive climate
- *develop* a consistent and responsive framework for assessment and instructional practices
- *value* multicultural and multilingual literature and materials
- *provide* pupils with meaningful experiences through which to develop their language abilities
- *build* informed home-school partnerships.

These principles guided teachers in making decisions about designing and providing for professional learning and development, purchasing and/or creating resources, and focusing their work. They provided the strategic directions from which thoughtful, informed action planning flowed and led to substantive changes that had a positive effect on the life chances of many students. In addition, involving all teachers and using an informed consensus process that ensured and valued the contributions of all greatly increased the commitment and engagement in the work that followed. Most important, the process empowered educators to participate authentically in pedagogical matters of fundamental importance.

As educators, we are committed to our pupils doing well. Pupil *achievement* (in its broadest, holistic sense, where students are viewed as both source and constructor of their own experience and knowledge and thus active participants in the development of their own identities, abilities, and autonomy) is the fundamental raison d'être of our work.[6] However, there is often a tension between locally developed goals and purposes and government programs and mandates. There is also often a tension between what we do in school and its fit with the needs, aspirations, intentions, competencies, and values of today's youth and families. Thus, one of the ongoing quandaries of the school leadership team is "How do we turn top-down mandates or innovations into bottom-up commitment in order to benefit all students?" How we answer this vital question begins with how leaders frame this quandary.

Where to Start with Change

Schools live with change constantly. New approaches to reading may be advisable or mandated, discipline policies may be revised and require implementation, or innovative teaching methods in math may become desirable or required. Regardless of whether change is mandated from without or identified as needed from within, leaders have three choices in how they implement it: to impose it as a new innovation or policy; to start with the teachers' desires and their current practice; or to start with the pupils and their aspirations, needs, experience, and intentions.

The relationship among the new innovation or change, the teacher, and the students can be portrayed in a number of ways depending on how the change is framed. Moving from left to right on the continuum in the first instance, we start with an innovation or imposed objective:

Innovation/Objective ⟶ Teacher ⟶ Student

Implementing change through a mandate or new innovation that has come down from on high is tricky because whether it's the district, the government, or some other stakeholder, the policymakers can't know the students, their needs, their culture, or their community as well as the school leader. There is no moral authority to mandate what is usually a one-size-fits-all policy or procedure. "Selling" change to teachers is unlikely to succeed.

In this next continuum we start from the perspective of the teacher.

Teacher ⟶ Innovation/Objective ⟶ Student

Teachers often become enamored with a new innovation or technique, and that is not necessarily a bad thing. However, the challenge occurs when teachers try to entice colleagues to buy into the same innovation. Sometimes colleagues can't see the benefit in terms of their pupils. Others feel threatened by the zealousness of their colleagues. Most fail to grasp the compelling purpose behind the innovation. Implementing change with teachers and their passions may work when there is a high degree of trust throughout the organization and when the promoter of innovation already commands respect from all colleagues. However, this is fairly rare; schools where there are pockets of innovation and excellence that have not spread throughout the building are typically driven by teacher perspective or interest.

In the third example we commence the change process by focusing on the needs of students.

Students ⟶ Teacher ⟶ Innovation/Objective

Starting with students means being deeply informed about their history of learning, the experience they bring to the learning activity, their learning experience in the classroom, and their learning styles and abilities— all while recognizing that they have intentions in every learning situation. By grounding improvement in data about the experiences, needs, aspirations, culture, and community of the learner, we have the opportunity to uncover and mobilize the persuasive moral imperative that brought us to the profession in the first place.

In the reciprocal relationship shown in Figure 1.2, students' experiences and needs interact with the teacher's perspective and with a critical examination of the new program's ability to benefit the students' life chances. This stance enables principals and teachers to take a proactive, informed, and principled approach to innovation and change. It recognizes the diversity of learners' interests, experiences, intentions, and abilities. It questions the potential of the innovation to respond to the pupils' needs. It enables the participants in the change initiative to frame the challenge in ways that foster the emergence of a morally compelling purpose.

Let us look at these alternative approaches to innovation in practice through the lens of the questions that are implied:

- In framing a change initiative as an external innovation to be implemented, we might ask the question, "How do we implement this new reading program?" The focus is the program.

- When framed as a series of objectives, this new mandate might prompt the question, "How can the program ensure that all pupils read in a variety of genres, for a variety of purposes, and for different audiences?" Here the focus is on the program's utility.
- If a teacher arrives back from a conference or a school visit with a new program or teaching strategy, then this question might frame her new task: "How can I convince my colleagues that this is the right approach to teaching literacy?" Here the change initiative is to be marketed or sold.
- When a morally compelling purpose fostering children's literacy development frames the question, it might look something like this: "How and to what extent are our diverse readers engaged in reading, and how and to what extent do and might our practices encourage them to read in a variety of genres and for a variety of purposes?" In this scenario, the question is as much for the pupil as it is for the teacher. How and in what ways do you, the reader, engage in reading? Inquiry questions like these direct

Figure 1.2. Students' Experiences Interact with Teacher's Perspective, thus Critiquing Innovation

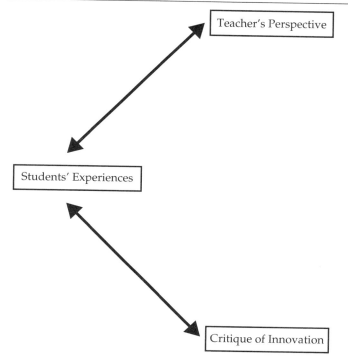

attention and frame our efforts toward that which is morally compelling about our work. The questions are about the needs of the students.

Working with Mandated Change

When changes are externally mandated, the astute leader needs to be mindful that teacher colleagues will not necessarily embrace such changes. Colleagues may wonder whether the changes are really appropriate for their students in their community. They may wonder if the changes are really geared toward improving the life chances of all students or whether they are politically motivated. They may have already implemented previously mandated changes with a passion only to find a few years later that the change or innovation is forgotten or overturned. Despite this skepticism, it is possible to work with colleagues to reframe mandated change as an opportunity to gather data and to intimately learn about and move to productive action for all students. Data-gathering practices are described at length in Chapter 3 of this book.

Purpose and Its Paradoxes

Uncovering compelling purpose in the work of the school these days is like walking through a minefield. Moral purposes representing the compelling needs of our students are often in conflict within a context of contradiction and paradox. Policy and curriculum frameworks at times appear to ignore student needs. For instance,

- Our pupils are different in terms of their interests and intentions; they are different experientially, linguistically, socially, and intellectually, yet expected outcomes are becoming more and more standardized.
- Our pupils learn best when they can go deeper and deeper into compelling topics, yet our curriculum is so full that teachers feel obliged to race through it in order to "cover" the curriculum.
- Our pupils are computer literate; they are capable of simultaneously sitting in class, texting friends and family from their cell phones, and accessing information like never before, yet, for the most part, technology is not effectively used as a teaching tool.
- Lifelong learning is about increasing control over and responsibility for one's own learning, yet from kindergarten on, pupils have less and less control over what and how they learn.

- We all learn well when we have a vested interest (ownership, intentionality) in the topic, yet our pupils have little choice or voice.
- Our pupils have differing learning styles, yet we teach to the "average" student.
- Learning is holistic, yet, for the most part, learning in schools involves the accumulation of discrete parts or pieces; supposedly when one knows the parts one also knows the whole.
- Our pupils need to learn collaboratively, yet most classroom learning is an individual encounter between textbook, pupil, and teacher.

Raising the question of moral purpose confronts these contradictions and raises a fundamental question: Are we merely employees of a school district or government who are responsible for managing prescribed policy, or are there higher purposes and responsibilities of meeting pupil needs requiring innovation and adaptability that are equally or more compelling?

Perhaps educators should take something akin to the Hippocratic Oath requiring that we do no harm to our pupils. If we did, interesting questions and tensions would arise:

- Do we harm when we fail to respond to the varied needs of our learners?
- Do we harm when we knowingly accept that students who regularly get low grades eventually stop trying and give up on seeking help?
- Do we harm when we give grades (especially failing ones) to pupils as young as age 5 or 6?
- Do districts or states do harm by heavily emphasizing testing, standards, and high achievement while also accepting high dropout rates?[7]

It seems to me that the moral purpose has to trump all others when leaders and teachers (who are also leaders) make decisions about youngsters in school. We need our own Hippocratic Oath to go something like this: *In assuming significant responsibility for the learning and social development of other people's children, educators have an ethical duty to improve the life chances of all and to take or support no action that may be construed as harming these same life chances.*

Duigan and Macpherson tell us that "the moral knowledge on which educative leaders base their actions and judgments about whether something is right or wrong, is not a separate and distinct form of knowledge.

Rather, it is part and parcel of their total pattern of knowledge, understandings and beliefs."[8] Evers et al. argue that most decisions made by educational leaders have a moral dimension and suggest that they be judged by the following criteria:[9]

- Their ability to develop and maintain an effective inquiry and problem-solving culture in their domain
- Their respect for and tolerance of different points of view and an acceptance of criticism as the key ingredient in the growth of knowledge within the organization
- Their ability to adapt to challenges and provide for change in policy or practices through feedback and reflection
- Their concern for ensuring that people have the freedom to fully participate in this process of learning and growth
- Their commitment to the holistic belief that their decisions can be defended because of their contribution to the benefits of long-term learning within the organization.

This book is about how to lead in ways that persuasively meet these criteria. Improving the engagement and life chances of all students involves much more than improving test scores. Ruddick and Demetriou point out that schools have changed less over the years in their deep structures and patterns of relationships than young people have.[10] We now have whole schools of computer-literate pupils facing an uncertain and ever-changing future attending schools with deep traditional structures. Simultaneously, these same students may play significant roles in their families, sports teams, and communities. Rethinking school with a view to finding a responsive fit between the institution and the youth who attend it has to be one of the most morally compelling tasks facing educators today.[11] Talisman Park Secondary School provides one example of how a school can begin to approach this vital responsibility.

Case Study: Talisman Park Secondary School

A neighborhood secondary school finds that its past role in the community is no longer practical. A new purpose and identity has to be forged with the community's participation.

Talisman Park Secondary School had for decades been the only secondary school to serve its large community, and even in the 1950s, as more schools were built in surrounding areas, it had maintained its reputation as "the" academically prestigious school to attend. Recently, however, the school found itself competing for pupils and searching for identity. A neighborhood school, Talisman Park was eventually surrounded by three magnet schools, each offering distinct programs to lure the best and the brightest from the community. As a result, Talisman's staff found their very purposes, reputation, and survival under threat.

In response to this new reality, the principal formed a school design team that was representative of the entire staff. The team was charged with uncovering moral purpose, strategic planning and actions, and the professional learning of colleagues. With the help of the team, the principal organized a school-community dialogue that she titled "Looking to Our Future." She brought together 65 business and political leaders from the community, parents, community agency representatives, and Talisman Park faculty and students for a one-day conference. The attendees were tasked with reviewing the schools' purpose and developing a strategic plan to achieve common objectives. In preparation for the conference, these stakeholders were given readings about varied contextual issues. For example, they examined the Conference Board of Canada's Employability Skills,[12] a list of skills young people must learn to gain employment in the modern knowledge economy. More than a third of the staff joined a reading club that discussed, among other works, Margaret Wheatley's book *Leadership and the New Science*, engaging with her powerful insights into transforming how we organize work, people, and life.[13] In the morning, a visionary keynote speaker addressed the theme of the day by describing the process of organizational transformation in a rapidly changing world. He then raised questions for the delegates regarding new government standards, including the new curriculum, compulsory credits, tracking (streaming), standardized testing, and accountability.

In the afternoon, heterogeneous groups of six to eight people discussed three questions:

- What is our mission as a school?
- Where do we want our school to go?
- How can we get there together?

A teacher was present in each focus group to record its conversation and report to the whole group at the end of the day. The principal facilitated the afternoon session and arranged for a group of Talisman Park teachers to analyze the discussion's key themes and identify next steps in a public report. This process opened up a vibrant discourse of renewal that enabled all stakeholders to reflect on the school's mission, its future, and their all-important role. It compelled the teachers to action!

What I find significant about the approach at Talisman is that:

- The principal worked with her representative design team to plan processes that engaged stakeholders from the entire community.
- The principal was open about the outcome but determined to move her colleagues forward.
- There was a sense of urgency about the work.
- The process enabled all to contribute equally.
- The dialogue was informed not only by a visionary speaker and professional readings but also by inside/outside expertise and, most importantly, by the students themselves.
- Context matters! Information and dialogue included the local and broader context of the district, province, and workplace.
- Provision for the dialogue to continue was essential.
- The process led to strategic action planning and specific actions.
- The principal's role was facilitative; her responsibility was to press for and then act on the coherence that emerged.

In summary, the principal's role was to energize her colleagues by developing a coherent purpose and bringing meaningfulness to the lives of students, teachers, parents, and others who had a stake in the school and community. Sergiovanni reminds us about schools like this: "Meaningfulness leads to an elevated level of commitment to the school, greater effort, tighter connections for everyone, and more intensive academic engagement for students—all of which are virtues in themselves but which have the added value of resulting in heightened levels of student development and increased academic performance."[14] With renewed clarity of purpose, the principal was able to forge ahead with her colleagues and community to enact decisions and programs that reflected the values, will, and commitment of the various stakeholders. As a result of the principal's efforts and the participation of staff and community members, the school was well on its way to regaining its standing in the community and dramatically improving teaching and learning.

GETTING AT THE CORE OF MORAL PURPOSE

Understanding the importance of moral purpose in developing wholly accomplished, successful young people is fundamental to school leadership. However, uncovering and enacting moral purpose seems to be a difficult thing to do well. What has helped me over the years has been to reduce the idea of moral purpose to four essential questions. The morally persuasive answers to these questions make the necessary actions more apparent and achievable. The questions are:

1. Who will get to learn?
2. What is to be learned?
3. How is it to be learned?
4. What counts as progress?

Simple questions—but hard to answer well! To find satisfying solutions, it is necessary to create an informed collective dialogue that brings stakeholders together and fosters the development of a true consensus. Moral purpose resides within the very real needs of our pupils. It is uncovered through inquiry and reflection. It is mindful of the larger and local context. Imposing moral purpose from without is futile. What's needed is a robust dialogue that takes place among stakeholders who are knowledgeable about the students themselves and their needs and informed by a vision of the future leading to a strong consensus supported by all. More about these processes will be discussed in later chapters, particularly Chapter 7.

How Moral Purpose Ignites the Work of the School

I don't think I know a teacher who came into the profession without a love for his or her subject and/or a commitment and passion for making a difference and improving the lives of learners. Teachers new to the profession bring energy and often an intimate and more immediate sense of why we come to school each day. In doing so, they add an important dimension to the work of the school. Often, during a teaching career, whether it is the constant change, the lack of supportive professional community, or the ongoing drain of emotional labor, teachers sometimes lose heart, direction, and passion for their work.

Helping one's colleagues rekindle their passion and build commitment begins with collectively uncovering or redefining the purposes of the school. It is about returning to those very basic questions of what we can do to improve the life chances of all pupils, of how we can collectively make a difference. The vehicle for uncovering moral purpose is one of inquiry, in which an intellectual, social, and emotionally supportive collegial community (see chapters 3 and 5) is charged with identifying and addressing the needs of all our pupils. It is as Sergiovanni tells us:

In successful schools, consensus runs deep. It is not enough to have worked out what people stand for and what it is to be accomplished; a binding and solemn agreement must emerge, one that represents a value system for living together and forms the basis for decisions and actions. This agreement is the school's covenant. When both the value of vision and the value added dimension of the covenant are present, teachers and students respond with increased motivation and commitment, and their performance is well above the ordinary.[15]

Developing Deep School Purpose

Most schools have a mission or vision statement. It tends to consist of general comments with which it is hard to disagree and within which most educators can find enough substance to feel they are indeed enacting the mission. The phrase "lifelong learning" often appears in these declarations. It's hard to argue with, and it is easy to find something we are doing that promotes lifelong learning, such as enabling students to learn to work cooperatively.

Nevertheless, are we really promoting lifelong learning? Educators committed to this goal should ask themselves and others the following questions:

- How do we prepare our pupils to be lifelong learners?
- Is lifelong learning central to improving the life chances of all pupils?
- What would a graduate who is well on the way to becoming a lifelong learner actually do?

Students who are becoming lifelong learners would be

- taking increasing control of their learning by gathering and reflecting on data; by defining content, outcomes, and demonstrations; by taking risks; and, especially, by asking mindful questions;
- increasingly self-directed and resourceful in questioning, extending, and improving their own ideas and the ideas of others and in working collaboratively to express their emergent understandings (theories), predictions, and outcomes in a variety of media to a variety of audiences; and
- able to articulate their intentions and, most important, to be effective teachers of others.

When we think about the objective in this way, even schools with the most visible posters and letterheads proclaiming lifelong learning fall short. With a few wonderful exceptions, most pupils experience diminishing control and ask fewer questions as they progress through the grades. Most kindergartens and primary classrooms provide an environment that fosters lifelong learning. Kindergarten children typically have more opportunity to pursue their interests, to articulate what they think to all, and to follow their curiosity by asking questions at will.[16] Something fades on the way to graduation! It is clear to me that pupils' natural curiosity, their opportunities to be co-researchers and co-decision-makers in the learning process, their opportunities to pursue their own interests and passions, and their opportunities to seek novelty and innovation diminish rather than burgeon over time. Why is that? Is it the rush to cover the curriculum, the teacher's need to control the class and its work, our reluctance to change the deep structures and patterns of relationships, or simply outdated pedagogy?

Working with colleagues to prepare your pupils for lifelong learning is a morally compelling task, but one that takes fearless actions and courage to pursue. It's not only about unleashing the passion of your colleagues and building capacity of all to teach and learn in new ways, but also about working with your community and school district to enable them to be part of the journey. In short, it is about *taking charge* of the all-important learning agenda.

Built on the informed participation of stakeholders, a compelling vision should

- clarify and bring coherence to the purposes and activities of the school;
- create meaning in students' and teachers' lives;
- paint a persuasive picture, often through narrative, of what the future could be;
- attract commitment while energizing and motivating people;
- define the capabilities of graduates;
- improve substantially on current practice; and
- evoke sustained and strategic directions and actions by faculty and the school.

Michael Fullan made popular a very important lesson about vision with the "Ready-Fire-Aim" metaphor. You don't have to get it perfectly right before starting the journey. If the journey is to be a successful one, then it will mean that participants (teachers and pupils) are gathering information that not only informs classroom practice but also deepens the meaning and clarity of the vision. In the case of Talisman Park, it's not that facilitating a community event for stakeholders produced the perfect vision and clarity of purpose so much as it provided a place to start and a direction to pursue. It is in the active pursuit and execution over time that clarity and cohesion emerge.

Imagining the Learner

Creating an image of the graduate is a powerful way to identify a preferred future and express the vision for a school. The following is an example of an image that a group of colleagues and I constructed together.

An Image of the Learner

Our learner is an increasingly self-motivated, self-directed inquirer and problem-solver, aware of both the processes and uses of learning, who derives a sense of self-worth and confidence from a variety of accomplishments.[17] Our learners have intentions, asking many questions, creating, challenging, and improving on their own knowledge and that of others as they engage in sustained community-improving projects. Their work is characterized by improvisation,[18] surprise, technological sophistication, and a diversity of outcomes as they communicate using a variety of media to share and teach their discoveries to others. Our pupils, in learning, working, and playing together, learn to act as caring, contributing members of a dynamic, pluralistic community and planetary society.

This definition represents the vision of one school in one community and one context. Other schools undoubtedly would construct somewhat different images.

Having developed an image of the learner, the question arises of what to do with it. For me, it's always been the basis for explaining, telling, and/or describing the work of the school to teachers, students, parents, and others. In Neil Postman's words, "Without a narrative, life has no meaning. Without meaning, learning has no purpose. Without a purpose, schools are houses of detention, not attention."[19] Leading with moral purpose, for me, has been about storytelling, wherein the stories capture or imagine a future for all the learners in the school. My former teacher colleagues tell me that coming to parent evenings was always interesting and inspiring because teachers and parents would see and hear visions of learners—their experiences and their learning—and understand how we (the educators) were striving to engage, challenge, and extend the accomplishments of everyone. My stories were always of a work in progress, frequently illustrated by the work of pupils or by the pupils themselves. I used the classroom examples, storyboards, and student work that we educators learned from (see Chapter 3) as the basis for my storytelling and strove to capture a future that was slightly ahead of our current practice.

TAKING CHARGE:
THE PRINCIPAL'S ROLE IN UNCOVERING MORAL PURPOSE

Moral purpose cannot be mandated or imposed from without; rather, it emerges with nurturing from within. Uncovering moral purpose is the key to developing coherence and focus. Significantly, it is the first step in building commitment and fostering ownership for the work of the school. Working with your colleagues, pupils, and community to establish a local voice, broad contextual perspective, student-centered values, purpose, and commitment (in many cases in a context of overwhelming mandates and external micromanaging of your school) requires courage and fearless actions. When external policies and pressures challenge the very moral nature of educating young people, then school leaders, more than ever before, have to provide valiant leadership and *take charge*. You can achieve this by executing the following actions:

- *Know your pupils well.* Moral purposes are rooted in the intentions, interests, and experiences of your students, as well as in their physical, social, emotional, and intellectual needs. These purposes are made apparent through the process of evidence-gathering (described in Chapter 3), and through participatory consensus-building processes (described in chapters 5 and 7). This requires teachers to spend more time with individual pupils in order to know them well.
- *Create a culture of inquiry.* Such a culture begins with reconceptualizing the leadership role by *building the capacity of yourself and your colleagues in order to create a sustainable and purposeful culture of inquiry*—a culture within which the aspirations, abilities, and very real learning experiences of your pupils become the basis for transforming and building knowledge about teaching and learning.
- *Collect sweeping data from current research and exemplary practice to inform the process of uncovering purpose.* Data about community needs and values, employability skills, cultural and linguistic needs and values, and global influences and directions, as well as information about classroom teaching and the day-to-day learning experiences of pupils, help ensure that you and your colleagues are truly on a path of improving the life chances of all pupils.
- *Account for the larger and local context for education.* Work with your colleagues to bring the broader perspective of the knowledge society to bear on the work of the school, but also document, examine, conceptualize, and act upon the unique needs of the pupils in your

community. Pupils bring a rich history of experience and diversity to the learning stage. Whether they are multicultural, multilingual, socially unique, or living in poverty, they all are influenced by a culture, a set of values, and a social experience that is unique to them and to their community and school. The important thing is to see diversity as a valuable resource, not as a handicap.

- *Actively support and broaden the experience of teachers as learners.* You and your team must develop the understanding that *the lives teachers lead—their very selfhood—is very much intertwined with how they teach* and with the quality of pupils who graduate from their school.[20] This is about you and your design team *planning to deepen and sustain the lives that teachers live.* Teaching is much more than a technical job; the improvement of students' life chances directly links to the values, experiences, passions, and perspectives that teachers bring to the classroom each day. If our pupils are to be lifelong learners, so too must be our teachers and principals. If our pupils are to be literate, so too must our teachers and principals live, model, and demonstrate their use and love of books and authorship. If our pupils are to be curious, creative, ingenious risk-takers who are able to question, hypothesize about, and constantly improve ideas, then so too must be teachers.

- *Model what you value.* School leaders lead by example, *demonstrating their curiosity and wonderment about the learning process.* As Roland Barth has taught us, being a principal is less about being the head teacher and more about being the *head learner.*[21] If you want teachers to be inquirers who have a thirst for data and information about learning and teaching, then you, too, had better exhibit and demonstrate these qualities. If you want your colleagues to value and revel in the challenges and excitement of working with and responding appropriately to diversity, then these values and behaviors have to start with you.

- *Encourage and foster participation, diversity, and multiple perspectives.* A school's greatest potential lies in the diverse experience of its teachers and their facility in bringing a broad perspective to the compelling issues of teaching and learning. Participation builds coherence, commitment, and ownership. Perspective enriches learning by moving between general and specific, shifting points of view, from the context and the curriculum to the teacher and to the experience of the learner[22] Perspective enables learners to view information and their practice by seeing and experiencing it in different contexts, through a variety of media, and through shifts in time—from the immediate experience to the life history of the learner.

- *Assertively support coherence in planning and pedagogy.* Coherence is about providing a consistent set of expectations for pupils and their learning over time. Coherence is also necessary for teachers and their practice and parents and their understanding about the purposes and actions of the school. Coherence cannot be mandated; it is built through participation and the continuous development of shared meaning.

- *Make decisions and take actions that are deeply embedded in the agreed-upon purposes of the school.* Principals work with many different individuals and constituent groups. It is tempting and foolhardy to try to please them all. Meaningfulness that emerges out of moral purpose gives principals an informed and fair basis to make decisions about people, strategies, and resources that are coherent and strong on integrity. When the purposes are agreed upon and compelling, it is much easier to say no. It is also easier to lead with integrity and to sleep well at night.

- *Move toward and speak out about purposes and moral issues in educating young people.* Principals are valued and recognized leaders in the education and local community. Contributing to the broader educational debate is an important part of the leader's role. Work toward building an acceptance of the idea of schools developing a unique local identity that is forged through partnership with community. Participative leadership means urging and facilitating the move toward school-based decision-making. It is about speaking to the need for pupils, teachers, schools, and communities to have more say over what is taught and what is to be valued in the community school. It is about capturing and representing the purposes of your school through narrative that is less about the jargon of policy and school improvement and more about the experiences, future, and hopes for all learners in your community.

In conclusion, let me say that the rewards and fun in school leadership are to be found in embracing quadrant four of Figure 1.1 above. Here the work of the school is focused and coherent, as is the role of the leader. Moral purpose is clear and drives the work and decision-making in the school. Teachers' ongoing professional learning is paramount and is driven by student needs and experiences. Classroom inquiry is continuous, transparent, and shared by all. Decisions and dialogue are deeply informed by students and their experiences and needs.

REFLECT ON THESE QUESTIONS

In considering how moral purpose underpins the work of your school/district, gather evidence to respond to these questions:[23]

1. If an outsider visits your school/district and asks each teacher to describe the purposes of the school/district, how will your colleagues answer?
2. What drives the purposes within your school/district? Outside factors such as policies, political pressure, and/or government mandates? Teachers within the organization? Students and their needs?
3. How and to what extent have your colleagues and students participated in the formulation of school purposes?
4. How and to what extent are you and all your colleagues truly engaged in the work of continuous improvement and capacity-building?
5. How and to what degree do the stated purposes of the organization focus the work on continually improving each student's learning and life chances?
6. How might leaders shorten or make more visible the "learning horizon" for teacher colleagues in order to make the consequences of pupil learning more direct and able to be learned from?
7. In what ways and to what extent does the school culture encourage and enable teachers as continuous inquirers into what they do and how they might do it better?
8. How often and in what ways do educators competently engage in a sustained dialogue in order to improve the quality of teaching and learning?
9. How and to what extent do you and your teachers consume, critique, and produce new knowledge?
10. How and to what degree do all your colleagues demonstrate through their day-to-day behavior a commitment to school purposes and continuous improvement?
11. How and to what extent do educators care about themselves and one another in the same way they care (or ought to care) about their pupils?
12. How and to what extent do classroom practices and assessment procedures demonstrate coherence from classroom to classroom?

FOR FURTHER READING

Fullan, M. (2003). *The moral imperative of school leadership.* Thousand Oaks, CA: Sage.
     Moral leadership can reinvent the principalship and bring about significant improvement in students' lives.

Hargreaves, A. (2003). *Teaching in the Knowledge Society*. New York: Teachers College Press.

When test scores serve as a proxy for school quality, this book builds an eloquent and compelling case for moral vision and social commitment in schools.

Sergiovanni, T. (1992). *Moral leadership: Getting to the heart of school improvement*. San Francisco: Jossey-Bass.

A seminal book about bettering the life chances of all students and the roles school leaders can play in that endeavor.

CHAPTER 2

The Principal and the Curriculum

How school leadership conceives of curriculum frames the work of the school. In this chapter you will learn

- to challenge underlying assumptions about the nature of curriculum and what this means for students;
- to rethink how we understand curriculum and to frame it in ways that are helpful for all learners;
- to debunk many myths about curriculum and how youngsters learn;
- important lessons about enduring understandings, meta-cognition, rethinking time, and broadening perspective on curriculum and teaching; and
- to uncover students' intentions as a basis for negotiating the curriculum with a view to meeting the learning needs of all.

Laura, a principal of great vigor and passion, strode down the hallway propelled by purpose and determination. Her love for her work and her belief in what she does was immediately obvious. Lest we be left behind, we visitors hurried to keep up with our energetic host. This delightful country school, Calgarrick in Victoria, Australia, is a popular visitor site because its teachers and pupils use technology in creative and meaningful ways. Laura excitedly described and showed examples of the electronic portfolios all pupils maintained, the graphs they made with Excel, the artwork they created and scanned, the stories they wrote, and an informative school website where parents could access their child's page. She produced a range of impressive samples produced by every pupil and teacher.

Visiting from overseas, I was curious about the kinds of questions my fellow visitors would ask. The first was, "How do you get the teachers involved with all this technology and the website?" Laura's answer raised interesting questions about capacity. One highly motivated, technologically proficient teacher, she said, had brought about most of these achievements. This individual created the website, loaded the student work onto it, enabled parent access, set up the accounts, and provided training for colleagues.

The second question raised was about training teachers. By all accounts, staff development followed a commonplace approach of providing workshops and some specific training by the technologically enabled teacher. Workshops, perhaps useful for building awareness, by and large do not have a very good record of affecting learning and practice of teachers.[1] Even if effective in engaging participants in the short term, workshops alone cannot support or sustain the ongoing learning that is required. Teachers need to build deeper understanding of their craft knowledge.

Calgarrick School, like many others, was incorporating network communication into the work of the classroom. From what I could tell, this model school uses the Internet merely as a library of resources for pupils producing reports and projects. Visitors raised more questions:

- How and to what degree does using the Internet transform, fundamentally change, improve, or inhibit effective teaching and learning?
- How and to what extent does the use of the Internet change or improve classroom discourse?
- How and to what extent does student involvement in Internet-related projects enable or promote higher-level cognitive work of goal-setting, planning, questioning, synthesizing, problem-solving, and monitoring?

As interesting as these questions are, of equal importance were the many questions not asked during our visit:

- How effective are electronic portfolios, and how does the school measure their effectiveness?
- How do they compare, and in what ways are they different from or better than, regular portfolios?
- How and to what extent has embracing technology changed, improved, or inhibited student learning, and does the school know what effect technology is having?

Often when we're confronted with a new innovation, we become so enamored with the innovation itself that we seem to forget to ask fundamental questions such as these.

During my visit, the dynamic Laura explained to me that it was important to her that teachers and their pupils use technology effectively and often. She said, "I don't really care about the curriculum, or what specifically they do, as long as they are using technology." Her feeling that technology will have only a positive effect on teaching and learning if all learners use it frequently and consistently is an interesting assumption. To that end, it is fair to say that she has been entirely successful, although it was not apparent how this affected student learning. However, this points to a hypothesis that I have long held, that *the principal's conceptions of curriculum frame the work of the school.* In other words, what principals believe curriculum to be determines what they ask their teachers to do. In Laura's case, clearly, the way she perceived curriculum and technology framed the work for her colleagues.

CONTRASTING RESPONSES TO MANDATED CURRICULUM

In visiting a number of schools in Ontario when their principals introduced a new government-mandated curriculum to their colleagues, I observed other examples of the principal's influence.

Eagle Ridge Elementary's new principal, Margaret, called a meeting early in the school year to explain the implementation of the New Ontario Curriculum to her staff. Eagle Ridge is a very diverse, multicultural, high-immigrant, and multilingual school. Having just been appointed to the school, her second principalship in a kindergarten-through-grade-6 school, Margaret seized upon the new curriculum as the means of making her priorities clear. "Here's the scoop on the new curriculum," she said. "The government has mandated its implementation, so we don't have any choice in the matter. So here is what I propose. There are seven curriculum documents. I have assigned each of you to one of seven teams. Each team, over the coming months, is to complete a match/mismatch comparing the new curriculum with current practice between what we are currently doing and what we will need to do to implement the curriculum fully. Hopefully, you will also identify some things we no longer need to cover as well." Like many of her principal colleagues, for Margaret, the mandated curriculum is a given. It is non-negotiable, a question of compliance—of "covering the curriculum."

I found Margaret's arbitrary structure surprising, as the school, under Margaret's predecessor, had operated five inquiry-based teams that had been meeting to examine the experiences pupils were having with various aspects of the curriculum. Teachers were very committed to this work. When teachers asked about continuing this inquiry work, they were told they could continue the work on their own time if they wished, as the new curriculum would now supersede this inquiry stuff. This example of how one principal succeeds another raises some interesting questions about principal succession.

The principal raised no questions about the appropriateness of the curriculum, even though most educators were aware of just how quickly the curriculum had been assembled and that little of its content had been tested. There was no question about its length, even though most teachers have complained for years (particularly in the upper grades) about how rushed teaching and learning have to be in order to "cover" the curriculum. There was no question of adaptation, of negotiating the curriculum according to student needs. Margaret only wanted her staff to find out what was being and would have to be covered.

Margaret assumed that her vision of how her school should change was the one to implement. But any meaningful change requires individual implementers to work out their own meaning of the change.[2] By this I mean that it is hard for leaders to impose their own vision upon their colleagues when there is no value in or process for teachers collectively creating their own meaning, which they inevitably do. Astonishingly, for Margaret, there appeared to be no explicit relationship between the purposes of the school, the particular needs of the pupils who attended Eagle Ridge, the improvement efforts of the past, the interests and passions of her colleagues, and the new curriculum.

In nearby Harvest Grove School, which is similar in size and makeup to Eagle Ridge, Susan, a principal who has been at the school for 5 years, explained the curriculum to her staff somewhat differently: "The New Curriculum documents haven't all arrived yet," she said, "but not to worry, as we have three years to work with them. I am thinking our teams will continue with the classroom inquiry-based work we have been doing. We can take this first year to get familiar with the documents. Let us see how and to what extent they will help further the goals of the school. Let us see if they really will support the needy and diverse learners we have in our community. Hopefully, as we delve deeper into teaching and learning, these documents will be useful in informing our discussions."

Susan clearly had a different conception of curriculum. For her, the paper curriculum was more of a road map, co-opted where appropriate to further the already clear purposes of the school. When I talked to Susan after the staff meeting, she explained that for her, the real curriculum was what went on between the ears of the learner in the classroom, and her role was to design the work of the school in order to improve that experience. For Susan, the curriculum was not a given. It was something more malleable, more negotiable, which truly informed, thoughtful practitioners adapt according to the purposes of the school and the needs of the learner. Susan clearly valued and was interested in promulgating teachers' professional judgment.

In secondary schools, during the same period, Ontario, like at least some jurisdictions in the United States and elsewhere in Canada, decided to mandate a literacy test for grade 10 pupils across the province in an effort to raise standards. This became a high-stakes test, as the results were publicly reported, school by school. More important, if a pupil failed to pass this standardized test even after possible retakes in grades 11 and 12, they would not graduate from high school. The implementation of this policy, enacted in a relatively short period of 18 months, provides interesting insights into how secondary school leaders view curriculum and assessment and respond to challenges on behalf of their students.

Devon was the principal of a large high school (grades 9–12) with a significant immigrant population. He met with his department heads, and they responded quickly to the testing initiative by first purchasing software for an adolescent skills-based reading program. They instituted a program in which each at-risk pupil was scheduled in small groups into the computer lab. The technology teacher received basic training in running the literacy program. They then planned to have the teachers of English rehearse all pupils' skills by having them frequently practice examples of the anticipated literacy test.

Helen, principal of a nearby secondary school, on the other hand, was more thoughtful in her approach. Initially, she decided it was important to find out about the reading and writing experiences of her pupils. On a given day, she had each teacher interview three pupils from each of their classes about their reading and writing habits and experiences. Collation of the results of these interviews by the school design team formed the basis for a lively discussion at the next staff meeting.

By having each teacher contribute to the data-gathering, Helen immediately began to frame the issue as one that involved all teachers. The results of the sampling surprised Helen and her colleagues. They discovered that there was very little reading and writing happening across the school and that what there was tended to be fragmented, isolated, and task-specific. By this they meant that most literacy activity was about reading or writing short paragraphs or sentences in order to answer a question or solve a problem. Moreover, the pupils' after-school employment and busy social and recreational lives left little time for reading and writing at home.

From the discussions, the teachers agreed to have the school design team significantly increase authentic opportunities for all pupils to read[3] and write.[4] The school implemented the DEAR (Drop Everything and Read) approach—for 30 minutes a day, teachers and their pupils read books of their own choice. Good authors recommended by the librarian and students were promoted, student book reviews shared, and pupil authorship encouraged and celebrated, with exemplary texts published for fellow pupils to read. Over time, excitement and commitment built around this activity. In emphasizing personal and social development and exploring the relationship between reading and writing, the program positively affected the kinds and amount of reading and writing students engaged in during their various subjects.

Two very different conceptions of literacy spawned two very different approaches to the task. In the first case, the tyranny of the test dominated the thoughts, views, and actions (reactions) of Devon and his department heads. They framed the task narrowly as getting their pupils through the test and proceeded accordingly. In a constructivist, proactive, and participatory approach, Helen first thought to engage her colleagues in finding out how and to what degree their pupils engaged in literate behavior. Only then did she begin to work with colleagues in order to devise a plan to improve literacy for all pupils. Helen framed the task more broadly by responding to the literacy issues identified by staff during their data-gathering. Clearly, in these cases, how the principal conceived of curriculum shaped the work of their school. Of course, it is not only school principals who have different conceptions of curriculum; often, school districts will respond to mandated curriculum policies from varied conceptual bases.

THE PRINCIPAL'S CONCEPTION OF CURRICULUM

How principals understand and represent the curriculum depends significantly on their understanding of what they perceive the curriculum and learner to be. If they perceive the pupil as an empty vessel, then the work of the school is just a question of covering the curriculum, stuffing the empty vessel full of knowledge, and urging and supporting the pupil through the test. A principal with this belief might be attracted to workshop training for his/her teachers such as "Teaching for Transfer," "Reinforcing Positive Learning Behavior," and those that focus on subject content. They would welcome standardized, one-size-fits-all, prepackaged programs. They would see the task of curriculum much as Margaret and Devon did in the examples above. Miller and Sellers define this viewpoint as the "transmission position."[5] They have found that educators embrace one of the following three positions, or meta-orientations, regarding curriculum (See also Figure 2.1):

- *Transmission Position.* The purpose of education is to transmit facts, skills, and values to pupils. This orientation stresses learning of traditional school subjects through traditional methodologies, particularly textbook learning, and an emphasis on basic skills and particular cultural values necessary to function in society. The teacher is the expert who by covering the curriculum imparts knowledge to the novice learner. For example, in teaching reading, teachers who hold a transmission position use textbooks, provide the student with little or no choice of topic or material, regularly engage in direct instruction through whole-group teaching, and see little value in the students' opinions, interests, or passions.

- *Transaction Position.* Here the individual learner is seen as rational and capable of intelligent problem-solving. Education is viewed as a dialogue between the pupil and the curriculum in which the pupil reconstructs knowledge through the dialogue process. Transactional teaching emphasizes curriculum strategies that facilitate problem-solving, the application of problem-solving to social and democratic contexts, and the development of cognitive skills within the academic disciplines. When teaching reading, teachers who hold this position foster student choice in topic and material while personalizing instruction according to perceived student need. At times individual and group instruction may be specifically directed toward helping students learn new skills as they require them. The teacher models good literate behavior by providing examples of exemplary texts and reading behaviors and facilitates dialogue about the meta-cognitive aspects of the task. Topic, resources, genres, and means of representing knowledge are negotiable but skills and strategy, when required, are not. Teacher and student tend to share control for the learning.
- *Transformation Position.* Here the focus is on personal and social change. It encompasses three particular orientations:
  - » teaching pupils skills that promote personal and social transformation;
  - » a vision of social change as a movement toward harmony with the environment rather than as an effort to exert control over it; and
  - » the attribution of a spiritual dimension to the environment, in which the ecological system is viewed with respect and reverence.

  Here, there is more overlap between the curriculum and the student's needs and intentions and more negotiation between teacher and pupil over the shape of the curriculum. Students have more voice in choosing topics and what they find compelling in the curriculum. In teaching reading, the transformative teacher will rely on the student to set goals and choose topics, materials, genres, and audience. Control over learning remains with the students wherever possible. Learning is very much a social affair. Teachers' interventions are focused on supporting the students in reaching their goals.

Figure 2.1. Summary of Teaching Positions

	Transmission	Transaction	Transformation
Aims/ Objectives	Behavioral Content Oriented	Complex Intellectual Skills	Integrated Objectives (e.g., Cognitive and Affective)
Content	Knowledge viewed atomistically as "objective"— content should reinforce traditional values	Knowledge is related to mental processes and cognitive frameworks— social content focuses on public policy questions	Personal knowledge is as important as public knowledge—social content stresses identification and resolution of pressing social concerns
Teaching Strategies	Structured teaching approaches— transmission of facts and values	Focus is on problem-solving and analysis— teaching strategies are matched to student developmental frameworks	Focus on connecting inner life of student to outer worlds— divergent thinking is encouraged
Organization	Subject-centered Hierarchical	Problem- centered Developmental	Learning-centered Integrative

In enabling pupils in her school to find a place for personal interests and topics through reading and writing, Helen is surely approaching a more transformational approach to learning in her school. Susan, by viewing the curriculum as malleable, co-opting it for school purposes, and adapting it to the needs of the individual, is taking both a transactional and a transformative approach. In being aware of and examining these three positions, principals can begin to clarify their own conceptions about curriculum.

LEADERSHIP AS MEANING-MAKING

Leadership is about taking the risk of managing meaning. Zaleznick was among the first to draw the distinction between managers and leaders, noting that managers pay attention to how things get done, while leaders pay attention to what events and decisions mean.[6] Bennis and Nanus take this a step further by arguing that leaders concern themselves with the organization's basic purpose and general direction and with articulating these ideas to others.[7] Others, such as Louis Pondy, emphasize that leaders' effectiveness resides in their "ability to make activity meaningful for others." Leaders give colleagues a sense of understanding of what they are doing. "If in addition, the leader can put [the meaning of behaviour] into words, then the meaning of what the group is doing becomes a social fact. . . . This dual capacity . . . to make sense of things and to put them into language meaningful to large numbers of people gives the person who has it enormous leverage," Pondy wrote.[8]

To be an effective leader today, principals must understand how to function as informed managers of meaning. The skill required to manage meaning is called "framing," and it has three components: language, thought, and forethought.[9] The language component is the most tangible of these. It helps us focus, classify, remember, and understand one thing in terms of another. Through framing we select and highlight one or more aspects of the issue while excluding others. Framing requires initiative, which includes both clarity of purpose and a thorough understanding of those for whom we are managing meaning. Values play an important role in the kind of framing that we do and the way in which we (and our frames) are perceived.

In the examples of Margaret, Devon, Susan, and Laura portrayed above, we can see how different leaders in a variety of school settings frame curriculum for their colleagues. Principals frame the curriculum in ways that reflect their beliefs and understanding. Occasionally, some might represent curriculum as framed by others, such as the district or government. Principals, in framing the curriculum for their colleagues, also define the opportunities for teachers to be more or less *empowered*, adept, and confident in *exercising* professional judgment; *capacitated*, because their workplace is the center of their own learning and development; and *committed*, with a sense of ownership, control, and voice in the curriculum decisions of the school. Participatory leaders, of course, develop frames with their colleagues and use them constantly and consistently to guide the work of the school.

RECONCEPTUALIZING CURRICULUM AND TEACHING

For many years now, evidence has grown progressively stronger for the claim that students adopt one of two quite distinct goals or orientations toward their own learning:[10] an intrinsic, or mastery, orientation; or an extrinsic, or performance, orientation.[11] Students with a performance orientation focus on getting good grades, cramming for tests, outperforming others, pleasing parents, winning approval from peers, and conforming for teachers. A performance orientation evokes the kind of superficial, rote learning that, over the long term, depresses both school achievement and the construction of personal meaning. Performance orientations fall within the transmission framework described above.

Students with a mastery orientation, in contrast, aim to increase their "competency, understanding and appreciation of what is learned."[12] When this orientation prevails, students are motivated to learn by engaging in the learning activity itself and the related feelings of novelty, competence, self-determination, and satisfaction of curiosity. Mastery approaches favor "deep-level, strategic processing of information which, in turn, leads to increased school achievement."[13]

Self-initiating, mastery-oriented pupils become actively engaged in analyzing the demands of school tasks, planning how to complete those tasks, and monitoring (that is, evaluating) their own progress. Mastery orientation falls within the transactional and particularly the transformative framework of learning described above. As one might expect, the orientation pupils take toward their learning is context-dependent in that how teachers present the curriculum and orchestrate classroom pedagogy over time largely defines how their pupils construe the learning task. Of real concern is evidence suggesting that when pupils are given extrinsic rewards for engaging in activity that is initially intrinsically interesting to them, they show a subsequent decreased interest in engaging in that activity. Figure 2.2 depicts a number of pupil characteristics that may be thought of as a continuum. With respect to the three teaching positions described above, transformative teaching would be at the far left side of this continuum, transactional would be somewhat to left-center, and the transmission teaching position would fall toward the right side.

Referring to the chart, on the first dimension, for instance, we see the student having complete ownership of topic and learning at one end of the continuum and being completely disenfranchised from learning at the other. Yet these positions are not absolute and, obviously, learners find themselves at different points on the continuum at differing times. However, the making of a lifelong learner requires pupils to experience an ever-increasing control over their own learning and to develop and maintain an intrinsic mastery orientation. Lifelong learners also seek patterns across their learning experiences, making connections to theories, ideas, and understandings they already have, and thus an integrated, multidisciplinary, and cosmopolitan approach is indicated. Students' orientation to curriculum, then, is not a pedagogical issue that can be ignored or left to typically eclectic approaches found within and across schools or, for that matter, the ideological whims

**Figure 2.2. Students' Learning Orientations as Exhibited by Their Behavior:
An Orientation Continuum**

Intrinsic Mastery Orientation Characteristics	Extrinsic Performance Orientation Characteristics
Ownership	Disenfranchised
Independent and interdependent	Dependent
Active learning	Passive learning
Inner-directed	Outer-directed
Pupil control	Teacher control
Empowered	Disempowered
Sense-making	Rote learning
Real applications	Contrived applications
Choice	Control
Negotiation	Arbitrary
Risk-taking	Risk avoidance
Students' theories and hypotheses	Experts' theories
Approximations	Standard forms
Context	Decontextualization
Development of multiple perspectives	Reliance on the expert's perspective
Integrated	Fragmented
Big ideas	Small parts and steps
Community-oriented	Textbook-oriented
Cosmopolitanism	Narrow-mindedness
Diverse perspectives	Limited perspectives

of the government of the day. I believe that an approach to curriculum is a deeply moral, ethical, and professional task, one that fearless school-based leaders and their communities must *take charge* of in an informed and mindful way.

Countering Popular Myths About Learning

In her book *The Power of Mindful Learning*, Harvard psychologist Ellen Langer identifies seven pervasive myths or mindsets (frames) that undermine the process of learning and describes how educators can avoid their debilitating effects in a wide range of settings:[14]

1. *The basics must be learned so well that they become second nature.*
   Learning basic skills in a rote, unthinking manner almost ensures

mediocrity. However, if we can learn the basics but not overlearn them, we can vary them as we change or as the perspective and/or situation requires.

2. *Paying attention means staying focused on one thing at a time.* We have all taught pupils who appear inattentive and distractible and are told to pay attention, focus, or concentrate on the specific task. Many of these same pupils have little problem paying attention when they have a choice in how they learn or explore a complex aspect of play, as in an extended computer game. Langer suggests that we reframe the concept of distraction by conceiving of it as being otherwise attracted.[15]

3. *Delaying gratification is important.* Implicit in the concept of delayed gratification is that work activities (including school) are necessarily arduous and unpleasant. Langer's studies show that work can become more like play when choices open up for the learner and when the learner's interests and preferences are honored.

4. *Rote memorization is necessary in education.* Memorization is a strategy for taking in material that has no personal meaning. Students able to do that successfully pass most tests on the material, but when they want to make use of that material in some new context, they have a problem. Learners need to know about the tentative nature of their learning and to be mindful and active in applying it to varied contexts and through varied perspectives.

5. *Forgetting is a problem.* It is easier to learn something the first time than it is to unlearn it and then learn it differently. In her experiments, Langer was able to show that subjects shown examples prior to a task came up with far less innovative solutions to problems than participants who were shown no examples.

6. *Intelligence is knowing "what's out there."* Many theories of intelligence assume that there is an absolute reality out there, and the more intelligent the person, the greater his or her awareness of reality. Langer proposes an alternative view in which individuals always define their relationship to their environment in varied ways, essentially for themselves creating the reality that is out there.

7. *There are right and wrong answers.* Langer argues that the capacity to achieve an outcome is different from the ability to explore the world and understand experience. Trying to solve a math problem in a way dictated by the teacher is different from attempting to test one's own hypothesis. There is an important place in learning for estimation, informed guessing, and hypothesis-building that is often squeezed out of the classroom in the pursuit of standards, preparing for tests, and covering the curriculum.

Mindfulness Versus Mindlessness

It is important, in addressing myths such as these in education, to take (collectively) a more *mindful* approach to the curriculum, teaching, and learning. In Langer's definition, "A mindful approach to any activity has three characteristics: the continuous creation of new categories; openness to new information; and an implicit awareness of more than one perspective."[16] She compares this to *mindlessness*, which, in contrast, "is characterized by an entrapment in old categories; by automatic behavior that precludes attending to new signals; and by action that operates from a single perspective."[17] Her studies raise important questions about pedagogy, especially as it relates to lifelong learning. In Figure 2.3, Langer further elucidates our understanding about mindfulness when she compares it to intelligence.[18] Intelligence, as she describes it, is a constrained worldview where the learner has less control, is reliant on others' expertise, and has little opportunity to construct meaning and alternatives for themselves. A more mindful approach to teaching, learning, and the curriculum is to me more morally compelling than a mindless, constrained, standardized approach as portrayed by Langer's notion of intelligence.

For example, I was observing a high school science class where a pupil was arguing for an alternative view of the theory of gravity. The young man was convinced that there had to be exceptions to Newton's laws of

Figure 2.3. Differences Between Intelligence and Mindfulness

Intelligence	Mindfulness
Corresponds to reality by identifying the optimum fit between individual and the environment	Controls reality by identifying several possible perspectives from which any situation may be viewed
A linear process moving from problem to resolution as rapidly as possible	A process of stepping back from both perceived problems and perceived solutions to view situations as novel
A means of achieving desired outcomes	A process through which meaning is given to outcomes
Developed from observing expert's perspective, which focuses on stable categories	Developed from an actor's ability to experience personal control by shifting perspectives
Depends on remembered facts and learned skills in contexts that are sometimes perceived as novel	Depends on the fluidity of knowledge and skills and recognizes both advantages and disadvantages in each

gravity. The teacher took the argument as an affront and declared it was impossible for anyone to challenge the universality of gravity. Later, I read in a science magazine that some theorists are indeed challenging the laws of gravity.[19] This example raises the ethical and pedagogical question of how important getting the right answer and covering the curriculum can be if the cost is disabling the learner's facility to question and develop his or her own hypothesis.

Coming at this discussion from an entirely different perspective, that of the arts in education, Eisner argues that the major outcomes of good education are not test scores but rather the willingness of students to explore ideas on their own.[20] These are the kinds of critical skills students are able to employ in tasks outside classrooms, through the strength of their curiosity in pursuing the issues they will inevitably encounter over the course of their lives.

In working with the curriculum, principals today are required to bring a critical edge to deciding how to use curriculum within their schools. That means collectively asking and answering hard questions:

- How and to what extent does the curriculum enable, engage, and excite *all* pupils?
- How and to what extent does the curriculum and the experience it engenders promote and develop improvisation, novelty, and diversity of outcomes (as Eisner unabashedly endorses[21]) as educational virtues?
- How and to what extent does it support the agreed-upon purposes of the school?
- How and to what extent does it promote equity, success, and satisfaction for the socioeconomically varied, multicultural, multilingual, and diverse learners in your school?
- How does the student's orientation to the curriculum foster or hinder the development of an intrinsic and mastery orientation to learning?

This plea for more creativity and ingenuity presents a tall order for schools. Innovation is rare. According to Marshall this may be "because it relies on one of the great imponderables: imagination. We're talking about an extraordinary thought process—the dedicated, persistent application of a free thinking, rule flouting, boundary crossing, convention busting mindset."[22] Mindset is developed in the early years and, arguably, our graduates are not likely to suddenly become innovative as adults if they haven't had many opportunities to be creative and seek alternative hypotheses during their formative years.

Strategies for Making Meaning in an Overloaded Curriculum

Curriculum overload and fragmentation are a challenge in most districts in Canada and the United States, where we have experienced the "add-on" curriculum—one that has been constantly expanding over the past 50 years. Mindlessly rushing to "cover" an ever-expanding curriculum leaves the learner with little lasting understanding and promotes a reliance on transmission-type teaching. In an effort to manage and find meaning within the overloaded curriculum, the following strategies have proved helpful to me.

Identify Enduring Understandings. One promising approach is to identify enduring understandings, or "big ideas," that underpin the curriculum in order to establish priorities. The purpose of enduring understandings is to help teachers identify those expectations that are of greatest priority and intrinsic value so that pupils can better identify "where they are going." Enduring understandings focus our learning and reduce overload. They are the learnings likely to spawn higher-order thinking skills, creativity, and ingenuity. Enduring understandings need not replace curriculum documents. Rather, they provide a selective lens through which to view the curriculum for the purposes of identifying that which is most appropriate/important for the pupils in your community.

When determining what constitutes an enduring understanding within the curriculum, educators consider the following:

- What has long-lasting and intrinsic value in the broader local, ecological, and planetary context beyond the classroom?
- What resides at the heart of the discipline (knowledge, skills, applications), and how can these be applied in a cross-disciplinary approach?
- What would engage pupils in learning? What is relevant to their and their community's needs?
- What lends itself to exploring more interdisciplinary and cosmopolitan patterns when teaching?

Focus on In-Depth Learning. My experience says that learning less material better, rather than rushing to cover a curriculum, will in the long term improve the learning of all. Pupils who are steeped in questioning, inquiry, hypothesizing, and improving ideas in one context find no difficulty in applying the approaches and, in particular, the understandings they've gleaned, to another. Choosing less follows the identification of and focus on the enduring understandings in order to spend time examining, exploring, arguing, improving, presenting, and teaching one's discoveries and theories to others. This strategy enables learners to engage in approaches that privilege higher-order thinking and strategic processing of information and are associated with the intrinsic mastery orientation described above, and to behave as a lifelong learner might.

Adapt Instructional Time. Most curricula that reach the classroom learner are structured around time. Particularly in secondary school, courses are equated with seat time (time spent in the classroom studying the course material), as they have been for the past 100 years. Curriculum defined by time is easier to schedule and it makes it easier to equate the accomplishments of one learning experience with another. The assumption that all pupils require the same time to learn and accomplish similar outcomes is spurious. Differing pupils who exhibit differing strengths, learning styles, aptitude, language, and cultural experiences obviously require differing amounts of time.

In terms of curriculum, it becomes a question of how the school can adapt instructional time: by providing additional tutorials for those requiring more time or by negotiating augmenting activities for those who require less. Schools where it is commonplace for teachers to negotiate goals, topics, and outcomes likely have greater flexibility in adapting to specific needs.

Foster Meta-cognition. Meta-cognition is about understanding what it takes to be a learner, a problem-solver, a lifelong learner, a reader, a writer, or a scientist. David Olson tells us that it is about developing a deep understanding of and the appropriate language to determine the nature of the learning that is required to complete a task.[23] It is about making transparent how one learns through critical self-reflection. Developing meta-cognition requires deliberate opportunities for learners to discuss the way they process knowledge—how they go about learning to read, write, speak, listen, and so forth. Meta-cognitive learning is key to enabling one set of understandings to be transferred to other contexts and disciplines. It is vital in enabling students to understand learning tasks and teacher expectations.

Encourage Interdisciplinary Teaching. Interdisciplinary teaching enables teachers and their students to look across subject guidelines and find commonalities, compelling relationships, and natural fits between varied topics and outcomes. It is not only efficient but also, more importantly, encourages students to explore these interrelationships. It mindfully fulfills every student's natural quest to find pattern and meaning in what can at times appear to be a curriculum that dishes up isolated and fragmented bits of knowledge and skills. It parallels the real world, where work is no longer defined by single disciplines but by multidisciplinary tasks. Interdisciplinary teaching lends itself to developing the planetary perspective I discuss below.

Incorporate Learning in the Real World. Classrooms, at best, provide limited representation or simulation of the real world but are no substitute for it. Youngsters need to be out in their world, working directly with experts in the community to study and solve real and practical problems and learning to collaborate with people of all ages. Activities such as class trips, class exchanges between rural and urban classes (where students get to stay with families in a completely different context from that which they normally experience), visits to science laboratories, community improvement projects such as cleaning up a habitat or protecting a bog, and working with younger pupils or with the elderly are just a few examples of what should be commonplace rather than once-a-year events.

Develop Community Perspective. Community, when engaged with and integral to school, contributes to compelling purposes and provides support for learners within and beyond the school. For many pupils, schools represent perhaps their first, and hopefully a constructive and lasting, experience with community. The curriculum and learning experience should provide pupils with opportunities to develop loyalty, fidelity, kinship, and a sense of identity, obligation, duty, responsibility, and reciprocity.[24] The curriculum must provide integral opportunities for communities to develop learning experiences that reflect their interests, needs, values, and aspirations, and that are responsive to the local context.

Embrace a Planetary, Rather than Global, Perspective. When creating an educational vision for the 21st century, a planetary perspective contrasts appreciably with a global perspective. The language of globalization is first and foremost used for commercial purposes, which are destroying the very natural resources that feed growth. Noted ecological economists Herman Daly and Joshua Farley call this a failure of the growth economy to respect the biophysical limits of its host, because growth demands ever-spiraling consumption—the purchase, use, and disposal of products.[25] In embracing a planetary perspective, educators can provide a counterbalance to globalization and raise questions that seek to uncover the interrelationships between learners, varied disciplines (including ecology, economics, biology, and geology), and the current state of the planet, with a view toward creating and envisioning structures and activities to address our most vital future needs.

Practice Sustainability in Education. Following from the planetary perspective, an environmentally sustainable economy is one directed by economic policies based on sound ecological principles: the unconditional commitment to healthy ecosystem services, protection of biodiversity, and recognition of the sanctity of water, air quality, energy, and nutrient and climate cycles.[26] Extrapolating principles of sustainability emerging from sound ecological practices has contributed to our understanding of sustainability in education.[27] Sustainability is the capacity of a system to engage in the complexities of continuous improvement consistent with deep values of human purpose.[28] In other words, continuous improvement, driven by morally compelling purpose, underpins issues of sustainability in education.

Curriculum cannot be cast in stone—it needs to be adaptable to the realities of the learners and their experiences, passions, and strengths. Sustainable educational practices are most likely to occur in schools that engage in sustainable living practices. One such school I visited recently has developed a remarkably large, successful, and sustainable garden using the principles of permaculture, which is permanent agriculture that can be sustained indefinitely. Permaculture effectively demonstrates examples of positive sustainable solutions to climate change, oil dependency, and potential economic decline. The attractive garden, designed to provide fresh food and herbs, contributes to school lunches. It also harvests and recycles water, keeps chickens on a bed of shredded paper left over from classrooms to form compost, and maintains a worm farm and beehives. All this in an inviting planned garden with fruit trees, berries, and a solar-powered waterfall and outdoor lighting. Students are truly learning in the "real" (or natural) world, where energy, resources, and food are regenerative and sustainable and little is wasted.

The principle behind this remarkable garden illustrates an important idea underpinning this book. How we live our lives acculturates in us important values that fortify our fundamental beliefs and behavior. In the case above, students and their teachers daily, through the life they live, embrace the principles of sustainability by way of their actions and talk. When it comes to sustaining gains and continuously improving the life chances of all their pupils, these teachers already have a deep appreciation for the principles involved.

The curriculum, then, is much more than subjects, lists of outcomes, high expectations, and test results. Teaching is not so much about delivering or rushing to cover a curriculum as collectively developing values, learning, and learners. It is very much about the kind of human beings and learners we want in our society. Teaching is about providing a counterpoint to the

knowledge economy and globalization by building character and fostering the values of community, democracy, humanitarianism, social justice,
planetary perspective, and cosmopolitan identity.

A WAY FORWARD:
THE NEGOTIATED CURRICULUM

In this chapter, I have identified many issues and opportunities relating to
the nature of curriculum and its impact on student learning. As I have discussed, a curriculum cast in stone, mindlessly covered, or applied without
adaptation to each and every diverse learner diminishes the life chances of
many. This has serious moral and practical implications for teaching and
learning. I am not arguing for the abandonment of centralized curricula but
rather for teacher, students, and, to some extent, parents to engage in a negotiation of experiences and outcomes that embraces the strengths, learning
styles, diverse abilities, and interests of all learners. This is not some laissez-
faire strategy, but a sophisticated, informed, motivating, and professional
approach to teaching and learning. Some 25 years ago, the gifted Australian
educator Garth Boomer proposed just such an advance.

In Boomer's rigorous model (see Figure 2.4),[29] teachers continue to
find worthwhile curriculum content and the appropriate enduring understandings that will enable them to develop the key principles and concepts
required for accomplished learning. These may be considered the non-
negotiable part of the curriculum. When initiating a new course of study,
the teacher talks openly with students about the topic of inquiry, why it was
chosen, why it is relevant, and what hindrances prevail. The talk centers on
what the pupils already know, what they would like to know, what varied
perspectives will assist, how the teacher thinks the new information and
understandings may be learned, how the necessary tasks may be shared, a
time frame, and what constraints the pupils have. The next step is for the
teacher and pupils to plan the unit, the activities, the broad outcomes, the
assignments, and the negotiable options. Collaboratively, a closely structured unit of work is prepared in which the class, the groups, each pupil,
and the teacher contract to contribute. Typically, rather than hiding the plan
in the teacher's planning book, it is posted in large print on the classroom
wall for all to see and for revisions to be collectively made.

Negotiation fosters the unforeseen learning related to the topic, the
serendipitous, the novel, and other incidental learning to be incorporated
along the way. The unit, however tightly planned, is open to negotiation
at all points by either the teacher or pupils. In such negotiation, the teacher
(who is extraordinarily knowledgeable about the student) is mindful of the

many important issues raised in this chapter. Specific objectives cannot be set in advance, for that would effectively sterilize the exploratory approach. Rather than the teacher and students proceeding down a narrow, direct path, a list of outcomes in hand, through negotiation they explore the expansive territory of the topic, related disciplines, and serendipitous discoveries. The power of Boomer's model lies in the uncovering of teachers' and students' intentions—and the responsiveness to pupil intentions, prior knowledge, learning abilities, learning style, and the ensuing intrinsic motivation and responsibility that follows.

Accomplishing the products of learning, whether written, constructed, modeled, painted, recorded, dramatized, or shared, enables teacher and pupils to carry out a critical process of assessment and reflection. This is when students share what they value in one another's work—when there is constructive comparison, informed response, respect for quality, and celebration of accomplishments. This is where teacher and pupils exhibit meta-cognition, making explicit their learning and their knowledge of how they learned. This model promotes clear thinking and self-aware, self-actu-alized teachers who believe in the learning power, interests, intentions, and resources of their students.

Boomer describes these kinds of effective teachers, who are able to rigorously negotiate the curriculum, as "hard headed, articulate theoriz-ers about practice, not plagued by guilt about what they cannot do, nor defenceless against attackers, armed as they are with both their theory and obvious quality of practice. . . . Their greatest allies are their students, and the parents of their students who are brought into the collaboration."[30]

Negotiating the curriculum honors teachers' professionalism by enabling them to respond personally and pedagogically to the varied needs of their diverse learners and to teach in a transactional and/or transformative way. It means deliberately planning to invite students to contribute to, and to modify, the educational program, so they will have a real investment in both the learning journey and the learning outcomes. The process goes a long way toward improving pupil engagement and intrinsic value in learning. Negotiation means that there are very real opportunities to adjust the time and support requirements for each pupil, depending on individual needs. It also means making explicit, and then confronting, the constraints of the learning context and the non-negotiable requirements that apply to it.

Let's examine an example of this process in action—just one small part of a study of weather and climate undertaken by some grade 5 students. Previously teacher Mandy at Southern Cross Public School has introduced her class to the unit by giving a brief overview of the inquiry and iden-tifying a few non-negotiables that she records on the whiteboard. These include a number of enduring understandings that she has identified and

Figure 2.4. Negotiating the Curriculum

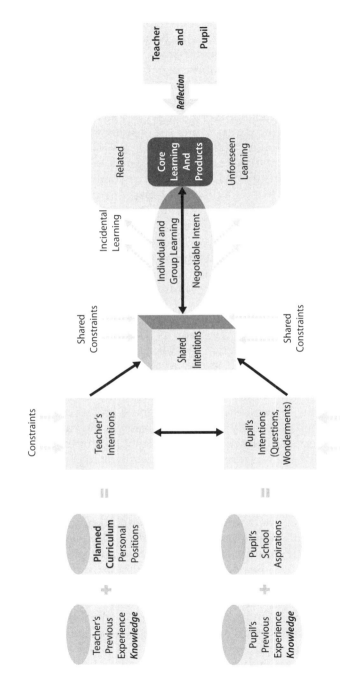

clear expectations about group work, individual work, and the variability and quality required in class projects and presentations. We pick up the story where Mandy introduces the class to some new ideas by way of a short video about the water cycle. She provides the class with a picture image of the cycle, illustrated in Figure 2.5. By this time, students who are working in groups have negotiated topics of interest and are working on a variety of projects. They take the cycle picture away to determine if and how they might be able to use the cycle to inform their study and eventual presentation.

One group of four girls examining the water cycle image in depth eventually come to understand how it works and how it would indeed enhance their particular project on how weather develops. Mandy had the girls (as she did some of the other groups) record their conversation on a tape recorder as part of her ongoing action research into her teaching and student learning. As shown in the diagram, the water cycle introduces some quite challenging vocabulary for these 11-year-old students. *Transpiration, evaporation, condensation, precipitation,* and *accumulation* are not only difficult words to understand, they are also difficult words to pronounce.

As we listen to the tape we find the group talking their way around the cycle. With the exception of Lisa, who although deliberate and slow

Figure 2.5. The Water Cycle

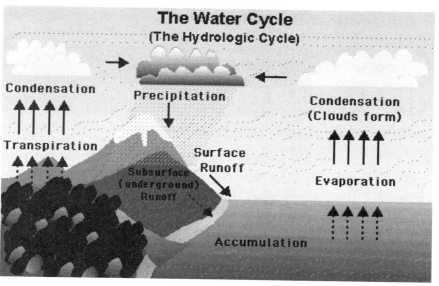

Source: Zoomschool.com

in her pronunciation is able to get her tongue around the words, the other three girls struggle.

They know that the cycle begins as water evaporates or transpires from trees and plants. Through the questions they ask, meaning is negotiated and uncovered. Mandeep says, " . . . and the water goes up . . . " Brigitta responds, "But how can water go up, it is too heavy?" Lisa suggests "It becomes vapor; it is not as heavy so it can go up into the sky . . ."Over a period of 40 minutes the girls continue talking their way around and around the cycle. Each time they have questions for one another. What is noticeable is that each time their pronunciation and understanding improve, although not all at the same rate. Mandeep, an English language learner, struggles, but her classmates help her as they, too, improve pronunciation and meaning.

At the end of the student-led talk Mandy sits with the group and listens as they explain their understanding of the water cycle. She questions their interpretation and explanations. The children answer with insight and poise. Mandy is mightily impressed with the depth of understanding and the confidence demonstrated by the group as they explain what they have learned. She then moves to discuss where they plan to go with this newfound understanding. The group has already decided that they want the water cycle to be at the center of their project and presentation. Mandy pushes them on how this will or will not deepen their classmates' understanding of weather and climate. She then introduces a new idea. She explains an experiment whereby they can replicate the water cycle. The students are to place a small container in the middle of a large, clear bowl. They fill the bowl with a little water, being careful not to fill the small container inside. Covering the bowl with plastic wrap and fastening the plastic wrap around the rim of the bowl with a large rubber band or string, they are to create a miniature weather system. A weight on top of the plastic wrap in the center keeps the space constant. The girls are then to place the experiment in the window where the sun shines and record their observations over time. The students observe as a mist forms under the plastic wrap that with time forms larger drops that begin to drip like rain.

The students have negotiated their topic and within that framework have considerable control over how they will proceed. They are decision-makers who make important decisions about their own learning. What is happening with the water cycle dialogue is that each time the students talk their way around the cycle, their approximations and representations of meaning become more accurate and precise. Initially they use words of their own limited vocabulary to try to explain what is happening, but with each recursive explanation they move slowly toward using the new vocabulary with closer approximations to correct pronunciation and more confidence in expressing the terms with meaning. With respect to teaching positions, this student-led process may be described as transformational learning. The students drive the process, each questioning and representing meaning in terms of their current understanding, each reaching further to extend their construction of meaning as the process continues. They are totally engaged! As we move into the experiment that Mandy suggests, we are moving into more transactional teaching.

THE PRINCIPAL'S ROLE IN THE CURRICULUM

In this chapter, I have shown that the principal needs to have a significant role in the school's curriculum—a curriculum that is not so much a deliverable product but, rather, a guide that enables us to proactively design, plan, and reflect on improving the learning experience and life chances of all our pupils. Used appropriately, curriculum ensures that each and every youngster has the chance to be his or her finest, regardless of talent and background. It promotes and supports high-quality teaching that is responsive to the different ways pupils achieve their best.[31] The key question for the principal is not how can we cover the curriculum, what program can we purchase to improve reading and writing, or how do we teach algebra but rather, how do pupils (and, for that matter, we teachers) learn? Answering this question is, in part, about understanding the learning pupils currently experience in your school. But it also requires a robust and informed theory of learning and curriculum.

Now, by "an informed theory of learning," I mean something other than being able to quote research findings on brain theory, multiple intelligences, learning styles, differentiated teaching and learning, knowledge-building, and so on. Developing an informed theory of learning doesn't mean attending a conference and adopting wholesale one approach or text, or cajoling your colleagues to improve scores on the league tables or standardized assessments. This is not to say principals shouldn't attend conferences or read research but rather that principals and teachers need to dialogue and act together based on their own best-educated understanding of how people internalize and apply new information and perform new operations. And they must do all of this in light of planetary issues, the knowledge society, and the local community they live in.

I am not arguing for the principal to be "the resident expert" in curriculum and learning theory. Rather, I want him or her to *take charge* by being a curious collaborator and a participant in a rigorous, robust dialogue with teacher colleagues around questions of how pupils learn and are learning, what they learn, and how this relates to the agreed-upon purposes of the school. Our children come to school in the early years questioning and theorizing about everything catching their attention. I suspect we lose much of the excitement and curiosity of the early years through the conformity, standardization, and sheer boredom of much of our schooling. Yet it is recognizing and valuing this very curiosity and hypothesizing that is necessary to approach the question of how our pupils learn, are learning, and might learn more effectively.

As innovations come along, it is important to understand and keep in mind the relationship between the innovation, the teacher, and the pupil. The innovation may take many forms. It may be a new resource such as a textbook, a new curriculum, new standardized measures, or new technology. Too often, we have let the innovation drive the change. As illustrated in Chapter 1, we have a choice of starting with the innovation or policy, with the teacher, or with the perspective and needs of the pupil. The implications are that school principals cannot merely be accepting of ever-expanding curriculum but need to bring a critical and moral edge to the judgment of how and in what ways the curriculum will support the purposes of the school and the learning of the individual.

Assuming a pedagogically informed approach to the curriculum in times of relentless pressures requires courageous, informed, and collegial leadership. How you as the principal, in dialogue with colleagues, frame the curriculum determines to a considerable degree the kind of learner who will graduate from your school. Pedagogical leadership roles require you to *take charge* by

- *Knowing your pupils well.* This includes engaging in many of the activities I will describe in Chapter 5. For example, in the primary school, this can mean having small groups of students bring all their work to share and celebrate. In the secondary school, it means meeting regularly with focus groups or classes of students and discussing their learning. In particular, I have always met with any pupil who is struggling with learning or social issues and typically get to know these individuals and their strengths, interests, and passions extraordinarily well. One key advantage of knowing students well is the ability to work closely with them to uncover their intentions in learning.
- *Engaging your teacher colleagues in an ongoing dialogue about purposes, curriculum, and pedagogy.* Come to know and enjoy the perceptions that your colleagues hold with respect to teaching, learning, and the curriculum. Encourage, nurture, and value the continuous informed dialogue necessary to build a deep understanding of teaching and learning. Informing this collective dialogue by incorporating the experiences of the students, data about how they learn, current

research, the perspectives of parents and students, and exemplary practices brings better judgment, passion, and commitment to the work of the school. Enacting purposes that will enable lifelong learning and facilitate a more intrinsic and mastery learning orientation while valuing novelty, improvisation, surprise, and diversity of outcomes is a monumental but rewarding task. It is ongoing, endless, and constitutes the real work of school leaders.

- *Framing the curriculum or innovation mindfully.* Intentionally or not, you will frame the curriculum for your colleagues. Better to examine it carefully, and if curriculum is not your strong suit (and it isn't for many principals), then seek expert help and guidance. This may take the form of a strong in-school design team, but also likely would include help from an informed mentor. Over the years, most of my mentors have been university professors.

- *Assuming the developers of the curriculum or innovation don't know your pupils as well as you and your colleagues.* Recognize that professional educators always mediate between the curriculum and the learner. Ensure that the mediation is deliberate, mindful, informed, and collective. Not all curricula are well designed; appropriate for your learning community; or supportive of the constructive, innovative, lifelong learner.

- *Capitalizing on those aspects of the curriculum or innovation that further the purposes of the school.* What is it about this new curriculum or innovation that will further the learning of all pupils? This is a key question for you and your colleagues to answer. Successful leaders learn quickly how to co-opt external innovation in ways that serve the articulated needs of their pupils and the purposes of the school and community.

- *Designing extensive support for inquiry and capacity-building.* Recognize that most innovations fail because designers consistently underestimate the quality and quantity of support needed to succeed. Recognize that building organization capacity requires teachers and their leaders to work and learn collectively more than individually.

- *Valuing the experience.* Recognize and plan for the experiential journey that professional inquiry and learning will provide for your colleagues. Positive experiences such as the joint examination of a critical teaching incident will further teacher relations, inquiry, professionalism, lifelong learning, and broadened perspectives; preserve continuity and security; and continue to build trust. The values, insights, curiosity, and excitement that characterize the professional lives of teachers can directly influence the kinds of values, interests, and excitement that pupils experience and the kind of learner your school graduates.

- *Involving parents, too.* A school that approaches the curriculum in the manner suggested by the arguments in this chapter needs to invest not only in the capacity-building of its teachers but also to seize every opportunity to educate parents. When parents develop capacity and commitment with regard to the work of the school, their interaction with their children can become increasingly supportive of school practices. Parents only know their own school experiences, and you can't embark on creating different experiences for their sons and daughters without their understanding and support.

- *Recognizing and acting with respect to the deep purposes of schooling that reach far beyond merely covering the curriculum, embracing standards, and getting test results.* This requires courage and fearlessness as you *take charge* and shape the work of the school around truly compelling purposes. It necessitates an understanding of the broader and local context, a mindful theory of learning, and profound appreciation for the learning needs of all your pupils.

REFLECT ON THESE QUESTIONS

1. How do pupils (and for that matter, we) learn? What is learning? Do we all learn in the same way?
2. Define how you frame curriculum in your school.
3. How and to what extent do you believe the curriculum to be malleable? Negotiable? For what reasons?
4. What evidence do you have that *all* pupils in your school have opportunities to develop improvisation, novelty, creativity, and a diversity of outcomes? To what extent?
5. How and to what extent does the curriculum enable and excite *all* pupils?
6. How and to what extent does the curriculum allow for diversity in learning styles, abilities, interests, linguistic ability, interests, and culture?
7. How frequently and for what purposes do all pupils get to ask questions of substance?
8. Can you define the relationship between specific pupil needs and the curriculum?
9. How are accomplishments in terms of curriculum assessed?
10. Is there provision for a diversity of means for pupils to express their understandings, accomplishments, hypotheses, and arguments?
11. How and to what extent are pupils and teachers able to make transparent and follow their intentions during the learning process?

12. In what ways and to what extent is the meta-cognitive aspect of learning made visible and accessible to all learners in all subjects and grades?
13. What evidence do you have that the curriculum supports all pupils in engaging in behaviors that prepare them for lifelong learning?
14. Given the diversity of needs, intentions, and aspirations of pupils throughout your school, what opportunities do or might they have to "negotiate" their experience with the curriculum?

FOR FURTHER READING

Langer, E. (1998). *The power of mindful learning.* Cambridge, MA: Perseus Books.

How students learn hugely effects how we should teach. Langer's profound insights show how we as a people can develop.

Langer, J. (2004). *Getting to excellent: How to create better schools.* New York: Teachers College Press.

This book provides powerful understandings into student learning and what makes highly effective schools.

CHAPTER 3

Using Classroom Evidence for Learning, Capacity-Building, and Accountability

Presenting an alternative to standardized testing, this chapter enables educators to use authentic information about students' learning experiences to inform and improve teaching and learning. In Chapter 3 you will learn

- how strong professional learning communities are social processes that turn information into knowledge and action;
- practical approaches to gathering data that inform teacher practice and student learning;
- how the frequent gathering of data about student learning experience underpins teachers' professional learning and development;
- that teachers who intensely and frequently engage with student data can transform the life chances of many; and
- an alternative way of responding to today's need for accountability by working more closely with students, colleagues, and parents.

Clarence looks more like a farmer than a principal, with his tousled hair, ruddy cheeks, bushy eyebrows, gnarled hands, and deliberate speech. Beneath this rugged exterior and demeanor, however, is one very savvy principal. Clarence, like many of his teachers at Dunkirk Public School, is troubled about the many students in his school who just do not seem to be able to get along. The staff is concerned about students' lack of engagement in classroom learning, as well as the constant playground disagreements and a disproportionately high number of altercations. Also worrisome are issues about the adequacy of the attention given by teachers to the needs of indigenous students. The consensus among Dunkirk staff was that cooperative learning, including increased engagement of pupils, improved interpersonal relationships, and better community involvement were sorely needed.

INITIATING COLLECTIVE PROFESSIONAL
LEARNING AND DEVELOPMENT

Clarence did many things most principals would do to improve the situation. He brought in consultants to present workshops, purchased resource materials on cooperative learning, and urged his teacher colleagues to try out some of the new approaches. He also took two actions that are less common. First, he committed one afternoon per week to personally teaching the school's most difficult class, using cooperative learning approaches. Second, he asked colleagues to share at weekly meetings their own and their students' experiences with cooperative learning.

I participated in Clarence's efforts as an external facilitator and advisor whose role was to support his work with colleagues on cooperative learning. I also met with Clarence monthly along with other nearby school teams working on school improvement when I provided training for principals and their staff representatives. I was privileged to witness the first sharing session at Dunkirk Public School. Clarence had cleared a wall of the staffroom, covered it with paper. and made two columns. The first he labeled "What I did" and the second, "What the pupils did." I arrived as he was documenting his first lesson in teaching the most challenging 7th grade class. By his account, it had been a disaster. He was teaching a geography lesson about the Canadian Shield. He had tried "Think-Pair-Share," a common cooperative learning strategy where students first brainstorm, meet with another student, then jointly share their efforts with another pair.[1] It was clear from what Clarence wrote on the chart that his pupils seemed to have little idea of how to complete the first part of the activity, brainstorming. The pairing activity worked reasonably well, except for a number of pupils who didn't want to pair with a particular neighbor. Finally, the sharing of his classroom teaching effort ended with his vivid rendering of how students, when meeting in groups of four, became totally confused, thus engendering pandemonium bordering on chaos.

Clarence's colleagues had many suggestions about how he might have improved his lesson, and the principal took this in good humor. He added a third column called "What I learned" while raising many questions of his own about classroom practice. Teachers described examples from classrooms, and two recorded their lessons on the chart that Clarence had prepared. He continued through the session demonstrating a genuine role of naivety, curiosity, and, above all, eagerness to learn.

A couple of weeks later, the sessions became even more dynamic. The wall chart was now full of teachers' lessons. A fourth column appeared between "What the pupils did" and "What I learned," titled "Consequences," which explored the actual accomplishments of the students. Teachers now brought samples of students' work from their classrooms. The teacher's narrative was energetic, with more faculty members contributing to the increasingly detailed charts.

Four months later, as I entered the school, the posting of weekly pupil awards for "acts of kindness" boldly stood in the foyer, and the staffroom walls were covered from ceiling to floor with teacher observations. Colorful documentation of student and teacher experiences now included photographs of classroom activity, samples of students' work and accomplishments, and two teachers' classroom videotapes. Teachers' stimulating discourse reflected opportunities to observe one another's lessons. New labels for the columns have evolved: (1) What I intended, (2) What happened, (3) Pupil engagement and interaction, (4) Achievements, (5) Questions we have, and (6) What we learned. These more specific categories demonstrated the growing sophistication in their observations and discussion.

In addition, Clarence had now posted a monthly summary of the number of behavior incidents by category recorded across the school over the 4-month period. A marked decrease in both verbal altercations and violence was evident. The sharing session now lasted for more than 2 hours. Clarence continued to evolve as a facilitator. More often than not, his questions started with "I am curious about . . . " With everyone enthusiastically contributing, the dialogue continued into the parking lot. What I find significant and like about Clarence and the role he played at Dunkirk are the following:

1. He abandoned the role of "the expert." He told me it took a long time to build the confidence to lead without having to speak as if he knew everything.
2. He modeled what he values for his colleagues. He was willing to take risks, to question, and to share his practice (both good and bad) and the experiences of his learners (information) as they adapted to new approaches.
3. He understands the importance of grounding teacher learning in the reality of and information about the learning experience of all their pupils. He values assessment for and as learning.
4. He appreciates and ensures that staff didn't merely collect information but, more important, made it communal knowledge to be interacted with (and, dare I say, interrogated) and acted upon.
5. He did not wait to develop the best model of teacher inquiry; he took action fast and worked with his colleagues over time to

collectively create a more sophisticated approach based on their experiences and needs.

6.   He urged his colleagues to articulate the lessons they were learning and enabled them to reflect on, extend, and improve their own and others' learning. In other words, he engaged his colleagues in a vibrant dialogue in which all participants were equal and listened with empathy while transparently challenging underlying assumptions.

7.   He valued and accepted the experience of his colleagues as a genuine representation of current work, and in doing so was able to use their experience (and his own) as a stepping-stone toward further growth and knowledge building.

8.   He perceived that his role was to make a difference in the lives of pupils and invested much of his time in actively participating in the professional learning of his colleagues and the organizational learning of his school.

In a nutshell, Clarence has developed sufficient confidence to demonstrate his own vulnerability as an effective tool to promote engagement and action with his colleagues. In fact, he "builds enduring greatness through a paradoxical blend of personal humility and professional will"[2]—a trait that describes a top-level leader in Collins's five-level hierarchy. Collins describes personal humility as demonstrating a compelling modesty, shunning public adulation, and acting with a quiet, calm determination that uses outcomes—not charisma—to motivate.

Attributes of a successful, professional leader include demonstrating unwavering resolve to do whatever must be done to produce the best long-term results and looking in the mirror to apportion blame and out the window to credit successes. In addition, Clarence clearly honors adult-learning principles in that he values the perspectives of participants, creates a criticism-free environment, builds on current experiences and questions of participants, and enables them to contribute to the developing agenda for their own personal and collective professional learning and development.[3]

HOW CAN PRINCIPAL LEADERS GATHER USEFUL INFORMATION?

School principals and their teacher colleagues have access to all kinds of information. They can purposefully gather specific information to improve their understanding of and practice surrounding teaching, learning, and the culture of the school.

Interviews and Surveys

Interviews and surveys can provide information, but their validity and utility are questionable. As principal at Lancewood Public School, a large K-8 school in Mississauga, Ontario, I worked with the professional growth (design) team made up of a representative group of teachers who had a passion for learning. Going out into the school as "explorers," we each met with about seven other staff members to complete interviews, the questions for which the team had worked on developing for several weeks and shared with the interviewees.

Explorers and their colleagues checked off a quantitative response after recording classroom evidence they brought to each descriptor. The checklist asked for frequency of the behavior: Few = 0–20%, Some = 20–50%, Many = 50–80%, and Most or Usually = 80–100%. These are the five areas of inquiry we used in the interviews and samples of the statements that we asked teachers to respond to:

1. *The Pupil as Learner.* The pupil has many opportunities to re-create, reconstruct, relive, and retell learning experiences. The pupil has many opportunities to talk to classmates and others about concepts he or she is exploring and about how he or she is learning the task at hand.

2. *The Pupil as Inquirer.* The pupil develops and asks clear and important questions about a topic. The pupil is adept at gathering a variety of data as a basis for hypothesizing and speculating about the questions at hand.

3. *The Literate Pupil.* The pupil reads voraciously and approaches reading with pleasure. The pupil sees him or herself as an author and a critic. The pupil understands reading to be a tool for growth and understanding.

4. *The Pupil and the Environment.* During the last few days, the pupil has investigated something he or she has observed in everyday life. The pupil develops and uses a variety of techniques for recording, reporting, and representing experiences with science (e.g., discussion, pictures, charts, graphs, drama, stories, models, newsletters, etc.).

5. *The Teacher and the Classroom.* The teacher encourages pupils to identify and pursue their own questions and interests. The teacher accommodates, through varied programming and expectations, pupils of differing abilities, learning styles, and experiences.

The explorers generated animated discussion and diversity of opinion as they met with colleagues to examine the statements. All teachers participated, generating close to 50 surveys to be analyzed by the design team. Although the schoolwide summary suggested a glowing experience for pupils across the school, my own observations of pupils' experiences indicated otherwise. For example, although teachers scored themselves highly on the literacy question, I observed many classrooms where there were no suitable reading books or evidence of pupils reading and very little evidence of engagement in writing activities. That being the case, what were the pupils reading voraciously? When and where were they doing this work?

The weakness of the interview and survey approaches, I believe, is that like most polls, they ask people for their opinions about an issue rather than getting at the evidence about and the nature of the issue or experience itself. Speaking to this last point, Carl Glickman, from his research, argues that in surveying teachers about their work, faculty in successful schools are less satisfied with regard to the adequacy of their teaching practice than are faculty in less successful schools, who are often unjustifiably positive.[4]

Language and Literacy Conferences

At Lancewood we continued to gather data. One of the most revealing activities we carried out was to have everyone on staff (including myself as principal) conduct language and literacy conferences with six students from each class, three who were identified as being successfully literate and three who were less than successful. This procedure was developed by Myra Barrs and others to enable teachers, even in the context of rigid curriculum and testing, to directly get at the experience and performance of students as they became more effective language users.[5]

The language and literacy conference gives the student the opportunity to discuss with the teacher(s) his or her experiences with classroom texts, as well as accomplishments and interests as a language learner.[6] The conferences usually occurred informally in a quiet part of the classroom, and the student brought a self-chosen selection of books or other texts that she/he had read recently. Students also brought some of their writing, both recent products and work in progress. The student would speak about him- or herself as a reader, writer, and language user, both inside and outside the school. The teacher's open-ended questions enabled the students to speak to their thoughts and feelings about their achievements, concerns, and areas requiring improvement in language and literacy. As the student read from a current text, the teacher noted the strategies used in approaching difficult words and the student's facility in comprehending and relating the meaning of the text to his or her own experiences and/or learning.

Depending on the purpose of the conference, the teacher may include an analysis of miscues to determine the strengths and weaknesses of a reader, a running record (a cumulative account of reading behavior over time), or other means to assess the pupil's ability to search for meaning. Teachers may also look for and record students' proficiency at picking up cues for meaning, structure, and visual and phonological information, as well as their strategies such as monitoring, prediction, searching, and self-correction.[7] Older students tend to be more private. However, they are usually very cognizant of their reading and writing habits. They are prepared to discuss their TV viewing habits, computer access, spare-time activity, their experiences with and use of story, and their leisure reading, including comic books and magazines.

At this point, we had enabled more than 40 professionals to spend quality time with 6 students each—that's a significant sample of more than 240 students from across the school. Initially, we shared our findings with teachers of similar grade levels. We then looked for patterns across grade levels—and several emerged. Perhaps what we found most telling was the rapidly diminishing opportunities for personal and leisure reading from grade 5 through grade 8. In addition, it was apparent that substantive reading opportunities were not available in the upper grades and that, for the most part, the range of expected genres in writing was not evident across the entire school.

These examples point to the importance of systemically and collectively gathering information to inform practice and learning across the school. However, we're not looking for just any information! The most useful information encompasses the bona fide learning experiences and accomplishments of each pupil.

GETTING TO THE HEART OF WHAT MATTERS

In Western societies, all kinds of information inundate schools: community, parent, teacher, and pupil surveys; standardized test data; checklists; portfolios; logbooks for literacy and behavior; curriculum guidelines; memos; and district or state/provincial standards and policy requirements, to name just a few. While some of this information helps efforts to understand and improve teaching and learning, much of it hinders or detracts from these efforts because it does not reflect the reality of the classroom and, in particular, the experience of students as they learn or fail to do so.

Pupil portfolios, audiotapes, videotapes, and authentic assessment measures are useful approaches to documenting the experience of the learner. However, what happens after this information is gathered is of vital importance. Information becomes knowledge only when it takes on a "social life."[8] Information not interacted with or acted upon is wasted. Persuasive information, particularly that which describes the experience of the learner, is often squandered by educators, not engaged with or used to inform the practice of the classroom and school.

Going Deeper Through Practitioner Research

We can go deeper into the information we collect by asking and answering hard but vital questions:

- What are the experiences of the learners in our schools?
- Are they adept at and confident in asking questions?
- How and to what extent do they define and solve problems? (Or do they solve problems at all?)
- How do they use texts?
- In what contexts do they read and write, and for what purposes and audiences?
- Do our students work independently? Interdependently?
- Are they becoming lifelong learners? How would we know?
- What are the practices that help or hinder the above? How would we know?
- How will we know if a new curriculum or innovation positively effects some or all of our pupils?

These are often troubling questions for school practitioners, and yet the answers are readily available, right in our classrooms. It is just a question of gathering significant information that all can interact with.

The professional learning capacity that Elmore seeks,[9] in order for schools and the practitioners who work in them to develop, incorporate, and extend new ideas about teaching and learning, is elusive. Capacity-building occurs through the continuous, deliberate, and systematic gathering, examining, and reflecting upon evidence that informs questions of pupil learning and/or classroom practice. Cochran-Smith and Lytle promote this view when they state that what is missing from the knowledge base for teaching is the inquiring voices of teachers themselves, the questions teachers ask, the ways teachers use writing and intentional talk in their work lives, and the interpretative frames teachers use to understand and improve their own classroom practices.[10]

This form of inquiry has been called *practitioner research*,[11] *action research*, and *classroom inquiry* to name a few. It can take many forms, but one helpful definition is provided by Kemmis and McTaggert, who define teacher research as

> a form of collective, self-reflective enquiry undertaken by participants in social situations in order to improve the rationality and justice of their own social or educational practices, as well as their understanding of these practices and the situations in which these practices are carried out. . . . The approach is only action research when it is collaborative, though it is important to realize that the action research of the group is achieved through the critically examined action of the individual group members.[12]

One significant part of evidence-gathering is the ongoing assessment procedures used by teachers across the school. By assessment procedures, I mean something other than marks, grade point averages, and percentiles. Earl argues that true assessment occurs when it informs teachers' instructional decisions.[13] It portrays images of teachers observing pupils, talking with them, and working with them to unravel their understandings and misunderstandings, transforming assessment into an integral part of learning that offers detailed feedback to the teacher and the pupil. When learners learn and move from neophytes to novices to experts, assessment *of* learning can illustrate models of performance and define what kinds of assistance, experiences, and forms of practice are essential to improve and extend students' performance.

The challenge for schools is to create a job-embedded infrastructure to enable the time, commitment, value, and passion required for this work. All of this ensures meaningful, morally compelling endeavors that are truly addressing the core issues of teaching and learning. Practitioner research has the potential to bring to light important theories about practice that have been long discredited as informal theory or "teacher lore." It can empower school practitioners by helping them discover their voices and resist attempts at de-skilling. It can build collegiality and a common community of learning among practitioners, which in turn provides a model of inquiry for students. But as Anderson, Herr, and Nihlen remind us, the promise of practitioner research is also subject to misuse.[14] But, if handled improperly, it can also become one more teacher in-service scheme that can be packaged and taken on the road, another implementation strategy cooked up by management to "build ownership" in schools for the latest centrally mandated reform. It can become just one more expectation, one more standard—one more thing teachers are expected to do.

Four Practical Strategies for Uncovering Learning Accomplishments

Effective teaching grounded in the intimate knowledge the teacher develops about the learner is essential in every classroom. By developing a deep understanding of each student's particular abilities, passions, and learning styles, teachers gather, examine, and question the most valuable and exclusive information available to schools. Below, I discuss four approaches to gathering this information. They provide a persuasive alternative to relying on standardized testing, as they focus on assessment for learning and, in many cases, involve students in a process that contributes to their own learning and appreciation of their own abilities and accomplishments. These strategies are depicted in Figure 3.1 and include:

1. Pupil Shadowing
2. Collaborative Classroom Inquiry
3. Taking a Slice
4. Following the Artifact Trail

Pupil Shadowing. Pupil shadowing is a powerful technique designed to deeply sample the experience of the few in order to better understand the experience of the many. The invaluable practice of pupil shadowing entails asking each teacher or a sample of teachers to spend a day or more per year observing and documenting the experience of a specific student in the school. This allows teachers to experience not only the teaching practice but also the culture of the school, deepening practitioners' appreciation for the life of the individual and the influence of the school. In designing this activity, it is important to consider whether to target a random sample student or a student from a particular category, such as an English language learner. In addition, it is important to orchestrate guidance and training for participating teachers to ensure that the observations are detailed, specific, and, to a degree, standardized. A simple observation sheet with two columns, the left being "observations" and the right being "interpretations," may suffice. Time at the end of the day enables the student to reflect with the observer on the observations (handwritten or typed) of what they are learning and how they might improve and adapt.

As a number of the documentations are completed, the observers need to meet with colleagues to discuss their notes and search for patterns across the observations. In larger schools this works well in small-group settings, where perhaps a half-dozen observational transcripts may be jointly examined. One method I have used is to have the observations photocopied, cut into idea-sized chunks, and then sorted by placing similar ideas together. Technology enables the same process. Using the naming technique described

Figure 3.1. Documenting the Experience of the Learner Leads to Improved Practice

UNCOVERING THE EXPERIENCED CURRICULUM
Going deeper with the information that tells

Practitioner Research
The action research of the group is achieved through
critically examined actions of the individual group members

Pupil Shadowing	**Classroom Inquiry**	**Taking a Slice**	**Artifact Trail**
Arrival-to-departure independent observer Older students are more participatory Pupil logs Analyze across cases	Journaling Observing Recording Photography Audio-taping Video-taping Interviewing Documentation Panels	*Sampling across age and subjects* All teachers All students A given time of day Standardized gathering Pupils can collect and contribute to the data	*The footprints that remain* **Pupil Work:** Explorations Investigations Demonstrations Applications **Teacher Work:** Plans Observations Visitations Mapping Documentation Panels

Engaging Information through
NARRATIVE IN TEACHER LEARNING, LEADING TO A GROWING SOPHISTICATION IN PRACTICE

Teachers as Knowledge Workers: Constructing, Improving, and Extending Teaching/Learning
Knowledge Building = Improved Practice, Collective Responsibility, and Accountability

in Chapter 7 (whereby participants seek to find an active phrase to capture the meaning of similar ideas), it becomes possible to quite objectively bring like observations together into patterns and to name or label the pattern. It is surprising how quickly a task like this can proceed when a group of six teachers works at it together. The results of this process require examination by larger groups throughout the school until everyone has had a chance to make sense of the data.

Pupil shadowing builds understandings among teachers about how students construe classroom and school life and how they have internalized, reshaped, or rejected institutional norms. In our 6-year study of secondary school reform in Ontario, in which we interviewed teachers many times during the project, it was surprising how few responses represented the student's perspective.[15]

Collaborative Classroom Inquiry. Teachers' observations, documentation, reflections, and writings, particularly when including all classes and students across the school, can be a primary means of deepening our understanding of student development over time, as well as building knowledge about teaching and learning. Unfortunately, perhaps because much of this research is private, it is often seen as an extra rather than as a core way of knowing the experience of the learner or as an underpinning for professional and organizational learning.

Classroom inquiry usually centers on a focus question. Often, the question will emerge from the ongoing dialogue and narrative that take place between knowledge-hungry colleagues. The focus question addresses something the teacher and his or her colleagues are genuinely curious about. Although this activity is fruitful when focusing on the experience of the learner, it is also very effective when teachers of similar topics, subjects, or age groups jointly develop lesson plans, teach lessons, and document and share the ensuing experiences and pupil outcomes. Commonly called "action research," it works well when associated with teachers' opportunities to take external curricular inquiry or teaching method courses with other institutions.

Taking a Slice. This in-school, cross-class sampling technique is useful in documenting the experience of curriculum learners in terms of the pedagogy they experience, and products or demonstrations of knowledge they produce. The "slice" may be *broad* or *specific* in nature. This is perhaps the most compelling strategy I know to help one's colleagues appreciate the journey learners take through the school and the impact classroom practices have on pupils over time. Learning is not an event but a journey—an ongoing process. This in-school, cross-class sampling technique enables teachers to move toward comprehending the student's experience through the ages, grades, and subjects over time. Here are some specific examples of the taking-a-slice inquiry:

- *A broad slice.* How much writing occurs in a school, and at what level, reflects the student's experience as an author, reporter, poet, critic, and researcher. At the end of a given day, all teachers taking a broad slice can have their students collect all of their day's writing and, with help from their teachers, display it by age/grade/subject/level on the floor of the gymnasium. Teachers review the writing but also form investigative groups to appraise the range of topics, genres, audience, ownership, response, quantity, quality, and so forth, that manifests across the age range of the school. Samples can be compared to exemplars, contrasted and analyzed for patterns, or grouped in ways that indicate similar or disparate kinds of progress.

- *A specific slice.* What evidence do we have that pupils in this school are able to support their arguments through research and inquiry? Teachers taking a specific slice would gather data on a given day demonstrating students' ability to build an argument. Samples might include visual and/or written projects, video or photographs of presentations, or interviews with representative pupils.
- *A literacy example.* Principals interested in inspiring improved literacy practices will want to be aware of the kinds and frequency of literate behaviors that pupils engage in across classes and subjects in their school. For instance:
  - » What is the frequency of fictional and nonfictional reading/writing across the grades/ages?
  - » For what purpose, in what genre, about which topic, for what audiences do students read in the school? In what ways does reading contribute to problem-solving?
  - » What strategies do successful readers use across the school?
  - » What strategies do less successful readers use across the school?
  - » What is the range of topics, genres, purposes, audiences, and choices in student writing across the school?
  - » How much writing occurs across the classes/subjects?
  - » What is the relationship between students' writing and content learning?
  - » What happens to the writing?
  - » What is the student's understanding of what it takes to be a competent writer?
  - » What is the student's understanding of what it takes to be a competent reader?
  - » In what ways does technology change or affect the development of writing competencies across the grades?

At Lancewood Public School, the first time we examined the literacy slice across the school we found that the quantity of reading and writing peaked in grade 5 and rapidly diminished to very little by grades 7 and 8. Evidence like this is very compelling and typically leads toward executing action fast. At Lancewood we instituted a personal reading time and a personal writing time for all students 4 days out of 5.

Recently, I worked with Estonian educators participating in leadership training.[16] They examined the questions that pupils asked in classrooms across their schools. The pervasive pattern was that most questions asked by pupils were found to be predominantly one category: procedural.

Questions such as, "Why do we have to do this?" "Will this be graded?" and "Where are the exercise books?" abounded. Participants found these data persuasive in examining their pedagogy, far more so than any lecture I might have given. They were able to work together to devise the kinds of questions they might well ask in order to challenge the intellect and thinking of their students while modeling the kinds of questions they would like their students to ask (see Figure 3.2).

Following the Artifact Trail. Artifacts are all those things that teachers and students collect, document, record, examine, and reflect upon. For example, reading logs are artifacts that show the number of books, authors, genres, reasons for selection, and book recommendations that students keep across the school. They provide an excellent basis to examine the reading habits of various classes, age groups, subject groups, or other specialized groups such as second language learners. Writing folders, and math, art, and teacher portfolios are other useful examples. As with taking a slice, organizing and displaying the artifacts from across the school can provide a powerful and compelling snapshot of the experience students are having in their classrooms.

Figure 3.2. Taking a Slice Activity: Try This

TAKE A SLICE ABOUT PUPIL QUESTIONS!

Nobel Prize–winning physicist Kenneth Wilson argues that the problem in physics is not that scientists can't do good research but rather that they don't do well at asking the right questions.[17] Furthermore, the problem with kids learning science in school is not that they don't learn the so-called scientific method or can't write up experiments, but rather that they don't ask thoughtful questions. Breakthroughs in science occur when the scientist asks the right question. "Why can't we have schools that are full of pupils asking substantive questions?" he challenged. Why not, indeed? It seems to me that lifelong learners are those who are extremely adept at and practiced in asking smart questions.

At the end of a designated school day, teachers can do the following:

1. Ask students to record, on a blank sheet of paper, their name, age, and grade level.
2. Have them write: "Questions I asked in class today."
3. Ask them to record all questions they asked in class. This can include whole-class and within-group discussions.
4. Older students can write *(W)* for questions asked within whole-class activity or *(G)* for questions asked within a group.
5. Have a student collect all papers, including incomplete responses, and take them to a designated teacher from the school design team, who will organize the responses by age/grade level. As teachers and parents examine a slice in the questions pupils ask, what do they discover?

I find the work of the Reggio Emilia schools in Italy, compelling in this regard. One of their core principles is *documentation* for the purposes of observation, research, and assessment. Teachers in Reggio Emilia constantly document and discuss meanings of photographs, recordings, and samples of children's work.[18] Mounting these onto documentation panels enables pupils, teachers, and parents to engage in an informed dialogue about the meaning of the experiences. Documentation panels capture the life in teaching and learning, and work well as a counterpoint to numerical data that assess learning metaphorically, never able to display it, only to approximate it. The panels use photographs, transcripts of children's words, samples of student work, and teacher comments about children's learning and their own practice. The panels permit us to think of teachers as producers of classroom culture with their children, rather than simply consumers and transmitters of curriculum documents. What is missing from the curriculum documents that teachers must deal with daily is the children's relationship to what they are learning.[19]

What we learn from engaging with documentation panels is that they take a long time to produce, for they require an inquiry process of mulling over and synthesizing classroom evidence, artifacts, student work, photographs, audio/videotape, and so on, consciously making decisions about what to show. Data reduction is the thinking process involved as we go from a lot of data to best illustrations of a learning event. However, once the documentation panel is made, it is a permanent trace of a fleeting process, making visible the learning in lived experience for the student. Panels can be used with other students to show previous students' work, thinking, and feeling. They model exemplary work for other students. They can be used with parents to show classroom processes (parents love them), and they can be used with other teachers to reflect on teaching and learning.

It is important that information be gathered and considered over time. We do this because we have poor memories, but also because students' growth changes (not always for the better or in a linear sequential fashion) during schooling. Graves, in studying progress in students' writing, asked independent authors to assess the quality of students' writing over time and found that there was constant variability. In studying the writing of many youngsters, the researcher's conclusion was that writing is a highly idiosyncratic process that varies from day to day. Many factors contributed to the variability, including familiarity with the genre, the topic, who chose the topic, and expectations about potential audiences, not to mention the student's health and well-being, how the writer perceives him- or herself, diet, degree of rest, and other factors.[20] What this means is that evaluation limited to a single effort or event on a given day is no basis upon which to make judgments.

INFORMATION AND ACCOUNTABILITY

Schools have available the most persuasive information about the learning of their students. If educators mobilize to use it, we can transform the ways in which we are held accountable to our stakeholders: the pupils, parents, community, and local educational authority. Somehow, we have entrusted what will count as progress to distant others on the state and national level, and as a result, we have ended up providing information to the public that can only be described as narrow, simplistic, and, debatably, unreliable. The shadow of progress has become confused with the substance of real student progress.[21]

Efficiency and the perceived need for objective measures drive what most districts and states gather in the name of accountability. It is unfortunate that tools of efficiency do little to inform educators about their practice or students. Parents also learn almost nothing about the students' learning experience, accomplishments, and needs from these assessments. The information we historically have gathered in the name of assessment and accountability is less than persuasive. Only when it authentically represents the student's experience with the curriculum and informs teachers' pedagogy can we have trust in the data we gather.

In Figure 3.3, I have represented the utility of the varied kinds of information about a student's learning experience in schools. The image portrays two dimensions: (1) from *distant* from the pupils' experience to *closest* to their experience, and (2) *minimum* to *maximum* learning that teachers, students, and their parents are likely to have from the information. Plainly, information that is closest to pupils' experiences and has a maximum chance of engaging them (quadrant 4) is the most useful and persuasive. Quadrant 4 represents activities that enable assessment for and assessment as learning. Assessment activities that inform and help youngsters understand the task, their accomplishments, and ways to continuously improve are the most powerful and useful.

Accountability in Schools

Legislators throughout the United States, Canada, and many other jurisdictions have taken control of education in the belief that education's problems could be resolved if only the people responsible for progress and working inside schools were more accountable. What goes on in classrooms in the name of teaching and learning remains a mystery for most people outside of schools and for some within. Consider this: What counts as students' progress, how it is assessed and evaluated, how information will be used and shared with whom, what information authentically captures

Figure 3.3. The Information We Gather: The Power of Engaging the Experience of the Learner

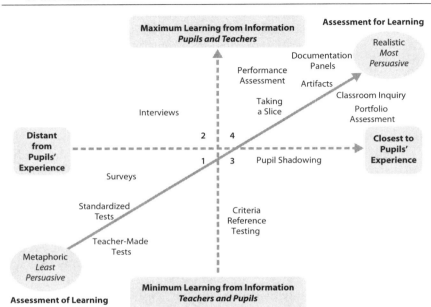

development, and what kind of young people emerge after about 13 years of public schooling are significant and serious questions. The answers have a lot to do with whether or not schools are able to improve the learning of their students and must come from the people who work in schools.

Externally imposed testing can apply considerable pressure to the purposes and learning that take place in school. Despite the reality of many pernicious testing regimes, it is extremely important that external measures account for the diversity of experiences, variation in abilities, learning styles, and interests of all students. This is a tall order given the meager role external measures can play. It is more important that every classroom and the schools students inhabit provide ongoing assessment information to be shared regularly with students, colleagues, parents, and the community. The purpose of sharing is not only to enlighten and educate the stakeholders but, more important, to inform the quality of teaching and learning. In short, assessment must serve learning.

I am arguing here for the idea that assessment is a fundamental part of learning and teaching. This notion is deeply rooted in a constructivist theory of learning that views education as a process of taking in information, interpreting it, connecting it to existing knowledge or beliefs, and, if necessary, reorganizing understanding to accommodate that information.[22] If people learn by constructing their own understanding from their experiences, then assessment is not only part of learning but also a significant component, allowing learners and their teachers to check their understanding against the views of others. Furthermore, as Earl and LeMahieu tell us, it enables learners to compare and contrast their understanding with the collective wisdom of the culture as it has been recorded in the knowledge, theories, models, formulas, solutions, and stories that make up the curriculum and the disciplines.[23]

Conversations that surround assessment in classrooms, such as those described in the following chapters, make transparent to the students and their teachers and parents the experience learners have with curriculum. In making the learning experience visible to others, we are creating an accountability that is an ongoing part of our day-to-day teaching and learning. This form of accountability differs from our traditional views. It is not so much about complying and sending a copy of our compliance to a distant supervisor, or relying on a limiting testing regime created by a remote other. Rather, it is about making an ongoing record of the learner's experience that is observable over time by all stakeholders, including the student.

Because it is ongoing, rich in texture and reality, available to all, and informs both teaching and learning, this assessment talk is arguably the most compelling form of accountability. In its broadest sense, this process uses assessment information closest to the experience of the learner to inform the ongoing thinking and judgments that teachers make about their practice and students make about their learning. Much more than school statistics alone, accountability is a deeply human enterprise. It depends on open sharing of information and continuing conversations among and between educators, students, parents, and the community as they interpret and make sense of available information and establish action plans.[24]

Case Study: Lancewood Public School

One school moves towards evidence-based accountability, equity in parent-pupil-teacher relationships, and participatory, goal-driven information about progress.

At Lancewood Public School my teacher colleagues and I designed and introduced an effective way of engaging parents, along with their sons and daughters, in meaningfully setting and assessing goals and accomplishments. What we did worked as follows: During the first few weeks of the school year, parents were invited to individual parent-student-teacher conferences in which their child led a discussion about potential goals he or she wanted to accomplish during the upcoming year. Parents had filled in an information profile identifying students' strengths and potential objectives to be achieved during the school year.

What the process achieved was to place the parent and student in the position of being the expert on the development of the individual. Parents responded extraordinarily well to the process, as many of them said that the conferences were the first time their experience with their youngster and aspirations for the future were acknowledged by the school. Teachers found that placing the parent and student in this role changed for the better the relationship between themselves and the family and enabled them to learn more about the student's history of learning than ever before. The outcome of this first session was a signed statement attesting to the student's strengths, past accomplishments, planned curriculum outcomes, and agreed-upon goals.

The team developing this process was very excited about its potential; however, other staff experienced various degrees of apprehension as they contemplated parents asking the impossible or impinging on their teaching practice. There were a lot of "what ifs" in the early discussion. What if parents wanted spelling taught differently? What if parents demanded impossible goals? What if parent, child, and teacher couldn't agree on the goals? The idea that a teacher would greet a parent with, "I have only known your daughter for a few days, whereas you have known her for 10 years—can you help me know her better?" seemed foreign to teachers' past experience and role.

In view of the worries, our drama teachers orchestrated a role-play whereby teachers rotated through various roles of teacher, pupil, parent, or observer. By the time we were through, all had practiced the protocol and dealt with the most obnoxious parent. The real experience was a breeze after this rehearsal.

Teachers were surprised because the goals that parents had in mind almost always had to do with social and work habit–related outcomes. Parents wanted their child to "complete things they start"; "speak with more confidence"; "get along better with classmates"; "write more neatly"; "be more polite"; "do more homework"; and "demonstrate more confidence in relating to others." Teachers were then able to relate these goals to appropriate curriculum and academic outcomes.

Three more conferences were scheduled throughout the year to review and revise the agreed-upon goals. The value of process was that it established the relationship between teacher and family early in the year. It enabled each student to reflect; to describe his or her own abilities, learning style, and passions; and to contribute to the overall planning for the future. It meant that goal-setting emerged from the need of the individual, as opposed to some outside source, and that assessment not only related to possible curriculum outcomes but also reflected the agreed-upon needs of the individual.

Whether a school has the capacity to improve student learning has a lot to do with the kinds of information that are routinely gathered, shared, and examined by and with professional colleagues, students, and parents. For example, as a principal I would want to know, and I would want my colleagues, parents, and community to know, the nature of books and other texts pupils are reading—how many, which genres, for what purposes. Documenting each student's experience with the curriculum is easy and essential for the complex decision-making that takes place moment by moment in the interactions between teachers and students. Equally important in improving the life chances of all is collating and sharing the information with colleagues, students, and community members.

Wide-ranging, crucial information informs teachers about context, innovation, the change process, and classroom pedagogy. Principals are in a position to promote, facilitate, or constrain the kinds of information teachers have access to. Principals of successful schools lead by designing the work of the school in ways that enable teachers to gather information—to collectively question, evaluate, reflect, and act on their practices and the learning experiences of children. They focus on assessment *for* and *as* learning. Principals of successful schools find ways of documenting and having stakeholders interact with this information as they effectively build knowledge about the learning of all and demonstrate accountability.

LEADING THE INFORMATION- AND KNOWLEDGE-RICH SCHOOL

School-based educators have not taken accountability seriously enough, and as a result, those outside the schools have imposed accountability measures by opting for strategies characterized as quantitative, simplistic, rarely informative, externally contrived, cost-efficient, and easy to administer. Courageous principals can take the lead in defining, observing, gathering, and documenting consistently over time the experiences, artifacts, demonstrations, performances, and theories that currently and realistically represent the development of each young person in their classrooms and across the school. School leaders and their teacher colleagues in knowledge-rich

schools can use information to inform and improve teaching and learning
and show accountability to their community and parents by

- *Gathering data frequently.* Continually and consistently gather and
  share data that are close to the learning experience and varied
  accomplishments of pupils as they explore, question, hypothesize,
  demonstrate, and represent their views and accomplishments about
  a meaningful curriculum within which they have negotiated control
  and voice.
- *Building knowledge through documentation and interaction.* Use
  documentation (e.g.,the documentation panels described above) and its
  examination as a basis for teacher development and capacity-building.
  Information only becomes knowledge when examined, questioned,
  and discussed—when underlying assumptions are made transparent
  and comparisons made over time. Professional learning communities
  collaboratively transform information into knowledge and action.
- *Defining what counts as progress with respect to purpose.* Use information
  that most closely represents the reality of the students' learning
  experience, along with available internal or external exemplars, to
  define what counts as progress.
- *Sampling progress.* Regularly sample reading, writing, inquiry, talk, use
  of mathematics, research, argument, frequency and kinds of student
  questions, knowledge-building, and so on across the school to inform
  teachers, students, parents, and other stakeholders about learning
  patterns and progress across the school.
- *Including parents and pupils ingoal-setting and in planning assessment of
  those goals.* Education is about the development of the whole child!
  There is no better way of enacting this than working directly and early
  with students and parents.
- *Building community capacity for accountability.* Use documentation and
  its examination as a basis to educate and build the capacity of parents
  about what counts as progress, what fairly represents growth over
  time, and how and to what extent their youngsters are improving.
- *Developing a school/community accountability pact.* School/community
  accountability pacts commit the school to sharing authentic data with
  the community regularly, demonstrating the diversity of learning
  and accomplishments, the strategies teachers intend to employ, and
  the capacity the school intends to build in order that growth may
  continually occur. Accountability pacts are a way of increasing the
  community's commitment to and involvement in the school, thus
  providing a more persuasive alternative to the often pernicious effects
  of imposed accountability measures.

- *Working with and educating stakeholders.* Work with districts, teachers' unions, parent groups, and other stakeholders to proactively move the accountability debate from predominantly outside/in policy and procedures toward more inside/out practices.

When you gather and collectively examine information, using the strategies described above, improving the life chances of all students is not a question, then, of motivating your teachers to act. When your collective data says your grades-5-to-12 pupils don't read of their own volition; when the reading they do is fragmented and limited in their range of genres; when the writing from kindergarten to grade 5 is predominantly about television and pop culture characters; when the pupils in your grade 12 science classes don't get to ask questions of substance; or when, in a secondary school with 500 Hispanic students, none of them take advanced math, there is a moral imperative to act.

In any of these examples, you don't need a policy or a mandate from government or the district to move to action fast. The data, if they reflect the actual experience of learners and the kinds of people they are becoming across the school or program, are always compelling. What you need is the facility to document and jointly examine it; the collective ability to *take charge* by forging and executing genuinely compelling strategic directions; and the courage, capacity, and fearless leadership to enact those strategies. A strong professional learning community engaging in the activities described herein represents a social process for turning information into knowledge and action.

REFLECT ON THESE QUESTIONS

1. What kinds of data are gathered in your school? For what purposes and for what audiences? How are they used?
2. How and to what extent are data about pupils' authentic learning experiences used as a vehicle for teachers' professional and learning development?
3. How might the school keep track over time of the books individuals read and their topics, genres, audiences, and responses?
4. In what ways and for what purposes might you regularly sample pupils' learning experiences across the entire school?
5. What are the practices and procedures that will enable the important information about pupils' learning experience that you gather to be collectively turned into knowledge, thus informing classroom practice and continuous improvement?

6. In what ways might you and your colleagues ensure that the entire staff is assessment-literate—that is, how can you foster a deep understanding of the purposes, practices, and strategies for authentically assessing the learning and learning experiences of all pupils?
7. How might the school keep track over time of the amount of writing individuals produce, the topics and genres they write about, the publications made, and the audiences they write for?
8. How might the school keep track of the kind of pupil talk that takes place in classrooms? The opportunities pupils have to express ideas, to clarify, extend and improve on the ideas of self and others? The frequency and kinds of questions they ask?
9. How and to what extent do parents have access to data useful in describing the accomplishments and growth of pupils across the school?
10. What opportunities do teachers across the school have to collectively gather authentic data about their pupils' progress with a view to sharing the information for continuous improvement?
11. What are the potential advantages and obstacles to you and your colleagues creating a community/school accountability pact?

FOR FURTHER READING

Anderson, G., Herr, K., & Nihlen, A. (2007). *Studying your own school: An educator's guide to qualitative practitioner research* (2nd ed.). Thousand Oaks, CA: Sage.

Practitioner research is now the vanguard of educational improvement. Learn to study your own school.

Bullough, R., & Gitlin, A. (2001). *Becoming a student of teaching: Methodologies for exploring self and school context* (2nd ed.). New York: Routledge.

Learning as we teach is implicit throughout *Taking Charge.* This book provides deep insights into these processes.

Earl, L. (2003). *Assessment as learning.* Thousand Oaks, CA: Sage

The concept of assessment as learning allows teachers to use their judgment about students' understanding to inform the teaching process while personalizing learning for each individual.

CHAPTER 4

Personal and Collective Professional Learning

Schools that are notably successful in improving the life chances of all their students are learning schools! In these schools, learning is for everyone, especially teachers and school leaders. It begins with the head learner: the school principal who visibly and avidly engages in learning throughout the day-to-day work of leading. In this chapter you will learn about

- rethinking the use of your time;
- two core strategies that underpin personal and collective learning—examining critical incidents and studying underlying assumptions;
- practical strategies for coming to know you pupils well;
- practical strategies for knowing your teachers well; and
- important lessons about professional learning.

I was sitting in my office with the door closed and my feet up on the coffee table, engrossed in a book about early literacy and, in particular, some thorny instructional issues with which my teacher colleagues and I had been struggling. Usually I do much of my reading in the school library or classrooms and at home, but that day, I felt the need to clearly focus on particular issues around developing genres such as mystery, science report, or travelogue in writing and reading that my colleagues and I had been trying to resolve for some time. As often was the case, I was surrounded by professional books; journal articles; samples of student work; my own hastily scrawled notes; several sheets of chart paper covered with circles, squares, arrows; and multicolored notes hanging from one wall. There was a knock on the door and, without waiting for a response, my school superintendent walked in. "Well, it's good to see at least some of us have time on our hands," he commented, somewhat in jest but also, I sensed, with a certain degree of criticism and seriousness. It was clear he didn't see this as a valuable use of my time.

But for me, providing schoolwide pedagogical leadership and sound moral judgment is very much about being a learner, about being informed of current research, about bringing a planetary perspective to issues, about thinking deeply on the issues of change and increasing complexity, and about self-reflection. It is about valuing, modeling, and enabling personal, collective, and organizational learning for my teacher colleagues. Fulfilling this role demands that you are broadly informed, knowledgeable about teaching and learning, and, above all, that you bring current and new perspectives to the work of your colleagues. It is simply not possible to fulfill this role if you are mired in detail, bound to your e-mail, constantly controlled by the immediacy of day-to-day events, and unaware of current developments. You have to step outside the business of school and your surroundings and have real, uninterrupted time to deliberate on ideas, perspectives, values, and research. You must reflect on the big issues and concepts that challenge you, your students, and your colleagues.

FINDING TIME:
THE 50-40-10% SOLUTION

As a young principal of the small (approximately 500 pupils) Conestoga Public School, my work plans were consistently superseded by problems of immediacy. The parent who walked in and wanted to meet about their son or daughter, the sick pupil, the discipline problem, the teacher with family needs, telephone calls, communications and questions from the district office, faxes, or e-mails seemed to control my time and attention. Over the years, I have visited and observed many principals who were also constantly caught up in the moment.

Effective leadership begins with *taking charge* of one's own time and learning. It starts in the school office, by building the competencies and confidence of your staff so that they can take the initiative to respond and solve the many moment-by-moment problems requiring immediate response or personal attention. When discussing with office staff what it is they value in their work, I find that most find rewards in acting with initiative, in assuming responsibility for and following through on projects and problems to be solved. As principal, it should be possible to leave one's school at any time and know that, regardless of what happens, the people in your office and in your school have the confidence and capacity to manage whatever issue or challenge walks through the door. This means that you have ensured that your support staff has the skills and, as required, the training to constructively handle their roles and the unexpected. This doesn't mean that, as principal, you are not informed and involved in the work of the school office; it just means that very little that happens in the school needs to be time-dependent upon you. It is important that you remain informed. As I write this, I think of Lucy, a vice principal who worked with me. She often repeated the phrase,

"Just so you know . . . ." And she taught me the importance of communication. Her phrase caught on, and eventually all of us in the office constantly used it. "Just so you know, I spoke to the district office and . . . ."; "Just so you know, Mrs. Brown was in and I told her . . . ."; "Just so you know, I spoke to Zhang about his behavior on the school trip . . . ." Informal as it may sometimes be, I can not overstress the importance of this constant communication with colleagues about the workings of the school.

In an attempt to become master of my own time in my work as a school principal, I have had to think deeply about my role and the purposes I need to fulfill. Clearly, for me, the major role is that of pedagogical leadership. Practicing pedagogical leadership begins by knowing your students', teachers', and community's experiences, their successes and struggles, extraordinarily well. Mostly, this work takes place somewhere other than the office. It means that principals are purposefully engaged in classrooms, gathering data and listening to and talking with pupils about their work, their experiences (or lack thereof), their goals and aspirations. It means frequently participating in the weighty discussions about assessment, teaching methods, values, and learning. It means building an understanding of the experiences and perspectives of learners, teachers, and parents.

Recently, at a training session for a large group of educators, a principal asked me a most common question about time. She said, "Look, I am so busy managing my school as it is, so how on earth can I find time for all the work that you describe pedagogical leaders doing?" My answer was this: It is impossible to layer on top of the administrative role that principals have traditionally played the new work of designer, lead capacity-builder, model learner, professional inquirer, data-gatherer and analyst, moral and ethical steward, informed and articulate vision developer and keeper. What is required is an entire rethinking of the nature of your work as principal and identifying those priorities that will truly make a difference to the life chances of all students. Once identified, these roles and activities become the priority, and then it's a question of finding ways of managing the less important work with more efficiency.

All of this led me to what I have come to call the 50-40-10% solution. This is a simple guide for how I used my time: Fifty percent of my time was for pedagogical leadership. Forty percent was reserved for administration, which includes dealing with discipline, meeting with parents, addressing issues of maintaining the physical plant, reading and preparing reports, and so on. Then there is the final 10%, which was sacred time for my own personal development. Over the years, I learned to quite ruthlessly protect the 50% and the 10%, as I know how easy it is for administrative activity to consume an entire workday. Now that we have set aside the time for personal development, let's turn to how we can use it.

PERSONAL AND COLLECTIVE LEARNING:
TWO POWERFUL STRATEGIES

Two valuable and related strategies underpin personal and collective learning, whether it is that of the principal or the staff:

1. Examining and learning from critical incidents
2. Studying practice by identifying and discussing underlying assumptions

Critical incidents, which occur in classrooms, schools, and districts, are situations that clearly demonstrate specific examples of learning and/or interaction between student and teacher. They are illustrative in that they open our behaviors to the scrutiny of ourselves and others. They clarify why some practices are exemplary and others ineffective in achieving our intentions. Judith Newman defines this process in this practical way:[1]

> Everything we do in the classroom is founded on a set of assumptions about learning and teaching, about knowledge, and what counts as legitimate (learning). That is, each of us operates on the basis of what Chris Argyris . . . calls our [action theories.[2]] Our beliefs about learning and teaching are largely tacit. We operate a good deal of the time from an intuitive sense of what is going on without actively reflecting on what our intentions might be and what our actions could be saying to students.

Our beliefs about learning and teaching can only be uncovered by engaging in systematic self-critical analysis of our current instructional practices. Using critical incidents to identify underlying assumptions is an extremely effective approach to examining the essential beliefs and meanings that underpin practice, particularly from the perspective of the learners or participants. These two strategies, which are by no means mutually exclusive, enable the participant to examine, question, reflect, and construct a deeper understanding of behavior and practice. When carried out frequently and collectively, they enable the participants to create a precise, informed, and shared language in order to create and define the nature and impact of exemplary practice.

For example, let's examine the assumptions underpinning a grade 8 history/geography class I recently observed during project work in Washington State (thanks to the district personnel who edited this summary for me):

> There were 35 students, 22 boys and 13 girls, of predominantly
> Black and Hispanic origins. The teacher explained that there were 9

students who were being withdrawn from class at times for English Language Learning (ELL) coaching. The class was sitting in rows, and the instructional period was 50 minutes in length. The topic was American history. The students were using a rather large textbook. At the beginning of the lesson, the teacher received homework and admonished those 7 students who had not handed in the assignment on time. If they didn't hand it in by the end of the day, they would score 0 on the assignment.

The instruction began with a review from the previous day's lecture on American colonization, particularly in reference to the American Indian tribes living in the Eastern coastal regions. The teacher asked questions, calling upon students who answered according to the notes they took the day before. The students' answers tended to be brief, often one word in length.

After the question-and-answer review, the teacher showed some slides and gave some narrative about what the slides depicted, while the students took notes in their notebooks. After about 20 minutes, the students were given a worksheet to individually complete on the topic. During the last 10 minutes of the lesson, the teacher discussed their answers and collected the worksheets. During this instructional time several students were called out of the room for various types of diagnostic testing. They did not return.

The teacher then announced that a quiz would be given the next day about the lectures and reading notes for the last several days. A homework assignment, which consisted of reviewing the notes from the last several days, was given. Students were told to contact those students who were either absent from class the entire day or were gone for the previously mentioned diagnostic testing to inform them of what was going to be on the quiz the next day. Absence was no excuse for not knowing the material.

Apart from the content and class composition, this lesson could have come from anywhere in the world. So, what assumptions does this teacher make here? First of all, regarding time, an assumption has been made that young adolescents have short attention spans and, therefore, learn best when instructional periods are short. Furthermore, she assumes that regardless of ability, language proficiency, or background knowledge, each student requires an identical amount of time to learn the same content. There is also the assumption that, despite their difficulty with the language, English language learners can learn the same content as the rest of the class, even though they are absent for a good part of it. On the homework assignment, the arbitrary score of 0 for late work presupposes that pupils of this age don't have lives and responsibilities outside of school and that each has the same opportunities, resources, and support to complete the work on time. Giving a 0 grade also puts forth the assumption that pupils can overcome such grades in achieving success in this subject.

Moreover, what of learning styles, abilities, prior experience, interest, passion, and engagement? It seems to me that this teacher assumes that all students are the same. She allows very little room for students to identify particular interests or questions that they would like to pursue. The teacher simply fails to recognize that pupils have intentions of their own in any learning activity. She assumes that all students bring the same experience, have similar abilities, learn in the same way and at the same pace, and are able to express their understanding equally well in one specific form— writing. Fragmentary teaching like this assumes that students are able to make connections between what they are required to learn in one context and what they learn in others, without support. Significant are the meta-cognitive (the language that explains how to learn, read, write, etc.) lessons students are learning about what it takes to be a historian and a learner, and what counts as progress. To be a successful learner in this class is to take and memorize copious notes. Historians are obviously people who learn information about the past mainly through reading. What counts in this class is how well you can do quizzes, get things done on time, and write things down. Being curious, searching for patterns, expressing your own views and opinions, arguing a point of view, taking on perspectives of historical figures, representing your understandings in varied media—apparently these learning styles don't count in this classroom.

Who gets to ask the questions is telling. Here, the assumption is that either students don't have questions or that their questions don't matter. Yet it is through student questions that we have a chance of knowing about the difficulties they have with the content, about the connections they are trying to make, about their interests and passions, and about their varied abilities and learning styles. Developing their ability to ask deep and thoughtful questions may well be the greatest gift we can give them in terms of improving their life chances.

I could take this analysis of underlying assumptions further, but it is clear that exercises such as this are not something this teacher and others in her school have ever imagined. When the collective examination of assumptions is a commonplace occurrence in the school workplace, carried out in a climate of high trust and support, then teachers (and principals) are able to think more deeply about practice and become motivated to move to improved action fast. An interesting follow-up task associated with this activity is to rewrite the lesson description in a way that significantly improves on variables identified with a view to going back and teaching an improved lesson. I have used this process by first of all training teacher colleagues to identify and question assumptions. This can be accomplished by jointly analyzing a video of a class lesson. Following that experience, teachers are then paired up and observe a lesson in one another's rooms, recording observations and then discussing the analysis the next day.

Transparent assumptions help us understand the impact of our teaching practice on our students' learning, attitudes, and values. But our practice can be even better informed and responsive to student needs if we know our students exceedingly well. In this next section we explore what this means for our practice.

KNOWING YOUR STUDENTS WELL

Throughout this book, I repeat the underlying principle of "knowing your students extraordinarily well" as a key to school improvement. This means teachers knowing students' social, emotional, physical, and intellectual/academic needs. It comes through developing an intimate relationship with each and every student and family so that over time, their needs, interests, and capabilities are identified and collectively addressed. Finding the time to know and relate to the student is frequently a challenge in larger schools. To accomplish this means structuring the school so that teachers and their students spend substantial chunks of time together, preferably over a period greater than a year, as I illustrate in Chapter 6. This is particularly important in schools where discipline, course completion, dropout rates, pupil and family mobility, and social issues are major issues. This implies strategies like block timetabling, subject integration, interdisciplinary teaching, and team teaching. Knowing students well means providing frequent opportunities to observe and interact with individuals and small groups. It means orchestrating teaching in ways that enable the teacher to engage in deep and sustained ways with individuals and groups, requiring other students to work more independently and interdependently without constant teacher supervision.

Frequent opportunities for all students to talk about their learning history and current experiences as learners are essential. This enables them to articulate their understanding of their learning intentions, strengths, abilities, and style. In participating in this kind of activity, they are in fact building their meta-cognitive understanding of what it means to be a learner, a reader, a writer, a historian, or a scientist, as explained in Chapter 2. Linked to a form of intelligence about school leadership known as *reflective intelligence*, meta-cognition encourages all learners, child and adult alike, to deepen their understanding of what it takes to succeed. MacGilchrist describes the process as follows:[3] Reflective intelligence covers the core skills and processes of monitoring, reflecting upon, and evaluating the effectiveness of the school in general and, in particular, the progress and achievement of the students. Reflecting upon the progress and achievement of students is a central concern, and as such it is closely interrelated with academic intelligence. This is because integral to this reflective capacity is an awareness of the dangers of low expectations for students on the one hand and complacency—for example, about their seemingly good examination results—on the other.

Knowing your students well also means advantaging the knowledge and expertise parents have about their offspring. It requires opportunities for students, parents, and teachers to spend time exploring learning strengths, needs, goals, and plans. In Chapter 3, I explained our innovative use of parent-student-teacher conferences at Lancewood Public School. Coming to know the student well, through frequent, lasting, and informative interaction, is important and made more valuable by having a knowledge base to assist in interpreting your observations and documentation. The knowledge base, in this case, is the psychology of childhood and adolescent development and learning, which teachers can use to interpret and inform the knowledge they are constantly building about each individual student and the efficacy of his/her practice. Part of the capacity that schools have to develop is fostering this expertise among the staff.

Capitalizing on Interests and Unleashing Passions

In low-income, multilingual, multicultural, new immigrant communities like those where I have chosen to spend most of my professional career, it is easy to come to believe that various forms of impoverishment inevitably lead to low motivation and are responsible for many students doing poorly in school. The problem with such assumptions is that we clearly have examples of students faced with these circumstances who succeed. Some of these, described in this book, occur when colleagues working together have capitalized on student interest and unleashed their passion, gathering rather extraordinary results. A key principle underpinning this idea of unleashing students' passion is called "choice theory." Choice theory argues for the opportunities and benefits of individual and groups of students uncovering and exploring their interests and passions through making informed and reasoned choices.

Choice theory rests on a simple axiom that "no one does anything, simple or complex, because someone tells them to do it."[4] As educators, we have often failed to appreciate this fundamental fact. In many secondary and middle schools, significant numbers of students make little or no effort to learn. For too long, we have believed the assumption that humans can be motivated to work by what we can do to them (fear) or for them (external rewards). Glasser identifies a number of fundamental needs that we all have, including the need to stay alive and reproduce, and four psychological needs: belonging (which includes love), power, freedom, and fun.[5]

Choice theory postulates that the more students can fulfill the fundamental needs of security, belonging, control (power), and freedom in their academic classes, the more they will apply themselves to their learning. The implications for the curriculum and teaching here are clear. There needs to be choice! There need to be opportunities for students to pursue their particular interests and passions; control how they might represent their learning to others; link their learning to what they have previously learned and the learning of others; and extend, improve, and build on the learning of self and others. Practically, this occurs when the curriculum and learning goals emerge by negotiation between an informed and caring teacher and student. Negotiating the curriculum means deliberately planning to invite students to contribute to, and to modify, the educational program so that they will have a real investment both in the learning journey and in the final accomplishments.[6] It is a process that students can become very adept at with experience over time.

Most schools have diverse populations. Diversity can be seen as a negative or a positive force within the school community. Diversity always raises the question of equity and what we mean by it. For some, it means treating all students equally—giving them identical learning experiences and support. For others (like me), equity is about leveling the playing field, which means recognizing that some students will need more time, more appropriate support, and to feel valued if they are to have an equal opportunity to develop confidence, become accomplished, and achieve improved life chances. Diverse pupils (and diversity itself) when perceived and valued as a resource, change attitudes and practices for the better.[7] Appreciating diversity can add richness to the texture, experience, opportunities, and perspectives of all, and it can only occur when we know our students extraordinarily well. Here are some practical strategies I have deployed and refined over the years in order to foster my colleagues' and my own knowledge of our students.

Classroom Observation

All principals spend time in classrooms. Some tell me they supervise by "going walkabout." Simply by frequently being present (as a spectator), they argue, they are constantly aware of the issues and challenges that teachers and students face. I argue that the role needs to be more active and participatory. There is a huge difference between participant and spectator. When I visit classrooms, I tend to very purposeful. As I sit with students, I ask questions about their current experience, their intentions, their understanding of and engagement with the task, their (meta-cognitive) understanding of the tasks of learning, and the substance of and their accomplishments in learning. For example, I may ask the following:

- What are you working on today? Who are you working with?
- Tell me about what you are trying to achieve.
- What have you learned so far? What else do you need to learn?
- What do you have to know (learn) to be able to do this task well?
- What strategies do you need to know to learn this well?
- How do you feel about this topic/subject? How important is this work to you?
- What has been the hardest part? The easiest?
- How will you know if you have been successful?
- Who will you teach your learning to?

These initiating questions are followed up by further questions aimed at helping the learner and myself deepen our appreciation for the task at hand and what it takes to learn it well. I am always curious as to who is going to learn from their learning (other students in the class or in other classes, parents, visitors, volunteers, community members, etc.), whether there is an intended audience other than the teacher. I chat with the teacher about her purposes, strategies, and, above all, what she is learning and wants to improve upon.

I am particularly interested in learning about and fostering constructive roles for students in their classrooms. By having opportunities to tell, retell, and reflect on their learning experiences, students can act as a source of data for the teacher in thinking more deeply about and refining the learner's experience. Thus, I am always curious about how and to what extent students have opportunities to explore their learning experiences, to identify problems, to be co-planners in identifying areas of inquiry, strategies to explore, and interventions to make. Essentially, I am looking for evidence of student voice and ownership (choice) in their learning and the learning of the class.

When visiting classrooms I am particularly attentive to the activity and engagement of students of diverse backgrounds. For instance, often students new to the language or culture play a very passive role in class, so I am interested in exploring with them their understanding of the task at hand, who they go to for help, and what they need in order to learn well. Teachers often need to provide ongoing direction and support to ensure that they are fully engaged and that they participate in class activities. In particular, I am interested to find out how and to what extent learning is being differentiated for these learners. Simply put, this is about beginning with where the student is in his or her development and requires the teacher to modify content, process, and products in order to accommodate each learner.

Vulnerable Students

One aspect of knowing your students well is to personally know, in the most constructive sense, all of the at-risk students in your organization. In each of the four schools where I was principal, I made an effort to know the work, experiences, strengths, and accomplishments of every pupil who appeared to be at risk. I did this by meeting each of these students, often in a group setting where all members, regardless of ability, had an opportunity to show their work and speak to their learning experiences. I was particularly interested in how they saw themselves as learners, what they identified (if anything) as accomplishments, strategies they used in approaching problems, and how they perceived themselves as readers, writers, and storytellers. In very large schools, I would share this work with my vice principal colleagues. I kept notes of my observations, discussed them with the student, and shared them with teachers and parents.

Focus Groups

Periodically, I conducted focus groups across my school, sampling a variety of students from different classrooms, age groups, and subjects. Topics usually generated a series of focus questions I used to scaffold the conversation. My role was one of an appreciative listener; in fact, the whole approach is based on the work of *appreciative inquiry*,[8] a strategy designed to search for the best in people, their organizations, and the relevant world around them. It is an attempt to view the world through the participant's eyes. Essentially, it is about bringing to light exemplary practices and learning experiences.

Literacy Circles

Literacy circles are small groups of individuals who share their impressions of, ideas about, and the problems they encountered in a particular text. It is shared reading. Collective dialogue enables clarification, extension, and/or improved meaning. Participants learn to appreciate the perspective of others while responding concisely and clearly with a view toward deepening or improving understanding.

The beauty of literacy circles is that they can work at many levels in a variety of contexts. In classrooms, students in literacy circles can further their appreciation of varied perspectives of others as they collectively construct new and improved meaning. Put simply, through dialogue, the students construct their understanding of what the author intended. Teachers in professional interest groups can participate in a literacy circle, as might parents and other stakeholders.

Identifying Strengths and Likely Successes

One activity that I find compelling is to work with my colleagues to identify anticipated accomplishments for each and every student. Initially, in exploring this activity, teachers would simply list some anticipated accomplishments for each pupil on a class list. This first experience was quite revealing, as it was easy to identify potential accomplishments for the students doing well in school, but for those who were low achievers or who were less engaged, it proved a very difficult task. As a group, we had to examine why this was so. We had to learn to think deeply about accomplishments that were both real and worthy for those who found school more challenging.

Classroom Inquiry and Data Collection

Action or practitioner research, in all its forms, when pervasive, can provide the educator with a continuous stream of data about the workings of the school and classrooms (see Chapter 3). University professors and graduate students who want to research, and who agree to share their data and its analysis with staff, add more information for learning and capacity-building. Whenever there is discussion about issues—from discipline to social activity to sports to parental involvement—there are always opportunities for teachers, volunteer parents, and students to keep a record of the activity of interest and to share that data. The idea that students and teachers can be co-researchers is a powerful one and a sure sign that students are having a voice in their schooling.

Figure 4.1 provides a summary of the strategies discussed above that contribute to knowing our students well. Individually, each activity helps us know the student a little better, but it is through the intensity of the knowledge-building that occurs when all strategies are being used that teachers and their leaders are able to really build a deep knowledge and understanding of each student's needs.

KNOWING YOUR COLLEAGUES WELL WHILE BUILDING CAPACITY

School leadership is about developing and mobilizing the talents, interests, abilities, and passion of your colleagues in furthering the clear and

Figure 4.1. Knowing Your Students Well—Summary

Activity/Purpose	Supporting Infrastructure	Underlying Strategies
Classroom Observation	Outside observers and/or in-class support to enable teacher participation	Recording critical incidents; collectively examining to clarify, extend, and improve understanding
At-Risk Pupils	Principal time, will, skill, and appropriate environment	Developing personal knowledge and informed insights, positive relationships, sharing the responsibility
Focus Groups	Principal time, will, skill, and appropriate environment	Skill in appreciative inquiry; judgment-free, problem-solving learning stance
Literacy Circles	Compelling text, time, commitment, and good working relationships	Collective learning, appreciating perspective, learning from one another
Identifying Strengths and Predicting Successes	Collective time, constructive dialogue, appropriate information	Knowing pupils well, examining learning through the eyes of the learner
Classroom Inquiry and Data Collection	Tools for inquiring and data collection, support for in-class activity, specific skills and/or training	Deepening our knowledge of the pupils learning experience

omnipresent purposes of the school. Just as teachers need to know their students well, so, too, there is a need to know your colleagues' current and future professional interests, issues, potentials, and accomplishments extraordinarily well. This does not occur spontaneously in the hustle and bustle of busy school workplaces without deliberate attention that emerges out of planned and focused activity. Here I describe some effective ways to form closer relationships with colleagues.

Fireside Chats

Depending on the size of the school, I try to have one or more personal meetings with each teacher per year. Many of us who embrace this practice call these conversations "fireside chats." The title conveys the idea of informality, of a discussion that is open ended and far reaching, yet deliberate. It is a conversation outside the realm of teacher evaluation that explores the purposes of the school and how the teacher relates to them as well as a review of how and in what ways students are making accomplishments in a teacher's class. In a fireside chat, the principal and teacher explore the ways and the degree to which current practices are actively engaging students in their learning. They are also helpful in discovering the capacities the teacher is developing and the professional accomplishments, aspirations, and personal needs the individual has. This is an excellent opportunity to acknowledge the teacher's current roles and accomplishments, and how he or she might further contribute to leadership within the school.

Classroom Observation

When visiting classrooms, I like to leave some form of feedback on what I observed. In my case, this is usually something written and is likely a fairly precise synopsis of an action or dialogue that may well be thought of as a "critical incident"(described above). The objective here is to provide the teacher not with judgments, opinions, or generalizations but rather concrete data that he/she can reflect on and learn something from. A principal friend of mine who is also an artist, frequently leaves a detailed pencil drawing capturing what she perceives as a critical incident from her observation. Her pictures are quite wonderful and capture not only a moment in time but present it in the context of furniture, equipment, resources, and the activity of students and teacher. The objective, then, is to leave some form of meaningful data that upon discussion the two of us can reflect on and learn to improve together.

Teacher Focus Groups

Once or twice a year I like to conduct teacher focus groups, including in each group a cross-section of the faculty. Holding focus groups is a deliberate capacity-building strategy, and the sessions are designed to be a learning experience for all who participate—especially the principal, who gets to yet again demonstrate his or her interest, curiosity, and eagerness to learn. The groups typically last about 60 to 75 minutes and have a clear topic about which participants are informed prior to the meeting. Focusing on a variety of issues over time, they always relate to and further the purposes of the school. For instance, in a secondary school I might ask teachers to share concrete examples and practices that demonstrate how and to what extent they are supporting literacy across grades and subjects.

Vulnerable Teachers

Schools committed to improving the life chances of all are responsive to the needs of their teachers to continually improve and grow. Not all teachers are created equal, and in most schools there are some who, due to any number of reasons, are at risk of not ensuring that every student has the appropriate opportunity to develop. Teachers at risk require ongoing support that may focus on their personal, intellectual, and/or pedagogical needs. Knowing the teacher well means that as a school leader, you have a deep appreciation for what the teacher does well and what he or she needs to do better. Aside from the other activities described in this chapter, additional support may come through finding your at-risk teacher a trusted mentor or coach,[9] support from district curriculum resource staff, inclusion on growth-provoking work teams, and visiting exemplary programs within and outside the local school. Differing teachers require differing levels of support, and the capacity-oriented leader will go to extraordinary lengths to bolster this sustenance.

Interest Groups

In all of my schools, my colleagues and I have constantly sought opportunities to learn more about our craft. Pursuing this quest, we have sponsored interest/inquiry groups on a multitude of topics, including the teaching of math, inquiry in science, and the development of genre and response theory in reading and writing. Self-nominating interest groups can explore a topic from varied perspectives, perhaps the most compelling of which is that of their own lives.

Whole Class Review

My first experience with whole-class review (WCR) goes back to my professional beginnings as a teacher. Every 6 weeks the principal required that I write a review of the needs of my class and how I responded to and planned for those needs. He responded with copious notes and suggestions. At the time, I remember wishing I could have a look at reviews of the more experienced teachers.

Over the years, I have refined the process to increase the number of people who contribute to and benefit from the growth-provoking dialogue that is so integral to the process. The purpose of whole-class review is to focus on the strengths and needs of the students as a whole and to broaden the responsibility for the experience of the class. The whole-class review is conducted by a whole-class-review team(s), which in larger schools should include a core group of educators and a selection of other teachers. In this way, each teacher is likely to contribute to at least one or two of their colleagues' class reviews. In secondary schools, the WCR team might consist of the department head, one other member of the department, a guidance counselor, and perhaps one or two teachers from other departments. Typically, particular groups of pupils would be reviewed in one subject area. Bringing in a district subject consultant, a teacher from another school, a university faculty member, or an administrator can add depth and perspective to the reviews and subsequent growth-provoking dialogue about improving students' learning experiences.

The purpose of the WCR is to provide support by way of expertise, strategic approaches, interventions, and goal-setting to enable the classroom teacher to effectively respond to students. The WCR considers the history of the students—their particular physical, social/emotional, and intellectual/academic strengths, needs, and interests as well as predominant learning styles. Widening the responsibility for the class beyond the individual teacher, breaking down the walls of isolation and professional privacy that characterize the teaching experience of many, and better informing each teacher about possibilities for improved practice are all part of the WCR process.[10] The whole-class review is about seeing ourselves through others' eyes, hearing ourselves "talk through or think aloud" what we are trying to accomplish, having the opportunity to share our joys and struggles, widening the circle of professional dialogue, and promoting multiple perspectives on student learning and classroom practice. It is very much about developing professional and organizational capacity because it involves varied players interacting across the organization and each participant is a contributor to and recipient of the collective wisdom of many.

We now move from a focus on the whole class to a focus on the needy individual learner that can be addressed through the process of an In-School Review.

In-School Review Team

An In-School Review occurs when an individual student's accomplishments, strengths, and weaknesses are reviewed by a multidisciplinary team with the sole purpose of improving the students' classroom learning experience. The process is closely akin to a shared case study or the type of review that takes place in some hospitals. The In-School Review Team (ISRT), will likely consist of an administrator, guidance counselor, school psychologist, social worker, special education teacher, and (where needed) specialists in health care, speech and language, and so forth—and, perhaps most important, a classroom teacher known for the quality of her pedagogy.

The team's approach is very much one of studying cases and is akin to interdisciplinary rounds in a hospital setting. The purpose of the ISRT is to contribute to the development of an Individual Education Plan/Program (IEP), which many jurisdictions in the United States, Canada, and elsewhere now mandate for designated pupils. The IEP has to ensure that resources are in place and, in particular, that capacity is developed within and beyond the classroom to provide the best possible opportunity to improve the life chances of the individual. Completing an IEP might be about complying with a district or government policy, but complying with a policy alone will not change the life chances of a particular student. What might change the student's opportunities is to improve the capacity of the teachers and teaching assistants involved to more effectively respond to the overall needs of the individual.

Figure 4.2 brings together these various strategies. They gain power and effectiveness when carried out simultaneously and collectively engaging the entire faculty.

CONTINUALLY BUILDING YOUR OWN
CAPACITY AND UNDERSTANDING

Exceptional principal leaders are also exemplary learners, using a precious 10% of their time to investigate and study the ever-present learning issues that confront their colleagues and students.

Understanding Teaching and Learning

Periodically, bureaucrats and politicians are enticed by colleagues, perhaps of a business persuasion, to think about schools with managers, rather than pedagogical leaders. They are perhaps attracted to the idea of the organization being securely managed, of budgets tightly controlled, of teachers being held more accountable, and so forth. This foolish thinking negates the fact that education, learning, developing personal capabilities, and building professional capacity within the organization are very human enterprises, dependent to a huge extent on relationships and values and requiring informed leadership in order to actively promote the life chances of all. Undoubtedly, strong pedagogical leaders who are continuously curious, informed, knowledgeable, and articulate about how students and teachers

Figure 4.2. Knowing Your Colleagues Well—Summary

Activity/ Purpose	Supporting Infrastructure	Underlying Strategies
Fireside Chats	Free time for the teacher; appropriate space, compelling questions	Overall approach of appreciative inquiry, capitalizing on the personal and the significant
Classroom Observation	Time to visit and to provide feedback	Providing a mirror in terms of feedback, constructive observations, building on strengths, and moving forward
Focus Groups	Clear purpose, time, and place for meeting; Opportunities to report findings back to all	Purpose is related to overarching goals of the school, going deeper into specific issues and accomplishments, skills in documentation, facility to share with all after completion
At-Risk Teachers	Principal and teacher time, clear agenda, access to district or other outside resources	Providing continuous support, additional focused training, every chance to succeed
Interest Groups	Clear purpose and time	Capitalizing on interests; personal learning on reflection can be generalizable to classroom and other contexts
Whole-Class Review	Finding time for stakeholders to participate, gathering appropriate data to discuss	Broadening the perspective about classroom pedagogy, capitalizing on strengths, sharing responsibility, appreciating and supporting colleagues
In-School Review Team	Orchestrating time of outside agents such as psychologist, social worker, etc.; finding appropriate time and space	Broadening the perspective on pupil need, enhancing teachers' response to that need, sharing the responsibility, building appropriate support

learn lead the most successful schools. Pedagogical leaders are focused on teaching and learning and are knowledgeable about and actively engaged in building personal, collective, and organizational capabilities.

One of my personal challenges was in being appointed principal when I was a relatively inexperienced teacher. This meant that I had to continue my personal development in teaching and learning from a stance of being more a spectator than a participant in the classroom learning process. There are advantages and disadvantages to being a spectator. As a spectator, you have the opportunity to observe closely the experience of students with the curriculum, and you can do this in many varied contexts. The disadvantage is that without the experience of truly engaging a room full of students, you don't really build an appreciation for the practicalities of working through learning experiences in a real context. One way I compensated for this was to visit with very gifted teachers in contexts outside my own.

Broadening the Network: Universities and Beyond

University faculty have always been influential and helpful in my learning. During my principalships, I always engaged with professors in a dialogue about my work in schools. Expressing a willingness to share their research and that of colleagues, they responded to my never-ending questions. Sometimes these relationships were reciprocal, and I was able to provide a setting for their research in return for the professional dialogue. But in others, it was purely one-way, allowing me to "pick the brains" of someone who knew some things extraordinarily well and gather pertinent professional readings while clarifying my own "muddy" thinking.

Teaching Is Learning

During my career I have learned to refine and clarify my thinking, bring language to my intuitive actions, and discover new interconnections between ideas through teaching others. Whether it's a workshop repeated many times over, an ongoing training program in some distant country, a keynote speech, or teaching a graduate course, teaching is a powerful tool for one's own learning, perhaps even more than for the learning of others. Having to explain one's actions, intuitive ideas, operating principles, deep understandings, and leadership behavior to others who question, refine, and represent their own understandings of important ideas enables a teacher to find more thoughtful language and constructs to represent his or her own thinking and behavior. In my diverse leadership roles, I am invariably teaching some course or other for various institutions. I have found that teaching constantly enables me to confront my deepest-held assumptions about teaching, learning, and leadership.

Collective Classroom Inquiry and Data Collection

Spending time gathering data is always informative. Whether we are merely noting the reading topics, genres, and audiences for reading in a class; conducting specific literacy conferences; or recording students' comments about their understanding of the learning task and levels of engagement, we cannot help but learn more about the process of learning. Obviously, the more deeply we understand learning in the local and classroom context, the more useful our comments will be to others. The advantages of this activity are considerable, not only for our own personal learning and understanding but also for modeling a very important activity for others.

Mentors and Mentoring

Doug and Hugh were extraordinarily fine young principals I met in my first principal training course. The three of us developed a professional bond that lasted for many years. We each worked in different districts, and once a year the three of us would spend a day visiting each of our schools. These days were extraordinary in that we had sufficient trust to be very frank in our observations and questions about what we observed. Hugh, in particular, had a way of questioning the assumptions underpinning the practice he observed. The importance of this mentoring is to be found in the high level of trust we established (we were equals rather than experts or novices, both mentors and mentored), enabling us to cut to the chase when responding to and reflecting on our observations. There was no evaluative component, and each of us could return to his workplace deep in thought and full of ideas and possibilities.

Other mentoring projects I have played a role in illustrate the principles of personal and collective learning described here. For instance, in the Peel Universities Partnership (PUP), a dynamic partnership between the Faculty of Education at York University in Toronto, the Ontario Institute for Studies in Education (OISE) at the University of Toronto, and the Peel District School Board (located west of Toronto), there were many projects through which teacher development and capacity-building were studied and supported. Looking across four specific projects in particular,[11] the following consistent lessons emerged:

1. Grounding teachers' development in tasks directly related to and rooted in aspects of work that preoccupy the participants works best.
2. Ongoing, focused, and informed teacher development is sustained by an infrastructure of purpose, time, process knowledge and expertise, strong support, modeling, and demonstrations by leaders (see Chapter 5).
3. Teacher dialogue is best informed first by the students' experience of the curriculum and evidence of teachers' practice, and only then by current research/examples of exemplary practice.

4. Teachers and administrators need guidance and support in the design and processes required to enable these "communities of practice" to emerge and be sustained. Knowledge-building dialogue requires a sizable allocation of time, clearly defined purpose, expert facilitation, the building of relational trust, and the means to move from having a good idea to collective action (see Chapter 7).

5. Although we have gathered little evidence about this finding, I am convinced that the kind of learning that is evident across these projects—practice-based, focused, going deeper and deeper into participants' understanding and actions—is the kind of learning teachers are most able to incorporate into their practice.

6. Teacher development in these projects is job-embedded; it creates and is supported by a culture of shared purpose, trust, inquiry, and collaboration.

7. Participants in the various projects have narrowed their purposes and have focused their energies and spirit, thus giving a sense of control over their work agenda, which leads to greater satisfaction.

8. The blurring of lines between teacher development (learning) and work creates a synergy that builds upon itself. When professional learning and capacity-building are incorporated into work, then the likelihood of the new learning transferring to everyday practice is high.

A FOCUS ON TEACHING AND LEARNING

In reflecting on my personal learning experiences described herein, I am somewhat surprised by my own preoccupation with teaching and learning. It is not that I didn't learn other things that were important to my role; it is just that to contribute constructively to the ongoing professional learning dialogue that permeated the work of the schools where I was principal, this was the area that I had to continually develop, refine, and improve. Although keenly attracted to leadership and improvement throughout my educational career, I found my formal studies pursuing the teaching of teachers and the learning of students far more rewarding because they related directly to improving the life chances of the students for whom I was responsible. In the next chapter, particularly in the case of Southern Cross Public School, we clearly see the elements described above in action.

REFLECT ON THESE QUESTIONS

1. How much and in what ways do you use your personal time for your own professional and learning development?
2. How do you learn best? What are the experiences that translate into improved practices for you?
3. If, as school leader, you are not deeply knowledgeable (and many of us aren't) about curriculum, teaching, and learning, how do you define and what is the important role you will play with regard to continuous improvement in these areas?
4. How and to what extent have you and your colleagues embraced the concepts of choice theory and its ramifications for student learning?
5. What strategies, both structural (e.g., time, space, and role) and relational (e.g., interacting constructively with others, building trust), have you and your colleagues enacted to ensure that all students are known extraordinarily well?
6. How and to what extent have you been able to put in place support structures and practices that ensure that the responsibility for class instruction and for meeting the needs of individuals is a shared one?
7. As a school leader, how and to what extent do you spend your time with respect to continuous improvement and improving the life chances of all students?
8. What specific practices and procedures are in place to ensure that at-risk students are known extraordinarily well over time by their classroom teacher(s)?
9. What specific practices and procedures are in place to ensure that the needs of at-risk teachers are transparent, supported, and continuously subject to constant improvement?

FOR FURTHER READING

Fullan, M. (2009). *Motion leadership: The skinny on becoming change savvy.* Thousand Oaks, CA: Sage.

Cycling from practice to theory and back, this book helps readers to understand problems, work with change, and mobilize colleagues to collaborate and focus on capacity-building.

Robertson, J. (2005). *Coaching leadership.* Wellington, New Zealand: NZCER Press.

Robertson's splendid book not only advocates articulately for the necessity of leadership coaching, but sets out practically what good coaching can and should look like.

CHAPTER 5

Capacity-Building: The Promise of Professional Learning Communities

This chapter seeks to make more explicit the complexity of how teachers work together in order to learn together—building capacity for all to incessantly improve. In Chapter 5 you will learn about

- the experiences of teachers as they engage in sustained ongoing dialogue about the documented learning experiences of their students;
- fundamental principles that underpin the work of a robust learning community;
- specific strategies to enable teachers to inquire and learn together;
- six core capacities that need to be developed in the successful school; and
- detailed plans of action and roles that leaders can deploy in building schoolwide capacity.

After leaving Cloverdale Public School, I spent a year working on my doctorate at the University of Toronto, which enabled me to reflect on my leadership practice and to plan to do better in the future. When I then was appointed principal at Southern Cross Public School, I was determined to create a structure embedded in the day-to-day work of the school that would permit the development of an informed continuous discourse among teachers about student learning. My purpose in attempting to do this was to build into teachers and my own day-to-day work a means of constantly gathering information about student learning so we could improve our appreciation of student experience and our classroom teaching. It was to be about collective knowledge-building. I envisioned deep, ongoing conversations involving all my new colleagues about teaching and learning, leading to a coherent, consistent, and rich experience for the youngsters at Southern Cross, a low-socioeconomic, high-immigrant, multicultural, multilingual community.

Our story begins with Andreas, a teacher in his fourth year of teaching who, like many of his colleagues, was working hard to fathom the intricacies of second language teaching. In a meeting with 15 of his teacher colleagues designed to explore the challenges of English language teaching, he played an audiotape of a writing conference from his grade 4 classroom. He was animated as he introduced the scenario: Yasmin, a 9-year-old recently arrived from rural Sindh in Pakistan, has written a story about her life in a small village in her home country. She has written it in Sindhi, a language unfamiliar to Andreas. He asks her to read the piece to her classmates. She is shy but seems pleased to be given an opportunity to share. Andreas struggles to find a response to her story in a language he doesn't understand. "Can you tell us what it's about in English?" one of her classmates asks. Yasmin knows very little English and struggles to explain. Andreas calls the school's office. Is there another pupil in the school who can speak Sindhi? Fortunately there is; his name is Zulfiqar, and he is in grade 5.

Zulfiqar attempts to read Yasmin's piece. He struggles, as he was only 7 years old when he immigrated to Canada, and before that he had attended a private school where the instructional languages were Urdu and English. However, Yasmin and Zulfiqar manage to reconstruct the story. It is about the beautiful orchards and market gardens in Sindh, which are watered by a canal fed by the Indus River. She tells of the camels and donkeys used to move the fruits and vegetables from the village to Hyderabad to be sold. Her classmates are fascinated. They want to know more about camels, donkeys, and fresh fruit. "What was it like to live in your village?" they ask. "Did you get to ride a camel? How big is a camel?" Yasmin is a bit overwhelmed by all the attention, but with help from Zulfiqar, she answers a number of the questions.

During this lesson, Andreas, who wrestles with his teaching of English language learners, stressed to his class the importance of children reading and writing in their first language. He responds to Yasmin by asking her to clarify her narrative and has tried to find out how well the story hangs together. He is aware of the importance of story in children's lives and that a sense of story is a potent indicator of literacy. For Andreas, diversity is a resource—a source of knowledge bringing novelty, improvisation, and a planetary perspective to his work and the learning of his pupils.

Andreas's presentation led to an important conversation with colleagues about the significance of first language learning and the appropriateness of encouraging and fostering first language, particularly with new immigrant pupils who initially are unable to read and write in English. His colleagues appreciate his struggles and are very positive about the value he places on first language learning. Fellow teachers share examples of their approaches to teaching English to immigrant pupils who have differing first languages. Essential questions are raised! For how long do we encourage first language writing, and when is it appropriate to stress writing in the second language, English? Is it appropriate to have a first language story translated into English? How would this help or hinder students' literacy development? Andreas clearly works in a context that requires him, along with colleagues, to examine and question his practice with a view toward improvement.

WHAT MAKES FOR EFFECTIVE PROFESSIONAL LEARNING?

Andreas's dialogue with colleagues portrayed above gives us a glimpse into the detailed collective examination of students' experience and their classroom learning. This attention to classroom practice and the assumptions that underpin it is required to begin to understand and appreciate the nuances and sophistication necessary for us to continually deepen our understanding of teaching and learning. We will learn more of the processes behind his experience later in the chapter when we examine the case of Southern Cross Public School.

Educators working in schools almost anywhere on the planet during the last 30 years have found themselves in contexts calling for improvement. A curious feature of this phenomenon is, for the most part, that school-based educators are typically positioned as objects to be manipulated and controlled from outside by distant administrators and politicians, rather than as professional creators of a learning culture within.[1] This chapter provides an extended example in which school-based educators, precisely the people who deal directly with the learning of their pupils, have indeed become the creators and sustainers of their schools, changing and improving learning culture. They have taken charge! In doing so, they reject manipulation by others by embracing a deep commitment to continuous professional learning to improve the life chances of all students.

In examining teacher development and learning through a very thorough meta-analysis of 97 studies of the relationship between educator development and substantive pupil outcomes, Timperley et al. reached significant conclusions in the four following areas:[2]

1. *The context of professional learning and development.*[3] Researchers identified seven elements that are important for promoting professional learning in ways that impact positively and substantively on student learning:
   - providing sufficient time for extended opportunities to learn and using this time effectively;

- engaging external expertise;
- engaging teachers in the learning process;
- challenging problematic discourses;
- providing opportunities to interact in a community of professionals;
- ensuring that content is consistent with wider policy trends; and
- having leaders actively lead the professional learning activities.

2. *The content of professional development.*[4] Successful professional learning and development include discipline knowledge and a focus on the interrelationship between such fundamentals as
   - new curricula, pedagogy, and assessment information;
   - knowledge of pupils, including their developmental progressions in relation to curricula and culture and their linguistic and cultural resources;
   - and theoretical frameworks and conceptual tools.

   This range of content can be examined best through collective teacher inquiry. The skills of teacher inquiry include
   - analysis of teachers' own practice and exploring new possibilities;
   - the ways in which practice impacts diverse learners;
   - and new possibilities for evaluating the adequacy and improvement of practice.

3. *Activities constructed to promote professional learning.*[5] The findings didn't support any particular kind of learning activity or form as being more effective than others. Rather, the researchers emphasized the importance of teachers engaging in multiple and aligned opportunities that supported them in learning and applying new understandings and skills.

4. *Learning processes.*[6] Changing practice in substantive ways is difficult. Timperley et al. found that few studies have directly addressed the processes involved in changing teacher practice. It is indeed a neglected area. Their findings, although far from conclusive, do suggest that teachers' responses varied according to whether new understandings were consistent with current practice or created dissonance with it. There were promising examples of teachers learning to regulate their own learning and that of others.

These findings will be useful in examining the case study of Southern Cross Public School that follows, and we will return to them later in the chapter. This case demonstrates both the challenges implicit in and the potential for creating robust learning communities.

CASE STUDY: SOUTHERN CROSS PUBLIC SCHOOL

The learning community my teacher colleagues and I created at Southern Cross Public School illustrates many of the key principles described at the end of this chapter. We jointly gathered information and developed through consensus a morally compelling purpose to which all could commit. Collectively, we designed an infrastructure for inquiry and knowledge-building. We learned to participate vigorously through dialogue, inquiry, and shared classroom practice as we sought to build personal, collective, and organizational capacity in order to improve the life chances of our pupils.[7] At the time, we called the more formal process and structure "professional growth," but more recently I have come to call it Continuous After-Learning Review (CALR).

Southern Cross was a needy school of approximately 530 students in grades K–6. Substantial numbers of new non-English-speaking immigrant students, a sizable portion of the population living below the poverty level, a high crime rate in the neighborhood, and a significant portion of families receiving govenment assistance and parented by a single parent meant that many youngsters came to school ill-prepared to learn. In the months prior to my actual appointment, I visited classrooms, met several times with the entire teaching staff, and facilitated a process of identifying student needs. From this data-rich process I was able to forge a consensus with my colleagues around "literacy learning for all" as the core purpose of our future work together. This gave me the summer to plan how to move strategically to enact this compelling purpose.

Strategic Actions Taken During the First 15 Months

On returning from summer vacation, I provided an individualized reading for each teacher with a personal note asking him or her to respond and to share the article with colleagues. I saw this as the first step toward creating a reading culture within the school. Professional learning cultures are also reading cultures.

Having established the professional growth design team of six teachers plus myself the previous June, we initiated the first CALR session during the first week of school. Each session involved every teacher for a 2-hour dialogue about student writing. As I describe in detail later in this chapter, during this first session each teacher was asked to read a short professional article about student writing development and bring a sample of student writing to speak about with colleagues. As anticipated, more questions were raised than answered. However, the first blush of an ongoing dialogue and inquiry was created. The example of Andreas used to open this chapter provides the reader with a feeling for how these sessions unfolded as time progressed.

During this first year together, teaching colleagues and I were able to utilize 30 to 40 hours of instructional time for each teacher, which amounted to approximately one third of the 100 hours we planned to provide for these professional growth-provoking sessions. The remaining time came from meeting times, professional activity days, and teachers' personal time.

All through the first 3 months, we restructured teachers' planning and professional meeting time from the traditional grade-level meetings to divisional meetings, that is, kindergarten to grade 3 and grades 4 to 6. The reasoning here was to lengthen the learning horizon so that teachers began to see development over time rather than just 1 year at a time. For teachers to see that what and how they practice affects the lives and learning of students in the future and is informed by students' past experience dramatically broadens their perspective on student learning and the responsibility they have for it.

By the second year, approximately 25 to 30% of the classrooms were restructured as multi-age classrooms (i.e., family-grouped, spanning 3 grade levels). All teachers remained with their pupils for a minimum of 2 years. In contexts where pupils and families have complex and varied needs, part of the secret to success is to structure the school in ways that build deep, sustaining relationships. Elsewhere I have called this investing in social capital. Teachers staying with their pupils for 2 or 3 years, multi-age grouping, and integrated subjects in secondary schools are strategies designed to build closer relationships between families, teachers, and pupils and, most important, to ensure that teachers know their pupils extraordinarily well.

During the first 15 months, many strategic directions were moved to action. These directions were driven by the overarching purpose of improving literacy for all and were interrelated. Together the following directions changed our structure, culture, and use of time in ways that increased our organization's capacity to respond collectively, effectively, and in an informed way to the varied needs of our diverse population:

- All classroom teaching moved toward enabling pupils to explore, inquire, demonstrate, and apply their knowledge about topics of substance and depth.
- All pupils engaged in personal reading and writing on a daily basis. They maintained personal reading logs and writing folders. In-classroom libraries were established.

- Team teaching was actively encouraged and supported. The timetable was structured to enable cross-grade teams of teachers to meet and plan together.
- Teachers actively engaged with and were responsive to the linguistic, cultural, and socially diverse needs of the pupils. In fact, diversity became an extraordinary resource.
- Special-needs students were integrated into the regular classrooms with some support.
- Representative cross-grade in-school teams met regularly to review and plan programs for exceptional students.
- There was an active process to engage and inform parents of program developments as they emerged. Often, we repeated for parents (with some modification because of time) sessions and our findings emerging from the continuous after-learning review.
- Parents had a choice of classroom placement whenever possible, and families with more than one pupil usually placed siblings with the same team of teachers.
- Decision-making was shared, and for significant tasks (e.g., developing school purposes, designing the professional growth process [CALR], allocating budget and other resources), all stakeholders were involved in finding consensus.
- Teachers were supported to take on leadership roles.
- Budget was utilized specifically to support the agreed-upon school purposes (e.g., school funds and funds raised were heavily invested in quality children's literature and nonfiction books for both the classroom and the library).
- University of Toronto and York University placed preservice teacher candidates in the classrooms for extended periods. These teachers were known as "teaching partners" and helped release the case study teachers to participate in professional growth and class reviews.
- Performing artists (art, music, drama, puppetry, theater, poetry, storytelling), including a resident artist, performed regularly in the school. These experiences were commonly linked to classroom programs. The arts became a major medium for instruction throughout the school, across subjects, ages, and classrooms.[8]
- An in-school bookstore was established by parents in order to provide wonderful children's literature and to enable books to be recycled and made available to all to have in their homes.
- I organized 50% of my time to be engaged in activities such as observing, facilitating, gathering evidence, researching, and planning toward the goal of providing pedagogical leadership.

- Stressful times of the year (e.g., evaluation and report card writing periods at the end of each term) were identified, and teacher time during these periods was protected from interruptions and meetings.

The actions my staff and I took at Southern Cross were strategic in that they actively furthered the agreed-upon purposes of the school, complemented one another by adding value that was greater than single actions, and transformed the learning culture of the school.

Collective Capacity-Building: A Continuous After-Learning Review Session

Seventeen teachers, representing one-half of the Southern Cross staff, gather in the staffroom. Teachers from all grade levels and subjects participate in each group, the makeup of which typically varied from time to time. Each teacher is expected to bring some form of concrete representation of teaching and/or learning from their classroom to share at these sessions. As soon as there is a quorum of about 10 teachers, Clare, an experienced "family grouping" teacher, begins to share her data. She explains that she has videotaped a number of writing conferences with her grades 4, 5, and 6 pupils. Typically, about five pupils at a time would meet with her in the classroom writing center for about 45 minutes, during which time two or three would read aloud a current draft composition. Clare describes the scene: Safreen is sharing a rather lengthy piece that she is writing for the school newspaper. She has interviewed a number of the teaching partners (student teachers) who are working in classrooms throughout the school and is preparing a report. Because the writing conference lasts for about 25 minutes, Clare only shows part of her video.

This is what we observed: Safreen has read her entire draft, and the video shows the way her classmates and teacher give her feedback. Robert responds first. He likes the piece but wonders if it can really be called classroom news, as it is about many classrooms. Safreen is adamant: This is classroom news, and her work will be published as such. Clare intervenes and says that the piece is obviously of great interest, and the editors of the school paper can decide where it best fits. Jennifer, who helped with the interviews, says the piece is excellent. She wonders if there should be more about the pupils' experiences working with teaching partners. Clare asks her students to think about the piece from the perspective of someone who does not attend the school. What would they want to know? What would they understand about teaching partners? These questions spark a lot of discussion. Eventually, Robert notes that in her piece Safreen has never actually said what a teaching partner is. Each pupil has some ideas about how and where Safreen should add this information. Some recommend including it in the beginning, while others think the end of the article would be the best place for an explanation. After much discussion and prodding from Clare, it is agreed the reader needs to have this information at the beginning of the piece.

Teachers eagerly responded to Clare's sharing. They were impressed—first by the comprehensiveness of Safreen's draft, the way she had turned her interviews into meaningful text (copies had been distributed with Safreen's permission), and the thoughtful responses of her classmates. They also liked the time and detail in Clare's response to Safreen's report. Andreas linked this quality of interaction to the work that Professor Gordon Wells had shared from his earlier research about teacher/pupil interaction.[9] The link was to findings that teachers were more effective and learning was improved when their conversations were focused and in-depth with individuals and small groups rather than the typical short interactions with larger groups. (Wells had visited the school earlier in the year, and this is a good example of informing the dialogue through research.) The discussion quickly moved to the challenge that Clare was working on: How and to what extent is it possible for a 10-year-old to place him or herself in the shoes of the reader? The ability to distance oneself from one's own text is something most adult writers struggle with. Yet here we had 9-, 10-, and 11 year-olds examining a classmate's text through the eyes of a reader. This process was carefully designed and built into the way we worked together at Southern Cross. Here is how we did it.

An Infrastructure for the CALR

The school's representative design team, made up of six teachers and myself, structured the Continuous After-Learning Review in an effort to have a predictable dynamic process where participants could anticipate expectations with respect to the value, response, and support they would receive from colleagues when contributing to the conversation and thus build trust in the process and in colleagues. The infrastructure for the process consists of four crucial parts.

Preparation. Approximately 1 week prior to each session, an agenda is published by the design team that includes the following:

- focus question for the session (e.g., What evidence do we have of pupils developing and using a sense of story in their reading and writing?)

- request for participants to gather particular evidence (e.g., student work, an audio-/videotape of a teacher/student writing conference) to bring to the session
- carefully selected professional reading, pertinent to the focus question (e.g., a paper from *Language Arts* or the *Reading Teacher* on the role of narrative in pupil learning)

Participation Time. Sessions last for 2 hours. Time for these sessions is culled equally from in-class and out-of-class work time. Participating teachers' classes were integrated with a colleague's class for the duration. I found that meeting teachers halfway, as in half from classroom and half from non-instructional time, has been an important feature for securing the necessary time. Each session involves teachers of all subjects and grade levels. Teachers typically engage in the CALR process for about 100 hours per year. I call it the 100-hour solution.

Session Structure/Process. Most sessions at Southern Cross engaged half of the staff at a time. Typically, sessions begin with each participant sharing data (artifacts, videotapes, audiotapes, stories, pupils' work, etc.). Teachers talk about their interactions (what they say and do) with pupils, the design of their program, and the learning experiences and responses to the learning made by their students.

As each session proceeds, the content of the dialogue often turns to the implications of the experiences teachers share. Many times, preferred practices are identified and a general agreement is reached for faculty to collectively try a new technique or procedure. In order to address issues surrounding trust and purpose among and between participants and the new principal, we designed each first-year session with time to reflect at the close. The reflection focuses on the process (i.e., how well we have worked together, what we have learned today, and what further questions we have).

Informed Dialogue. What informs teacher talk in a CALR? Here are some basic parameters:

- the classroom experience of the learner (both the teacher and the pupil)
- current research, through relevant reading and periodical interaction by means of visits or audio or video conferencing with acknowledged experts in the field
- regular opportunities to attend and present at conferences

- exemplary practices observed when my teacher colleagues and I visited outstanding classrooms and had specific practices modeled and demonstrated by other teachers

With respect to selecting professional readings, it was important for the design team to choose relevant papers that would inform the dialogue. It was common to release a participant to spend an afternoon in the university library searching for an appropriate text or to call distinguished professors to recommend material. Berliner et al. argued that schools of education have "turned out generation after generation of teachers largely devoid of research understanding and appreciation"[10] and so, as Bruer explains, research is rarely used to inform educational practice.[11] One of the impacts of the professional readings was to create a pervasive "reading culture" within the school. Many of my colleagues tell me that "teachers never read," which is a sad statement about the profession. My experience is that professional reading can easily become part of the culture of the school. The trick is to find readings that are accessible and relevant to the moment and purpose of the school and to provide an infrastructure whereby the readings are integral to teacher learning and practice.

CALRs also involved interaction with local, national, and international university faculty and other educators. Important here was the role visiting educators were asked to play in the process. They were equal participants, listening and responding when their experience or research could contribute to or clarify the dialogue. The use of audio conferencing allowed educators from far away to listen to questions from the staff and respond for all to hear.

We also informed our dialogue through viewing and learning about exemplary practices during classroom visits, viewing videotape, and attending and speaking at conferences. As described above, teachers brought evidence (artifacts) from their classrooms to share at each session. This process of evidence-gathering was at times spontaneous and varied and at other times deliberate and systematic. Clearly one of the outcomes of gathering and sharing evidence across all classrooms and programs is making classroom practice transparent and visible to one's colleagues, the students, and their parents.

Finally, an important means of informing and deepening the quality of dialogue was the time to reflect built into our CALR sessions. Having time to reflect on experience and learning (even when we plan for it) is often pushed to the end of the day and put aside as a meeting exceeds the promised closing time. Yet for the organization to grow and to build capacity, time to reflect is critical! Through reflection, we bring our personal reactions and feelings to the collective experience and shared data. It is through reflection that we deepen our understanding by making personal connections to other experiences, stories, research, events, and practices. Reflection might involve a written response to our learning or the learning of students, an oral review of our learning, or a deep discussion of how principles underlying the CALR session might impact our future practice. It might examine the implications for assessment practices or how and what we need to communicate to parents with respect to our changed practices. It may review how we would measure the effectiveness of new practices in the future. Alternatively, reflection might review the saliency of the CALR process itself.

The Focused Conversation Method

An approach I like to use during and at the end of our CALR sessions is the focused conversation method.[12] Carefully selected questions bring out important understandings in time-efficient ways. The questions asked by me, members of the design team, and/or our teacher colleagues lead and focus the conversation. School leaders or others within the group need great skill to facilitate the participative learning process. This skill can be developed through specific training or guides (see "For Further Reading" at the end of the chapter).

Complex, yet deceptively simple, the focused conversation method structures facilitative discussions around four kinds of questions:[13]

O. *The Objective Level:* questions about facts, and external reality or impressions
R. *The Reflective Level:* questions to call forth immediate personal reactions to data, an internal response, emotions or feelings, hidden images or meanings, and association with facts identified at the objective level
I. *The Interpretive Level:* questions to draw out meaning, values, significance, and implications
D. *Decisional Level:* questions to elicit resolution, bring the conversation to a close, and enable individuals or the group to make a decision about the future

Examples of the use of these types of questions within a focused conversation framework are provided in Figure 5.1.

Figure 5.1. Focused Conversation During the Continuous After-Learning Review: How Questions Can Help

Here are two examples of the focused conversation method at work at the end of a 2-hour Continuous After-Learning Review Session.

On how we are learning to participate in the CALR, the design team might ask the following:

O. What words or phrases describe how we participated today? What is one thing we each did today?

R. What were the high points of our time together? What surprised you about the interactions? What concerns you?

I. What can we learn from our experience together? What powerful learning principles did we see at play today?

D. What did we do today that we want to continue next time? What do we need to do differently next time? Are their specific things we as a group need to learn or have training for, in order to work together more effectively in the future?

In a discussion about what we are learning and improving upon in our practice and with regard to students' learning, the design team might ask the following:

O. Describe one story you heard during our work this morning. What practical examples were shared? What words or phrases do you recall from our conversations?

R. How did you feel about the content of our work today? What were you reminded of in terms of your own practice?

I. What practices caught your attention? What ideas might you extend? What are the main lessons you learned from the morning's work?

D. What did you learn that is important for your pupils? What practices would you like to try or refine in your classroom? What is one thing you will do differently? What questions remain to be answered?

Themes and Voices

The Southern Cross case study demonstrates some compelling shifts in the ways participants experienced teaching and relationships with teacher colleagues and students. We were fortunate to have independent researchers interview a representative sample of one half of the staff at Southern Cross after 5 years of experience with the CALR process, which was also at the time of my departure. The interviews about and documentation of teachers' experience pointed to eight themes underpinning the ongoing professional knowledge-building of teachers and their improving classroom practice. These themes point to the conditions necessary for participation in a high-performing professional learning community. They indicate what it means to participate, teach, build knowledge, renew ourselves, and develop organizational capacity within an inquiry-based community of practice.

1. *Shared and Morally Compelling Purpose.* Teachers in our case study were strongly committed to improving the literacy learning of all students. The frequent gathering of data, documentation, and assessment made the needs of the students extremely transparent, immediate, and thus subject to analysis and reflection. Addressing issues such as literacy development was morally compelling to the participants.[14] The teachers' high degree of commitment to the inquiry process and collective refinement of practice seems deeply influenced by the perceived importance of the work. The major preoccupation for all participants was the examination of and learning about classroom practice and pupil learning. As Clare explains, "People feel the need to confirm and reaffirm and touch base with each other. . . . I mean, we have a shared reality here. And we are in agreement as to what it is that we're trying to pursue."

2. *Craft Knowledge Becomes Visible.* Regular gathering and sharing of classroom practices, procedures, student work, and observations through audiotape, videotape, artifact, and narrative clearly made the experience of pupils' and teachers' craft knowledge visible to the entire staff, regardless of role or position. The observable nature of the data enabled participants to question, examine underlying assumptions, discuss, refine, and reflect upon their own and others' professional practices. Annette, a grades 3, 4, and 5 classroom teacher, explains:

> Sometimes you would share a concern or a classroom practice that was similar, a similar concern or practice as other staff members. And I felt this really made for collegiality . . . because we realized that we weren't the only person in the school wrestling with the same ideas, that we all have the same concerns as we're trying to grow as teachers. . . . That really added to the whole climate within the school for learning where we are all engaged in a similar process of sharing our practice . . . and I think it really put the focus on the teacher as a learner.

The focus on the observable behavior, as opposed to belief, was perceived by participants as enabling safe and comfortable treatment of difficult issues.

3. Knowledge-Building Deepens the Understanding and Learning of Participants. When CALR participants focused their talk on specific classroom incidents,[15] they had the opportunity to go deeper and deeper into the craft knowledge underlying specific practices and/or behaviors. Carolyn, a grade 5 teacher, describes this process:

> We have to realize what we considered the best way to teach yesterday might not be tomorrow. When we listen to colleagues, add, and extend their and our own understanding, I really think we are creating our own knowledge. You know, we have to sort of keep our eyes open and realize there are not simple answers to a lot of the things that we are addressing . . . as long as we keep our minds open, keep questioning and extending our thoughts, then we'll continue to learn along with the children.

Participants developed an appreciation and understanding of their own learning and how alike their experience was to their pupils.

4. Collective Responsibility for the Program Leads to Consistent Experiences for Learners. The CALR design team (a vertical, i.e., cross-grade, stakeholder team) steered and evaluated the process, created the focus questions, and set priorities for program implementation across the school. Participation in the CALR, the whole-class review, and the in-school review teams (described in Chapter 4) ensured that all staff jointly shared the responsibility for learning in the school. Clearly, the collective learning of the participants affected all classrooms and all students in systemic ways. As Debbie explains, "I think we really do support the notion that there should be consistent messages that are given from class to class from year to year." I strongly believe we do a disservice to students when expectations about what it means to be a reader, a writer, a speller, a problem-solver, or a scientist change from year to year depending on the luck they have in being allocated to a certain teacher. Many schools I visit and have worked in are eclectic in that each teacher does their own thing, that is, the teachers are strongly individualistic and professionally private at the expense of the pupils who are trying to figure out what it means to a reader, a learner, a risk-taker, and so on. I am not arguing for the ideological mandate of a controlled curriculum, but rather for teachers and their leaders to forge an informed and collective understanding about the continuous learning experiences they provide for their pupils over time.

One of the perceived benefits of this collective responsibility was that it was not dependent on any one individual. As all were involved in the construction of a shared reality, the knowledge, values, norms, and passion remained with the group even when some members of staff left.

5. Honoring Adult Learning Principles. In setting the agenda, choosing their data, developing focus questions, and reflecting on process and practice, participants were able to experience self-directed learning in a process that recognized their wide range of previous experience, skills, interests, and competencies. They were able to participate in a supportive environment, free from personal criticism or threat with respect to competency. Molly explains, "We weren't expected to know everything, but we were expected to make the effort to grow." Participants made reference to feeling calm and/or safe, by recognizing that each held a different position with respect to the practice under examination and that this was okay: "I think there's a kind of general consensus within the school that people are growing and that we're all at different stages and will continue to grow hopefully forever."

Trust was built through accepting diversity in experience and practice and by facilitating a process designed to focus on teachers' current preoccupations in classroom practice. As Marilyn said,

> In professional growth sessions, when we first met, there was that hesitance. People sat back and were wondering what was going to be accepted. What were people going to say? They didn't want to feel incompetent and they didn't want to talk together on a basic or common level. But I think I have seen such a growth in the quality and openness in sharing our practice . . . our talk has grown so relevant and important to each of us.

In many ways, participants were learning to regulate their own learning and the learning of others.

6. Networking Broadly. At Southern Cross, teachers and I frequently engaged with educators in other schools, within the district level, and beyond as well as with universities. Informing the ongoing focused dialogue were opportunities to examine exemplary practices through visitations, workshops, and conferences; to explore relevant current research through readings, expert visitations, audio (telephone) and video conferences; and to regularly collect and share evidence from classrooms across the school.

Networking was extremely important and had serendipitous consequences. Nadia, the librarian, captured it well when she stated,

> I think people have pursued other means of growth. Not just the professional growth but because of the professional growth. I think a lot of people, well, almost all staff, apply for conferences, we're always looking for places that we can get money to develop ourselves professionally. . . . And I think that's maybe because of what's going on at school. People are always off on conferences and workshops . . . always reading and passing articles around. I mean, a good professional paper goes through this school like a dose of salts . . . just about everyone is taking a course of some nature. And I think the impetus for this has come from the professional growth.

7. An Inquiring, Collaborative Workplace Culture. The professional inquiry processes described above contributed significantly to the creation of an inquiring, collaborative culture. This manifested itself outside the three structured processes in the form of continuing dialogue and reflection on practice, a natural questioning of school policy and procedures, spontaneity in the formation of representative groups to solve problems and manage the business of running the school, and a confidence in taking risks in classroom practice. As Marsha describes it,

> We were talking before about not realizing how much we do because of professional learning, or how much thought we carry over into our everyday lives or take away from the actual sessions. One of the things that happened last year was that we had an author come to the school. . . . We took him out for lunch. I guess there were five of us at the table and the author. We immediately sat down and started to talk about a learning incident that had happened at school that morning. And we then continued on and we started to talk about ideas — of philosophies. After about ten minutes, the author sat back, looked at us, and said, "I cannot believe how you people are talking. You're talking about philosophy. You are talking about things that are important to you in your jobs. I see a great deal of reflection." He said that he taught at a university and he and his colleagues did not have that kind of relationship. They didn't talk about those kinds of things when they got together.

A commitment to and preoccupation with reading, experimentation with practice, inquiry, reflection, assessment of progress, and continuous learning became embedded in the way the school did business. As Mike, a grade 5/6 teacher, explains,

> It always amazes me that after staff meeting, I find that we often sit around tables and begin to talk about the kinds of things we've done in our classroom, even though that might be not what we had talked about in the staff meeting. . . . Sometimes I find that after a professional growth meeting we've been talking about a certain subject. And a day or two later, an idea will come to me obviously because I've had time to reflect. And you see somebody coming down the hall and you say, "Remember what we were talking about yesterday? Well, I just had another thought." And so you have often good professional growth sessions standing in the middle of the hall. Or even on yard duty.

8. In-Depth Learning in One Area of Inquiry Transferred Readily to Other Areas of the Program. Literacy pervaded the entire day for students and teachers. Visitors to our case study site, indeed the participants themselves, wondered at the efficacy of focusing on literacy for such a long period. When the Provincial Ministry of Education (equivalent to a state board of education in the United States) mandated a new science curriculum, this was seen by the professional growth planning team as an opportunity to explore the genre of inquiry through reading, writing, speaking, listening, presenting, and reflection. For example, Brenda explained,

> We were getting lots of articles to read all the time. I was taking in all this input and trying to have it make sense intellectually as I began to work with the children and read more and talk to colleagues in other sessions. And I've worked with another girl in the same classroom. We team teach. So, all these things have been working together. I think it's just been within this last year that it's all kind of clicked. Things have really made sense to me. The theory is now practice. It's part of who I am and what I'm doing in the classroom all the time. I see what I learn about one issue can be applied to another. What I learn about reading also applies to math and so on. . . . And it fits together so nicely, these pieces that seemed to be all in different places at first.

What Brenda is explaining is that when our inquiry and learning go deep, they readily transfer to all aspects of teaching and learning. Literate students inquire, gather data, develop hypotheses, solve problems, and avidly convey their understandings to others in all parts of their learning.

In concluding the discussion on the key learnings from this case, I want to highlight the excitement, passion, energy, and commitment that grew around this rigorous work. I, for one, couldn't wait to get to work each day to find out what the next discovery or insight was going to be. Yes, the work was about process and about building personal, collective, and organizational capacity, but it was much more than that. It was about a way of being—about building a confident, intellectual, and resourceful identity through intense professional engagement and relationships with others. Perhaps there is no more-compelling evidence of the power of this work than the fact that 70% of the Southern Cross participants with just a few years of this experience went on to be promoted to positions of leadership and responsibility within and beyond the district.

Southern Cross represents many other breakthroughs! It answers the fundamental change question: "How do leaders scale up exemplary practice found in small pockets of their school to affect change in all classrooms?" It clearly addresses the challenges of teachers finding and having a voice in their own and the learning of others as well as the critical work of the school and raises the level of teachers' professionalism; it specifically addresses the need for hugely improving the quality and responsiveness of teachers' professional judgment; and, finally, it seriously addresses the question of how reliability and consistency (coherence) in teaching practice can be developed without falling into "groupthink."

The case of Southern Cross Public School may be examined in light of Timperley's meta-analysis described earlier in this chapter. Figure 5.2 shows how the strategies we employed at Southern Cross achieved the objectives for effective teacher development that Timperley identified.

HOW TO BUILD A PROFESSIONAL
LEARNING COMMUNITY

This chapter is about professional learning and development—capacity-building. Capacity-building is about developing powerful knowledge bases by moving beyond the sharing of information to refining, improving, extending, and transforming this knowledge as participants construct and experience it over time. All participants in the community are legitimate contributors to the shared, morally compelling purposes of the organization and take pride in the knowledge advances of the group.

The Continuous After-Learning Review Process was central to this work at Southern Cross Public School. Here is some information you may find useful in implementing the process in differing contexts.

Figure 5.2. Southern Cross Compared with Best Practices

Significant Findings	Timperley	Southern Cross P. S.
	Provide sufficient and effective use of time for extended opportunities for teachers to learn	The 100-hour solution (CALR enabled and intensified teachers' continuous learning.)
	Engage external expertise	Built networks with universities; utilized audio and video conferencing; impemented best practices from elsewhere
Context of Professional Learning and Development	Focus on engaging teachers in the learning process	CALR (All teachers engaged deeply with the learning process.)
	Challenge problematic discourses	Practiced continuous, sustained, and inquiry-based dialogue; critical incidents used to inform practice; assumptions uncovered and questioned
	Interact in a community of professionals (Content is consistent with wider policy trends.)	Southern Cross recognized locally and internationally for exemplary practice with regard to literacy learning
	Leaders actively lead professional learning activities	Principal participated and contributed to facilitation of every CALR session

Content of Professional Learning and Development	Uncover interrelationship between new curricula, pedagogy, and assessment information	Classroom inquiry in attending to the students' learning experience uncovered the reality of curriculum, teaching methods, and assessment data
	Cultivate knowledge of students and their developmental progressions in relation to curriculum and culture	The entire focus of teacher learning is grounded in knowing students well and, in particular, learning to respond to their individual needs and interests
	Use linguistic and cultural resources, theoretical frameworks, and conceptual tools	Professional readings contributed to the theory-building discourse
	Strengthen outcomes for diverse student learners	High-immigrant, culturally and linguistically diverse student population preoccupied our learning and improvement
Professional Learning Activities	Teachers engage in multiple and aligned opportunities supporting them to learn and apply new understandings and skills	Opportunities included CALR, whole-class reviews, in-school review teams, conference presentations, contributing to books and videos, book clubs, reading-response groups, and action-research groups, all aligned with the morally compelling purpose
	Teachers learn to regulate their own learning and the learning of others	Honoring adult-learning principles, use of representative stakeholder planning team placed teachers in the driver's seat of their own learning and knowledge-building
Learning Processes	Develop skills of teacher inquiry including action research, analysis of teachers' own practice, and exploring new possibilities	Practitioner research methods underpinned continuous review and reflection
	Use methods for inquiring into the adequacy and improvement of practice	Constant data-gathering indicated the efficacy of practice

Examining the Continuous After-Learning Review Process

On the surface, the CALR seems as easy as getting a group of teachers into a room and having them share and talk about practice. In fact, at North Ridge Secondary School I helped a group of interested teachers design some sessions that initially were this simple. In the design meeting, they told me that their colleagues were quite shell-shocked with the pace of change and were suspicious of imposed agendas. We could not use phrases like *data collection, action research, classroom inquiry, documentation,* or *reflection.* All these terms were associated with previous change initiatives and carried emotional baggage for the participants.

The model we designed invited participants to bring and share one story about a teacher–student learning moment in their classroom.[16] Judith Newman was the first to describe these moments as critical incidences, and they are very valuable when used as a basis to examine the assumptions underlying our practice. Asking participants to tell a story and to extrapolate a teaching lesson/principle from it has the potential to elicit a sophisticated and, in time, informed dialogue. Surprisingly, we had good attendance at our first session and some great stories were told. For the second session, we (the school's design team and I) asked participants to bring more stories, this time with a more particular focus on negotiating learning outcomes with students. In addition, we asked each teacher to embellish their story with some concrete illustration such as students' work: photographs, audio or video of teacher student interaction, lesson plans, or whatever. Session by session, we were able to build trust and develop a growing sophistication and focus in stories told and evidence gathered by participants. The questions modeled by the facilitators helped the group develop more mindful questions and responses to the stories that formed the basis for their learning.

As we saw above, getting started is one thing, but nurturing and sustaining this process requires thoughtful, sophisticated design and facilitation. The CALR method is not merely layered over a traditional structure or approach to schooling, as is all too commonly the fate of innovative ideas. In fact, I am sure that an attempt to layer this process on top of a traditional school organization would fail. The CALR requires an organizational structure that provides the time, a receptive place, roles, responsibilities, and supportive design to succeed: in short, a new and improved organizational capacity. Discussing new issues as they arise during the course of an inquiry requires deliberate and informed action. The beauty of the process in identifying issues related to school purposes is that the shared domains of personal and collective learning, as well as the relationships developed during the process, enable the community of teachers to respond assertively to schoolwide, classroom, and student needs.

Figure 5.3. Continuous After-Learning Review

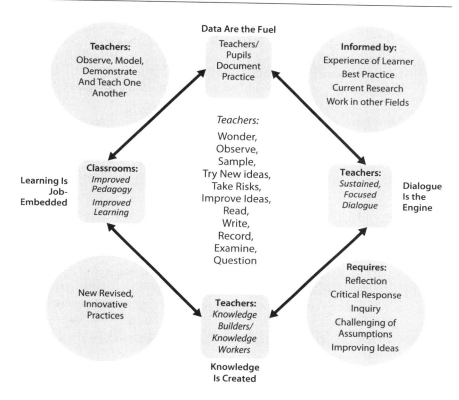

A Knowledge-Building Cycle. The Continuous After-Learning Review growth experience at Southern Cross is a cyclical process (see Figure 5.3). The capacity of participants is built through the gathering of data, which in turn fuel and inform the engine of growth via the sustained, focused dialogue of participants. Out of this lively teacher discourse emerge new understandings, knowledge, and innovation. The outcome is substantially more than new information because it is constantly questioned, documented, enacted, and reexamined. It is continuous knowledge-building at its finest. Some of my teacher colleagues describe the ongoing dialogue by the acronym GHOST: Good, Honest, Open, Sustained Talk. Others have expanded the acronym to GHOSSST, standing for Good, Honest, Open, Safe, Sustained, and Synergetic Talk.

A New Workplace Culture. Professional learning and development require teachers and other participants to talk intensely about their classroom reality by sharing their most fundamental beliefs and specific behaviors of themselves and their students. Constructive discourse requires:

1. Equality and the absence of coercive influences
2. Listening with empathy
3. Bringing assumptions into the open
4. Rigorous engagement with information for the purposes of knowledge and capacity-building
5. More time than most educators think[17]

These requirements demand a radically new workplace culture with new, sophisticated, and highly effective roles and responsibilities for principals, teachers, facilitators, and students. This change means:

For principals

- modeling participation, inquiry, and nonjudgmental reflection
- placing oneself in the shoes of students and/or teachers in order to appreciate the meaning that learning experiences and events have for the individual or group
- relinquishing the role of expert and embracing one of curious, vulnerable head learner—a major shift for some principals

For teachers

- having the confidence to share concise documentation of learning events from their classrooms
- having the trust and assurance in one's colleagues and leaders to expose personal classroom practices
- being prepared to appreciate and value the experiences of others as legitimate representations of their current thinking and learning
- thinking deeply about classroom practices and student learning experiences in order to uncover and understand the underlying assumptions
- valuing the intellectual nature of this collective, practical, and theoretical work

For external facilitators working in someone else's school

- abandoning the stance of outside expert who has all the answers and enabling everyone's experience and practice to contribute to collective development of expertise

- honoring and valuing the learning experience of others and helping them to think deeply about practice and underlying assumptions

For students

- learning more than the mindless completion of tasks assigned by the teacher
- examining for themselves and others the value, utility, and effectiveness of each learning experience
- contributing to the documentation of their learning experience so they and others may examine, reflect, and think deeply about the assumptions underlying this learning experience
- participating in the design and assessment of their learning and the learning of others

High-performing professional learning communities arise through the continuous, focused, informed, sustained, open, professional dialogue of all its members. Effective professional learning communities significantly improve the capacity of its members to do their tasks well. In education this begs the question, what capacities are needed?

What Kinds of Capacity Are Needed?

Michael Fullan has identified six core capacities,[18] and I have taken the liberty of adapting them and providing examples of activities to build each capacity. In some schools in which I have worked, we found it effective to identify "resident experts": teachers who have built deep knowledge and understanding about a single capacity and are responsible for bringing that perspective to the design and work of the school. These roles are noted under each category below.

1. Uncovering and making transparent "moral purpose," then moving quickly to informed action (Teachers and principals need to appreciate the importance and power of finding the moral purpose that will steer the improvement work of the school.)

Examples of capacity-building activities

- frequently sampling and examining students' learning experiences
- habitually engaging stakeholders in informed inquiry and dialogue about purposes

- establishing and continuously refining purposes
- constructing an "Image of the Learner" with all stakeholders
- designing and enacting strategic directions
- gathering ongoing information in order to evaluate progress in achieving desired purposes
- gathering broad-based information about pupil achievement, dropout rates, discipline incidents, course completion, and post-school outcomes
- identifying individuals to bring the "moral purpose" perspective to all discussions

2. Knowledge of professional and organizational learning (Teachers in effective schools understand what it takes to continually improve their practice and that of their colleagues. They contribute this knowledge to the design of and work of the school.)

Examples of capacity-building activities

- engaging in ongoing classroom inquiry (practitioner research)
- having time and means to reflect on classroom practice and the experience of the learner
- contributing to knowledge-building with respect to all aspects of the work of the school
- establishing norms and expectations for professional and organizational learning
- encouraging teachers to connect and interact with the broader educational community
- designing a powerful infrastructure for supporting school-based professional and organizational learning
- identifying individuals to bring the "professional and organizational learning" perspective to all discussions

3. Knowledge of participation/relationship-building (Educators need to know how to participate and how to build trust with their colleagues through lasting professional relationships.)

Examples of capacity-building activities

- providing specific training in facilitation skills
- bringing together a stakeholder design team with the capability to orchestrate events

- building in time and an effective process for reflecting on groups' participation
- building consensus to honor and thrive on a diversity of views
- documenting, questioning, and examining classroom practice thoughtfully
- becoming familiar with and able to honor adult learning principles
- identifying individuals to bring the "participative design and process" perspective to all discussions

4. Knowledge of context (Educators need to understand their context, which includes the community's needs, the students' needs, and the program needs; It is definitely not one size fits all when it comes to improving the life chances of all students.)

Examples of capacity-building activities

- gathering information from and about the community through surveys, focus groups, and personal conversations
- examining deeply and acting constructively on understandings of the community's cultural, linguistic, and social characteristics
- creating partnerships with social agencies, universities, arts groups, recreational agencies, and businesses in the community to broaden support for the school's activities and engagement with and understanding of the broader community
- plugging into local, national, and international networks of ideas, resources, and practices
- practicing positive politics
- constructing a shared school/community accountability pact
- identifying individuals to bring the "contextual" perspective to all discussion

5. Knowledge of the change process and sustaining change (Teachers need to appreciate and understand how successful change occurs so that they may constructively contribute to improving the learning of all over time.)

Examples of capacity-building activities

- initiating change despite the system; structures, policies, traditions, and values often deter opportunities for growth, so leaders need to learn to work around them

- understanding and managing the implementation dip: When making change, things typically get worse before they get better
- undertaking explicit training in the design and management of the change process
- monitoring and sustaining improvements
- building lasting organizational capacity and human capability
- understanding and creating a sustainable school environment where pupils and their teachers daily engage in sustainable living practices
- identifying individuals to bring the "change process" perspective to all discussions

6. Pedagogical knowledge about the practice of teaching and learning (Effective schools have teachers who are extraordinarily knowledgeable about effective classroom practice—teachers who are constantly learning and teaching their colleagues about their new learning.)

Examples of capacity-building activities

- challenging fundamental beliefs and assumptions about learning and teaching
- gathering and sharing authentic (evidence-based) assessment information in order to know students well and design assessment activities that enable student learning
- understanding and using the interrelatedness of students' development in order to support each individual in the learning process
- being knowledgeable about and able to act on the implications of child and adolescent psychology, multiple intelligences, brain theory, cooperative group work, and learning styles
- being able to document and examine classroom practices and learners' experience, then articulate them to colleagues
- developing meta-cognitive knowledge about learning and the relationship between teachers' own and their students' learning
- deepening content knowledge
- identifying individuals to bring the "teaching and learning" perspective to all discussion

Given these capacities, we move now to specific strategies school leaders can use to improve the professional and organizational learning of their school or, for that matter, the district.

Strategies to Improve Professional and Organizational Learning

Growth-provoking strategies, when aligned to school purposes and enabled by a supporting infrastructure for teacher learning and development, facilitate powerful professional and organizational learning. Many strategies made possible by the infrastructure for learning described in the Southern Cross case study support capacity-building within the school. Here are a few examples over and beyond the CALR sessions described in this book that could serve as an additional ingredient in enabling a school to improve the capabilities of all teachers:

- *Sponsor and participate in a book club* where a new, informative book about teaching and learning is shared every few weeks. Participants sign up for a book that interests them and meet weekly over lunch to respond to the chapters they have read.
- *Audio/video conferencing.* When important issues of teaching and learning emerge, consider going to the source of current thinking. Often, a university professor or other educator, particularly from another part of the world, is happy to respond to questions over the phone/Internet for an hour. In many cases, the only cost is the charge for the long-distance call. Purchasing the audio conferencing equipment helps technically. Don't forget to tape the discussion for future use.
- *Present at a conference.* With colleagues, plan a presentation at a national or international conference a year ahead. The content should be about where you think you will be in your practice a year from now. For instance, six of my colleagues presented at a conference on improving students' writing through broadening their experience with new genres. At the proposal-writing stage, we were not yet engaged in this strategy. The gathering of evidence, developing and drafting the concepts and ideas, rehearsal, and anticipation are all powerful capacity- and knowledge-building strategies.
- *Visit work contexts in the broader community.* Research laboratories, production houses, automobile assembly plants, and other workplaces offer the potential of broadening teachers' perspectives. For instance, the principal of Talisman Park Secondary School in Ontario took a group of teachers and department heads to visit a television sitcom set. Her colleagues were able to meet actors, set designers, and camera operators, among others, learning about the uncertainty and lack of predictability in their work lives, as well as

the multiple skills and long hours required when they did get to work. This experience fed into the school's effort to forge and clarify its purposes and relate them to the Conference Board of Canada's guidelines for workplace skills. This led teachers to broaden their perceptions of curriculum and to jointly find specific ways to help students build better work habits, find more varied ways of conducting classroom inquiry, and present learning through more varied media.

- *Contribute to a book.* At two schools where I was principal, teacher colleagues contributed to books and videos that were professionally published about our work in classrooms.[19] The preparation, collective writing, redrafting, and clarification of practices were enormously growth-provoking and important. Part of developing perspective with your colleagues is helping them to understand the importance of contributing to the profession's knowledge by creating and documenting their practice in ways that are accessible to others. As a professional, I believe we have a responsibility to inform and educate our own members, and the knowledge base of classroom practice needs to be valued and shared with other educators.

- *Form a reading response group.* When professional growth came to focus on "reading response," participants realized they were collectively weak in their knowledge about response. As a result, an elective group met regularly to attend arts events and made time to respond to their experiences. Some responded to colleagues in the group, others through journal-writing. As these experiences were shared with others, a deepening understanding of response theory emerged.

- *Form a research study group.* Many questions arise in busy schools about everything from best practices or the role of the arts in students' learning to the paradox of a standards-based curriculum imposed upon a diverse community of learners. Study groups can meet regularly, gather current research, meet with university professors, try new practices, and visit other schools and workplaces as they deepen their understanding of the issue. Study groups need an infrastructure of support that includes time, resources, and, above all, a means to interact regularly with colleagues about their discoveries.

- *Build university partnerships.* Hosting preservice teacher candidates, involving university faculty in research and development work, hosting teacher education courses at your school, and moving toward the idea of the professional development school are all powerful capacity-building strategies.

There are many more strategies out there, and I am sure you have many to add from your experience. The point about using activities to build school capacity is for the strategies to be numerous and ongoing, and to permeate the very fabric of workplace culture. The strategies and projects must be aligned with agreed-upon school purposes and thus collectively create a capability greater than would be expected. Capacity-building activity becomes a way of life. It is not an add-on! Perhaps the most important point about strategies like these is that they contribute to a coherent vision—that of morally compelling purposes underpinning the work of the school. I have visited schools that are extremely busy, where teachers and community feel pulled in many and sometimes conflicting directions. Successful, capacity-building schools use procedures such as those described above to contribute to the coherence and purposes. This is where systemic and courageous leadership becomes so important.

Challenges/Obstacles to Capacity-Building

With this much promise, it is hard to imagine why it is so difficult for schools to embrace the idea of school as a professional learning community. However, creating a learning organization presents many threats to the status quo of most schools:

- It asks school personnel to form closer and more collaborative working relationships and networks.
- It requires vast transparency.
- It demands closer relations with students.
- It requires a new and more pervasive infrastructure, including a serious rethinking of the use of time in schools.
- It demands a drastically more intellectual and critical approach to teaching and learning.
- It presents a paradox of more responsibility and collective action on the one hand, versus a loss of independence on the other.
- It potentially challenges the adequacy of current practice with the vibrant embrace of the new.

Schools that choose to become learning organizations will need to develop processes that acknowledge and minimize the threats while maximizing the promise of such significant change.

The idea of colleagues learning from one another runs counter to much of our experience as teachers! Typically, our training is short, and often we are left virtually alone to sink or swim in our first years of teaching; our workplace fosters isolation and professional privacy.[20] Indeed, a Royal Commission on Learning in Ontario, which devoted an entire volume to the professional learning of teachers, found that the way in which schools and school days are organized actively promotes this isolation and professional privacy.[21] Their recommendations with respect to the professional learning and development of teachers included ongoing professional development as a requirement for continued certification.

In many countries, including the United States and Canada, where I have worked, much of teacher learning takes place outside the workplace, in discreet and isolated activities such as workshops, additional qualification training, and graduate courses. These experiences may or may not be well received by the individual and may or may not affect personal classroom practice and procedures, but it is clear that they do little to contribute to schools' collective and organizational capacity to adapt and respond to the diverse and changing needs of students and society in general. Experiences such as these are based on a set of questionable assumptions,[22] suggesting that an expert is required in order for teachers to learn. Further dubious assumptions, such as that workshop and course designers know best about what teachers need to learn, that learning should occur in contexts isolated from the teachers' work, that teacher learning takes little time, and that new innovations can be learned in one or two workshops with little follow-up are commonplace in teacher development work. These doubtful assumptions need to be challenged.

PEDAGOGICAL LEADERSHIP:
ENABLING PROFESSIONAL LEARNING COMMUNITIES

Improving the learning of all pupils, particularly in the contexts of multilingual, multicultural, and lower socioeconomic settings, represents a complex challenge for leaders. It requires focused and sustained attention to the purposes of the school as they pertain to student growth. Principals are often tempted to view themselves as experts, people who have all the answers. School leaders who succumb to this temptation tend to play the role of program implementers, where curriculum lies within policy documents and is addressed through "programs" that exist in texts.

Rather than being the program implementer, the successful principal practices pedagogical leadership by investing in the development of teacher colleagues' capacities and by bringing focus and coherence to the work of the school.[23] Notwithstanding the demands and complex pressures arising from the agendas of others that are part of a principal's normal workday, effective leaders stay focused on designing strategies to address the instructional purposes of their school. They engage in and foster regular, ongoing dialogue with teacher colleagues about student need and related beneficial pedagogic practices. Their actions are strategic inasmuch as they advance the purposes of the school in a systematic way. In Chapter 6 we learn more about the setting of strategic directions and carrying through on strategic actions.

REFLECT ON THESE QUESTIONS

1. Describe the current pressures your school faces, as well as activities designed to change, innovate, and continuously improve your school.
2. Describe the frequency and kinds of opportunities teachers have to collectively learn within and beyond the school.
3. How and to what extent does teachers' professional learning and development directly relate to and invigorate the fulfillment of school purposes?
4. Respond to this statement: Most educational organizations seriously underestimate the time, resources, and quality of collective learning necessary to innovate successfully. What are the implications for your workplace if this is true?
5. How might you and your colleagues gather useful data about student learning in order to examine, learn, reflect on, and improve the life chances of all?
6. The ideas espoused in this chapter are powerful and have been replicated in a number of contexts. How might you implement them in your context? What are the dangers?
7. In moving toward more collective, informed, and school-based professional learning and development, what are the implementation challenges you face?
8. Look at the six kinds of capacity adapted from Michael Fullan's work that are outlined in this chapter. How and to what extent do these capacities permeate the classrooms and work of the school/district? If it is the case that these capacities are sporadic or nonexistent, how would you go about building them?
9. Professional learning and development take time—more than most educators think. How and to what extent are you prepared to work with colleagues to restructure time in your school/district? How might you include all colleagues?

FOR FURTHER READING

Nelson, J. (2001). *The art of focused conversation for schools*. Gabriola Island, BC, Canada: New Society Publishers. Available from the Canadian Institute for Cultural Affairs, 579 Kingston Road, Toronto, M4E 1R3.

This book is invaluable, as is the training that the ICA in Canada and the United States provide to support the book. I use the methods described and illustrated in this book formally and informally throughout my facilitation work. Check out the website: www.icacan.ca. See also the website of the National Staff Development Council: www.nsdc.org.

Retallick, J., Cocklin, B., & Coombes, K. (Eds.). (1999). *Learning communities in education*. London: Routledge.

This book provides a comprehensive examination of the issues, strategies, and processes, as well as cases from Australia, Great Britain, Ireland, and Canada.

CHAPTER 6

Thinking and Acting Strategically for School Improvement

Moving quickly to strategic action characterizes the principals in the four cases presented in this chapter. In Chapter 6 you will learn about

- how strategic directions informed by student experiences and contextual data lead to constructive and coherent actions;
- how multiple strategic directions and their consequential actions, when related, add value and power to the work of the school and to school improvement; and
- four schools and the actions that were taken during the first 15 months of new principals' tenure.

Strategic thinking evolves from vision and purpose: It requires creative, informed, and systemic methods. Strategic thinking is useful only when it leads to strategic action and implementation. Strategic directions arise out of strategic thinking.[1] Put simply, strategic directions are a course of related actions that lead to the achievement of the goals of an organization's vision. In schools, they demand that teachers examine learners' experience in the classroom—beyond the limited perspective of test results, the curriculum, or teacher assumptions about learning and the learner.

Strategic thinking that guides the creation of strategic directions gains power when participants value the perspective and lived experience of the learner in classrooms across the school. The experience of the learner, when documented, ought to be viewed from the perspective of the students' interests; social, emotional, physical, and spiritual needs; and development. Moving from identified strategic directions to action is where plans often go off track in schools. Strategic directions flow from the agreed-upon school purposes, and each strategic direction requires a multitude of related small decisions, actions, or projects to bring it about. Typically, implementing a strategic direction involves many players, and getting stakeholders involved from the beginning is the preferred way forward.

Strategic directions address broad tasks and are directly responsive to the overwhelming needs dictated by the school's context and uncovered moral purpose.[2] Effective strategic directions represent judgments and decisions made by the group that consequently advantage the future. They are broad directions or proposals that deal with underlying obstacles that separate one's intentions from the current reality, the space between what we want to do and how we can get it done. For instance, at Conestoga Public School (described below), improving the life chances of all was undoubtedly about the strategic direction of improving language learning, particularly oral language in all classrooms. The traditions of professional privacy, isolation, low expectations for professional learning, and practices that were unresponsive to language learning were obstacles that were addressed. Actions the school carried out stemmed directly from jointly constructed strategic directions.

Obstacles, real and imagined, are always present. Contracts, policies, timetables, roles, responsibilities, traditions, workplace culture, public acceptance, and resources are just a few examples. It often requires a fearless principal committed to improving the life chances of all pupils to *take charge* by having the courage to move beyond obstacles toward improved practice. Having a good and informed idea and doing the right thing require the unleashing of passion and energy and the building of commitment. Strong participative processes can go a long way toward energizing teacher colleagues for renewed engagement. They lead to informed planning and action. Plans don't have to be perfect or overly detailed to begin, as they are always modified and embellished as the work progresses. Strategic directions defined in the four case studies described below emerged out of an ongoing dialogue with colleagues and other stakeholders, who were constantly informed by current research, the examination of exemplary practice, and ongoing documentation and review of the experience of the learner. Figure 6.1 represents this process in action.[3]

Strategic planning led to the strategic actions taken in each of the four cases and took place during the first 15 months of the principal's appointment. The first 15 months are critical in terms of the newly appointed leaders' opportunities to positively impact the learning of all students and teachers. I strongly believe that a school leader must make an early, compelling statement about the importance of improving the life chances of each and every student through planning, decisions, and actions that emphasize

- knowing each student extraordinarily well;
- collectively building capacity to appreciably improve teaching and learning; and
- valuing the importance of responsive and cohesive pedagogy across all classrooms.

Figure 6.1. Strategic Directions Emerge from the Documented Experience of the Learner

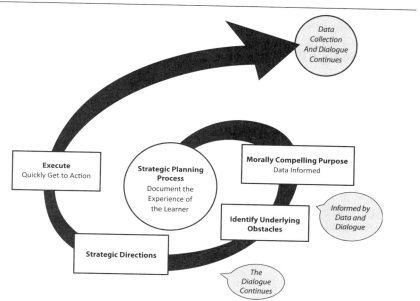

With new leadership comes the expectation of change. Seize the moment through informed action—don't disappoint!

CASE STUDY: CONESTOGA PUBLIC SCHOOL

A young, naive, enthusiastic principal and a professionally private and isolated staff learn to work collegially in order to improve the language learning and life chances of all students.

It was my first school. I had been principal for 4 months. Conestoga Public School was unusual, inasmuch as it was composed of 500 kindergarten-to -grade-3 pupils in a small village, with more than half of the students bused in from rural areas reputed to be the poorest in Ontario. A year prior to my arrival, closing many of the one- or two-room schools in the rural areas had led to the students and teachers amalgamating in this central village school. Some of the teachers arrived with an abundance of books and resources. Others had little. There was no central library. The school and its resources suffered from years of neglect. My mandate, as advertised in the classified

ads of a national newspaper, was to modernize instruction, respond to low
achievement (especially from low socioeconomic rural pupils), improve
teamwork, and develop innovative approaches to the use of a variety of
flexible spaces available in an historic old building.[4]

Restructuring and Reculturing the School

Clearly, the work was to be about building a new learning culture for
teachers, improving and diversifying classroom pedagogy, and addressing
the overall poor language development of pupils. Throughout this early
period, I had urged my colleagues to plan together, share their ideas with
one another, and apportion their resources (in particular, book collections)
in order for all students to have equal and plentiful access to reading and
resource materials. The teachers were very experienced, many of them having taught in their one- and two-room schools for 20 or 30 years. However,
they were very used to working by themselves. During the first few months,
it was clear that my pleas for collaboration, teamwork, and the sharing of
resources, with a few exceptions, fell on deaf ears. Like many new principals,
how to move from having and articulating a good idea to actually executing
it was becoming a very big challenge for my leadership.

Winter break was soon upon us. Being the eager, newly appointed
principal, I used this time to catch up on some paperwork and to reflect
upon my first 4 months as principal. Dismayed as I was by the variety of
teaching methods that I observed in differing classrooms across the school,
it was a struggle to conceive how to begin to build coherence in the experience of the students. In visiting the school the previous June (the end of the
school year), I was surprised to find that one kindergarten teacher had her
children sitting in rows. She explained to me, "I'm getting them ready for
grade 1; they have to be able to work in rows then, you know." Comparing
her approach with that of a 62-year-old 2nd- and 3rd-grade teacher who was
running one of the most child-centered, active, inquiry-based, and innovative classroom programs that I have ever seen demonstrated the range of
pedagogy and beliefs within the school. Most perplexing was my inability
to mobilize the teachers in ways that would enable them to learn from one
another. Evidently, merely talking the talk was not effective.

Contrastingly, more pleasing was the progress three teachers in grades
2 and 3 made in planning and teaching as a team and in using varied
classroom spaces in innovative ways. Early on, I had invested much time
in supporting their efforts. I contributed to their planning, participated in
classroom activities, arranged for them to visit exemplary teams elsewhere,
and ensured that they had the resources to create a hands-on, active, and
inquiry-based learning experience for their pupils. I saw the work with this

team as creating a "lighthouse" or "beacon" that others could follow. The problem was, nobody was watching!

During these few days in reflection, my only company was the many-talented and vocal observer Tom the janitor. "Well," he suggested, "if the teachers are not going to share their resources by themselves, then why don't we organize the resources for them? "Together, we conspired to construct a resource room in the basement of the school. We had lots of space, and all we really needed to build was a small wall, a door, and lots of shelving. Within a few days, we had succeeded in constructing a marvelous resource room. Over Christmas break, with the help of my and Tom's children, we moved all of the excess classroom supplies out of the individual classrooms and down to the new resource room. It was incredible. It was impossible to believe, but stashed away in some of those classrooms were simply truck-loads of paper, crayons, paints, brushes, and markers and hundreds of old textbooks. The youngsters had a great time classifying and organizing the materials.

Earlier, I had become enamored with the idea of creating a library for the children. I convinced the local school district of the necessity, which was not difficult because Conestoga was the only school in the district without a library. Now, it so happens that during the Christmas break, all of the library shelving and boxes of new library books arrived. Again, thanks to the help of Tom, we assembled library shelving in a central area on the second floor, which although not large was the best space we had available to build a library. Again our children helped as we brought all of the library books from the classrooms to the newly created library. We organized the books the best we could on the new library shelving.

Inspired by all this physical restructuring, I decided that in order to open the school up to more sharing, teamwork, and transparent classroom practice, I would remove all the interior doors not required for fire protection. The nice thing about the old Conestoga Public School was that most classrooms had two doors, and they were typically adjacent to the doors of another classroom. In the spirit of openness, I removed the door from the principal's office as well.

On our first day back after break, the teachers were preparing their classrooms, and there were whispered conversations throughout the building. With a taste for melodrama, I provided no explanation about what happened to the teachers' resources, doors, and library books. Word soon got around about the library books, as the teachers on the second floor found them immediately. Where did all the supplies go? At first recess, a delegation of teachers approached me. Yes, I told them, I would be happy to meet with the staff. We agreed to an informal staff meeting at the end of the school day.

Staff members arrived promptly! I said, "Follow me." We went down to the basement and unlocked the door of the new resource room. The teachers were amazed at the quantity and range of supplies. "Where did all this come from?" one teacher asked in disbelief. I spoke briefly of the benefits of centralizing resources, but in retrospect little needed to be said, because the materials spoke for themselves. Next, it was on to the library. Again, some teachers were delighted with the quantity and selection of books. They had many questions. Where did they come from? Who would look after them? How would they be catalogued? Who could use them? Finally, the discussion turned to the matter of the missing doors.

The above strategies are hardly transferable! In fact, when I tell this story I always feel like introducing it with the usual television commercial warning: "Do not try this at home (or in your school)." However, the actions were successful in bringing a sense of urgency and action to a by-and-large complacent situation. The changes created a very real and, in my view, necessary tension between a new vision of collegiality and inquiry and the status-quo individualism, professional privacy, and isolation that pervaded the school—a tension between past eclecticism and the need for more coherent, responsive, and informed classroom practice. Schlechty argues that during the initial period of a change effort everything must be done with sufficient drama and flair that people believe things are going to change.[5]

The boldness and visibility of the actions required my colleagues to respond. As a result, we transformed conversations in the school from the hypothetical and general to the real, specific, and practical. Within a few weeks of these actions, more than 90% of my teacher colleagues had forged working teams of their own choice, with some combinations (e.g., cross-grade and/or varied philosophies) turning out quite differently from what most might anticipate. I found myself spending most lunch hours, teacher preparation times, and after-school meetings with the varied teams as they began to experiment with new pedagogies, team teaching, and studying the language learning of their pupils. My ongoing participation enabled me to be the encourager, supporter, and problem-solver in implementing teamwork and ongoing professional learning and development. It became the norm for teachers to wander in and out of one another's classrooms, and conversations about teaching practices and creative uses of resources began to permeate the hallways and staffroom.

Strategic Actions Taken During the First 15 Months

Here are the essential actions my newfound colleagues and I took during this exciting time of change:

1. I initiated an ongoing conversation with and among colleagues about the particular language needs of our community. We collectively gathered information about the students' language (particularly oral language) learning. Together we planned strategically to respond to the documented language needs.
2. I centralized resources, set up a school library, and physically opened up the school in ways to promote shared and transparent practice.
3. I invested my time in initially supporting one very effective team. They truly were a model for others. I moved onto other teams as they expressed their interest and readiness. My work was to model and demonstrate shared practice and the collective examination of the students' work and classroom experience with a view to documenting and describing pupil progress.
4. Teachers grouped into teams of two, three, or four across a minimum of 2 years of students' ages (e.g., grades 1 and 2, or grades 2 and 3) and thus were able to sustain a caring, stable, and knowing relationship over time. Responsibility for teaching and learning now became a shared effort.
5. We revised schedules to enable clusters of two to four teachers of like mind to have time to plan, problem-solve, share practice, and reflect together.
6. We focused teaching and learning on students' talk. Children with impoverished language require sustained opportunities to use and develop their communication abilities.
7. We provided outside consultative support in areas related to language learning, including drama, storytelling, reading, writing, and integrated social studies.
8. We enriched students' learning and language experience by emphasizing planned and frequent excursions into the community, followed by hands-on re-creation, retelling, multimedia representation, and reporting of the experience.
9. We planned and prepared for the introduction of two new staff members and then implemented multi-age grouping (grades 1, 2 and 3) in many classrooms.
10. For the first time in the school's history, we opened the classrooms to parent visits and volunteer activity.

Reflections on My Work at Conestoga

Conestoga Public School presented unique challenges and circumstances. When I reflect back, I wonder if there might have been less dramatic ways to proceed. Of all the changes I made during that first year, nothing had the impact that the restructuring of teams, resources, and the opening up of classrooms to one another had in sending a message throughout the school. The message went something like this: "We need to work together as a team. This guy Shaw is really serious about this. He really wants us to share, plan, and work together on language learning and to make a difference in children's lives."

Initially, I was putting pressure on my colleagues to work more collegially, but it was only when I found ways to both structure and support the work (that is, to build adaptive and improved organizational capacity) that we began to make progress. Michael Fullan in many of his publications speaks of the need for both pressure and support for change to succeed. As a new principal at Conestoga, it was easy to provide pressure, but much more demanding and complex to find productive roles where I could provide real support for the work of my colleagues.[6] During this process, I, as a fledgling principal, struggled to explore the various supportive roles I could play. Eventually, I found that committing myself to the role of active team member helped me be most influential and supportive to my colleagues.

After the winter break, conversations clearly changed. Instead of the politeness and generalities about teaching of the first term, teachers began to talk more explicitly about what it means to work together and what it means to have children talk more in class. Teachers had very specific questions for me. If we work more together, are you prepared to spend as much time with our team as you have with the others? One of the potential problems with the lighthouse approach (where one program is highlighted and supported as an exemplary model for others to hopefully follow) is that by giving special attention to one group in terms of the leader's time and school resources, you run the risk of having the members of the lighthouse become balkanized from their colleagues. Successful leadership requires sensitivity to equity in terms of all teachers having opportunities to participate, learn, grow, and access resources. Fortunately, in this case the questions from my colleagues alerted me to this and I avoided the trap of playing favorites.

There were more questions: Can we visit classrooms where the pupils talk more? It is very important when embarking on new pedagogical approaches for teachers to have opportunities to visit classrooms demonstrating good practice. I typically arrange this for groups of teachers, with ample opportunity built into the experience for them to jointly share their observations and reflect on what they were learning.

How will we know if more student talk in classrooms improves their language? Schools typically embark on new innovations without building in ways of knowing how and to what extent the innovation improves or otherwise affects the life chances of students. How do you improve students' talk? How do we deal with the local language and idioms? Locals had some unusual ways of phrasing things, e.g., "We *bees* at the supermarket." Furthermore, my colleagues began to make their needs known. They said things like, "If we have more group activity and hands-on learning, then we need different furniture." We didn't have much success in convincing the district to purchase new furniture, so Tom and I made tables out of plywood, pipe, and pipe flange, which, along with some stacking chairs we found in the basement, became a great hit. A few months later the district trustees had a board meeting in the school and were upset about the furniture. Within 2 weeks, trucks arrived with beautiful new tables and chairs for eight classrooms.

Schools successful in improving the life chances of all their pupils communicate crystal-clear messages to their teachers and the broader community:

- This is our purpose.
- This is our strategy.
- This is how we are going to carry out our job.[7]

Our purpose and strategy, perhaps through our actions more than our words, became clear during the first year. We were focused on improving the language learning of all students, and our strategy was about teachers collectively learning and working together to improve our classroom practice. How we understood it and how we went about it, was addressed by the all-important role I played.

By meeting regularly with the small teams around the building, I was able to model, demonstrate, and foster teamwork. I was able to contribute to planning and problem-solving. In participating in the documentation of pupils' language abilities, I was able to explore the possibilities along with my teacher colleagues and demonstrate that I, too, was a learner. I was able to help frame and clarify the issues of language learning.

As we listened to hour upon hour of taped students' talk in classrooms and tried to analyze and understand how and to what extent our practices were improving their language, it became apparent that there were no simple or packaged answers. From my own perspective as a principal leader, I felt that Conestoga offered me a clear choice: Either I could spend my time and energy creating opportunities by building the capacity of colleagues to further the life chances of all pupils, or I could spend my energy managing and coping with the status quo. It never entered my mind to choose the latter!

After 4 years at Conestoga and feeling well pleased with the gains we had made in improving student language learning, I was ready for a change. A nearby district offered me the principalship of their largest school, and in looking for more of a challenge, I certainly found one.

CASE STUDY: CLOVERDALE PUBLIC SCHOOL

A junior-kindergarten-to-grade-6 school is failing as it has doubled in size to almost 1,000 students and the population has diversified, becoming predominantly multicultural and multilingual. Restructuring and reculturing improves behavior and brings coherence to expectations and classroom learning.

It was recess in the first morning of the new school year, and officially my first day at Cloverdale Public School as principal. Chaos had reigned for the first couple of hours as we struggled to register almost 100 new students. Cloverdale was a large school with high turnover of students and teachers. But despite having all secretaries, extra teachers, and older responsible students to guide new registrants to their new classrooms, watching this many new and unregistered pupils turn up on the first morning was overwhelming and surprising for all. Finally, I was relieved to take a break and go down to the staffroom to spend a few moments with my teacher colleagues. All too soon, it was time to go back to the office.

Recognizing Schoolwide Issues

Student Behavior. The office was now full of students. Forty-five young people milled around, making quite a racket as the last of the parents waited to complete registration. I could not imagine why the students were there, so I asked the head secretary. "Discipline," she said. "They are here for discipline." My summer chat with the vice principal, in which he described his job as predominantly discipline-oriented, should have warned me. However, I was unprepared, and I struggled to get my head around what I was witnessing.

The students were apparently sent from the playground without a teacher or a note to describe their transgressions. Clearly, teachers expected the principal to handle them. Little did they know! I am afraid my secretary was forming a bad opinion of me as she heard me mutter, "What on earth am I do with all these pupils?" Well, I marched them to the library and recorded their names and, where I could, those of the teachers who sent them and what they described as their transgressions (more often than not they said they had not done anything). Then I sent them back to the classrooms. By the end of this first 4-day week, more than 250 students from classrooms and the playground had arrived in the office in similar circumstances. Already the school superintendent's advice of taking the first year to get to know the school, to just "let the school run as it has, before you give thought to changing anything," was wearing thin.

Several other incidents during those first few weeks were quite memorable. The school, at the time, had two separate gymnasiums/auditoriums, neither of which was large enough to accommodate the entire student body. For this reason, monthly assemblies where students could show off their accomplishments and projects were repeated three times, each assembly for a group of grade levels in one of the auditoriums. When the older students had their first assembly, their teachers could not get them to quiet down. By the time I arrived, the whole assembly was out of control. Teachers were yelling. Students were laughing and jeering. For some reason, the arrival of the new principal managed to silence the group just long enough for me to send the teachers and their classes back to their classrooms with an admonition. The teachers were to have their students practice moving from classroom to auditorium quietly, entering the assembly silently, and sitting quietly until all were seated and finally listening politely to the information and performances.

A few weeks later, an unexpected early snowfall created more mayhem. Classes were warned about throwing snow during recess, as without a snow base it is easy to pick up gravel in wet packing snow and cause a grievous injury. However, within minutes, hundreds of students were chucking snow at one another and ignoring the supervising teachers, one of whom sent a student to fetch me. Her vivid description of the havoc on the playground proved entirely accurate.

Cloverdale had a very large playground that bordered on a park, and as far as the eye could see, there were students running, screaming, shouting, and throwing snow helter-skelter. There were students crowding around the duty teachers, and some children were crying and obviously scared. I contacted the office and had the bell rung to signal an end to recess. This had entirely no effect, as the pandemonium continued. It was only when I got all 70 staff out into the yard that we were able to calm things down and move the students back to their classrooms.

Perplexing problems around these severe discipline issues included the chronic lack of information about the occurrences. There were no records of previous incidents. The practice of teachers sending students to the office for discipline with little or no evidence of what had actually transpired, as well as the apparent understanding that this ended the teacher's responsibility, was seriously problematic. By the end of the first week of school, teachers knew that my vice principal and I would not speak to students without receiving specific information from the referring teacher. Even then, the information was vague and unhelpful: "Andrew was rude in class;" "Devon disrupted the class;" "Sukindar was violent to a classmate." What was clear was that a number of primary teachers felt intimidated by the 12- and 13-year-old students. Many teachers were failing to accept responsibility for dealing with discipline as it occurred, preferring to send the problem onto others. In addition, a familiar refrain from students was, "I don't have to do what you say. You are not my teacher."

Cloverdale had experienced rapid growth during the previous 4 years, morphing from a small school accommodating the children of White Anglo working-class families into what was now a predominantly new-immigrant, Black Caribbean (mainly Jamaican), East Indian, and Italian community. There were powerful tensions within the community, as the old and the new tried to reach some form of accommodation with one another. One evening during that memorable first term, there was a "rumble" in the local park, described as "the Italians versus the rest," where several hundred teenagers turned up with bike chains, pipes, and knives. Police called for 50 officers from other regions to reinforce local forces in restoring order. Although this incident did not involve younger children from Cloverdale, it certainly involved their older brothers and sisters and indicated some of the tensions in the broader community.

Structure of the School and the Implications. Cloverdale was organized just as it had been 5 years earlier when it was a small school. Each grade level, now including five or six classes, was located in a different part of the school, with a cadre of teachers who usually remained at the same grade level each year. The practice was to mix up the youngsters as they transferred to the next grade, so the odds were that students found themselves with a new homeroom teacher, in a different part of the building, and, given the high student turnover, with something less than about 20% of the same classmates from the previous year.

If you followed a student's trajectory through this school, then the odds were that they would have few classmates they knew well and little chance of relating to teachers with whom they were acquainted. In grades 5 and 6, each housed in a large, open-space area, pupils remained with their home teacher for only about 35% of their program. For parents with several children in the school, the odds were that they would relate to a different teacher for each of their offspring every year.

Classroom practices reflected this diversity and could be characterized as widely eclectic. Walking around the school, you might observe classrooms with desks in rows and the teacher lecturing at the front and other classrooms where the students were setting their own agendas, working in activity centers and cooperative groups. Variation in classroom practice within Cloverdale was greater than expected variations between schools. Examining this from the perspective of the student's trajectory through the school, expectations about what counted as progress, good citizenship, about what it meant to be a speller, a writer, or a problem-solver, varied significantly from class to class and from year to year.

For me, this lack of coherence and the superficiality of relationships between student and teachers were a major impediment to enabling all pupils (particularly the less capable learners) to succeed. More than 30% of the pupils in grade 6 had repeated one year (typically grade 1), and many of those had failed twice. I will always remember, in those first months, being approached by three 14-year-old Black immigrant girls who asked, "Why are Black kids always kept behind at Cloverdale?" This was a very fair question, about which there was no fair answer.

Faculty Divisiveness. The staff held a diversity of worldviews and, for the most part, they were willing to express them. Staff meetings were dynamic, surprising, and at times rowdy, as various factions fought pitched battles over many issues. It seemed that no matter the topic, we could never find agreement. Most disconcertingly, it became apparent that those who could not agree never felt an obligation to follow through on the final outcome. In part, I think this was due to the culture of the school and the teachers who worked there. Perhaps this had something to do with the kinds of teachers who came to Cloverdale, with the bulk of new teachers hired from other jurisdictions, provinces, and countries, due to the lack of local district applications to work in what was perceived to be a lower-class, diverse, and difficult community.

However, in part, it was due to my not having the skill, knowledge, or experience to deploy consensus-building procedures that were sufficiently robust to thrive on diversity and build serious commitment. For instance, getting over 900 students in and out of the building in a reasonably quiet, safe, and orderly manner was important, given the behavior issues in the school. My colleagues typically were split on their views of how to achieve this. There were those who wanted to line the students up (including at least two who wanted to segregate boys and girls) and march them into school only when they were silent. Others argued that if you wanted to avoid congestion of hundreds of students at each entrance and enable students to learn and act more responsibly, they should freely enter the building as they reached the door. One view was about control; the other was about teaching responsibility. Compromise was elusive!

Outspoken faculty such as this bring strengths and obstacles to the work of the school. On the one hand, it is useful and healthy to have the practices and procedures of a school constantly challenged and discussed in the open. It is in many ways easier to work with people whose beliefs and understandings are public, as opposed to being professionally private. On the other hand, teachers basing their opinions on belief or unsupported assumptions rather than the informed experience of the learner, exemplary practice, and current research is akin to religious proselytizing—a lot of preaching that leads to little persuasion or commonality in the outcome.

Consistent with this behavior was the failure of some teams to execute their responsibilities. For instance, given the diverse cultural and linguistic nature of our community and the importance of the arts to pupils' learning and lives, I saw the need for a dynamic performing arts program where artists visiting the school could model, demonstrate, and stimulate a passion for the arts across the school. I called for colleagues who had interests in this area to explore the possibility of designing, funding, and implementing such a program. "We are still working on it," was the response whenever I called for a report on the group's work. In my previous school, such teams always took their work seriously and applied a sense of urgency to such endeavors. However, at Cloverdale this was not the case. I learned an important lesson here: to differentiate between the mere delegation of responsibility and the need to invest in capacity-building.

Need for Capacity-Building. Investing in capacity-building of school teams means understanding that what a group can do with guidance and support today, they will be able to accomplish more independently tomorrow. This was a case requiring hands-on leadership on my part. In debriefing the arts group about their lack of progress, it soon became apparent that they were unclear about the purposes of performing arts in schools, had little connection with that community, and had absolutely no idea how to think strategically about planning and funding such an endeavor.

When I speak to principals' groups, perhaps the most controversial thing I say is to urge principals to "trust" their teachers more. I think the nub of their concern is this: In the case of the performing arts I could have designed a plan, found the funding, and implemented the program far more quickly and probably more effectively than my performing arts team. However, in doing so I would have deprived my colleagues of the opportunity to extend their capabilities and leadership by

- building a deeper understanding of the arts and performing arts in relationship to students' learning;

- sharing expertise, ownership, and responsibility for an important aspect of school life;
- providing the opportunity to think, plan, and act strategically;
- learning to build trust and work collegially; and
- improving their ability to provide future leadership.

Trusting your teachers to provide strong and effective leadership requires substantive time, expertise, and commitment to capacity-building. Capacity-building, as an investment, will, in the long term, pay extraordinary dividends.

Acceptance of the Norm. This brings me to Peter Senge's rendition of the parable of the boiled frog.[8] It goes like this: If you place a frog into boiling water, it will try and likely succeed in jumping out. However, if you place the frog in room-temperature water and slowly increase the heat, it will do nothing, becoming groggier and groggier until it is unable to climb out of the pot. Senge says that maladaptation to gradually building threats to survival is so pervasive in systems' studies of organization failure that it has given rise to this parable. The organization called school is no different from corporate organizations in this respect. From my own experience, I suspect that it is only in the first year of one's work in a school that we remain objective, as our perceptions are not yet colored by acclimating to the norm. As I build relationships with my colleagues, and as things begin to change, I find a greater acceptance of the reality of the school. I hope this is because things actually are improving and not because an adaptation to the new culture and the pleasant relationships with colleagues blinds me to impending disaster or systemic problems.

Cloverdale was a wonderful example of this parable in action. Systems and procedures that undoubtedly worked when the school was small, when everyone knew everyone, when a humanitarian principal could play the paternalistic role of managing discipline and supporting individual teachers, did not hold up as the school rapidly grew and the nature of the community changed. What was initially problematic for my colleagues and me, as described at the beginning of Chapter 1, was that I, too, in coming from a smaller school, continued this approach. Although many teachers were frustrated with pupil behavior, they also had come to accept it as normal for the community.

Solving the Systemic Problems Through Building Relationships

The enormity of the discipline issues at Cloverdale, in my view, clearly represented a systemic problem. By this, I mean they were not subject to a quick fix (although short-term, immediate action was necessary and taken) and required many policies, capacities, practices, and procedures to change and improve in an integrated way. Students' behavior is very much about the quality and strength of the classroom program, student–teacher relationships, student–student relationships, and the engagement of students by classroom teaching practice.[9]

On a systemic level, the behavior problems were also very much about relationships—or lack thereof. The very fact that students (particularly those in grades 5 and 6) were unable to build and sustain a relationship with a caring adult over time (more than 1 year) and that classrooms were deliberately structured to make it difficult for pupils to build lasting friendships mitigated against stability, consistency, trust-building, and the development of caring relationships.

Finally, the issues were systemic because of the great difficulty teachers had in agreeing and following through on consistent behavioral expectations and practices. This latter issue reflected a culture of individualism that pervaded the institution.[10] One cannot mandate cultural change. In order to change the culture of the workplace, one has to get at purposes, structures, and relationships. One has to make visible the issues and experiences students are living. One has to forge consensus and build coherence around discipline and classroom practices and procedures. In this case, building coherence required systemic thinking and action. In their book, Leithwood and Montgomery describe their level four (highest level) principal as the Systematic Problem Solver.

> Systematic Problem Solvers are distinguished by their ability to see relationships between the most mundane decisions and the growth of pupils . . . they are able to introduce an unusually high level of consistency (coherence) into school decision-making . . . their focus is largely unconstrained by established practices and their student orientation leads them to the invention and delivery of services (most) likely to realize the goals held by their schools.[11]

I was convinced that clear and significant actions had to take place to change the nature of the relationships within the school. Most importantly, the students required a lasting and consistent relationship with a few teachers who would know them, their siblings, and their families extraordinarily well. Almost as important was to structure the adult relations in a way that promoted teamwork, leading to consistent expectations about learning and acceptable behavior for students. In other words, the school clearly required massive investment in social capital as much for the adults who worked there as for the students and their relationships with one another. Acrimony between different factions within the building had to end. The strategic challenge was whether we could build coherence (in both academic and social capital) across the entire building and program or whether, realistically, it might only be possible across smaller units.

Given the size of the organization and its history of individualistic culture, my solution was to structure the school, at the beginning of my second year, into four teams. The first team comprised five classes of combined junior and senior kindergarten. Children arriving at Cloverdale could now expect to spend 2 years with the same teacher in the same room. The remaining three teams were vertically arranged (each team included grades 1 through 6) and parallel (meaning similar in makeup and numbers of students and teachers); see Figure 6.2.

Cloverdale had been a small, single-story school, onto which two-story additions had been added at each end. One end had two "open-area" pods, each accommodating four to five classes. The other end had many classrooms built on separate floors. Physically, the school divided nicely into three discrete areas: an open-space area at one end and two separate floors at the other, with the office, library, gymnasiums, and music room in the center.

Teachers were able to choose which colleagues they wished to work with. Through much discussion, we were able to allocate teachers to form the core of each new team. To address staff attrition, we involved

Figure 6.2. Cloverdale Public School: Restructured in Year 2

Team One (2-Year Reception Class for New Entrants)
Six Kindergarten Classes
Junior Kindergarten/Senior Kindergarten split where approximately 120 students remained with their reception teachers for 2 years.

Team Two *Grades 1–6*	**Team Three** *Grades 1–6*	**Team Four** *Grades 1–6*
Approximately 270 students spread over 11 classes. Students and their siblings and parents remain with the team for 6 years. Classrooms in adjacent areas of the school. Team responsible for discipline policy and practices, curriculum, and forging coherence.	Approximately 270 students spread over 11 classes. Students and their siblings and parents remain with the team for 6 years. Classrooms in adjacent areas of the school. Team responsible for discipline policy and practices, curriculum, and forging coherence.	Approximately 220 students spread over approximately 9 classes. Students and their siblings remain with the team for 6 years. Open-space classrooms on two floors. Team responsible for discipline policy and practices, curriculum, and forging coherence.

teachers in strategic hiring in order to hire prospective teachers for their team who shared their vision. This enabled each team to begin to clarify identity, purpose, and values that would underpin their work together. Schools were created within the school! For parents it meant they could choose which part of the school they most related to, that they would relate to a small number of teachers over time, and that their children could also be in the same small school within a school. For students it meant that they would have classmates that they would know over a sustained period of time.

Strategic Actions Taken During the First 15 Months

In light of the serious systemic problems underlying the work of the school, the following actions were implemented:

1. We initiated the careful, accurate, and descriptive recording of discipline issues and the follow-up taken by the teacher present at the time.
2. We devolved responsibility for all initial discipline contacts to individual teachers who consistently communicated and worked closely with homeroom teachers.
3. We restructured the school in such a way as to invest in social capital by fostering more intimate, caring, and lasting relationships between teachers and their students.
4. We restructured the school into teams where colleagues of like minds could forge common practice, where families could choose which team of teachers they wished to work with, and where families new to the school could visit the entire school and choose which approach they wished their children to experience.
5. We planned and implemented a process of creating an inclusive climate for new-immigrant families and their children.[12] Children arriving from other countries found the very large Cloverdale School an overwhelming experience.
6. We deferred any decisions about children repeating a grade (failing) until at least the end of grade 3. On examining school records, it typically appeared that pupils were asked to repeat grade 1 because they were not reading well enough by the end of grade 1. However, it is not unusual for some children to begin reading later, and certainly children learning English as a second language may come to reading later than at 6 years of age. Not surprisingly, far fewer children were having difficulty with reading by the end of grade 3.

7. We devolved specific practices and procedures to the school teams with a mandate for them to build coherence within their teams for classroom instruction (e.g., in their language arts and math teaching) and discipline (e.g., getting their students in and out of the building safely).
8. We began to design some compelling ways of gathering information to inform our discussions. For instance, by logging all behavioral incidences in the school, we were able to begin to define the nature of the behavioral issues across the school.
9. We initiated a vigorous professional development program for teachers focusing on the learning needs of our multicultural, multilinguistic, and rapidly changing student population.
10. We designed and implemented a rich and multifaceted performing arts program.
11. We refocused the physical education and sports program from one that was competitively oriented to one that was more inclusive and participation-orientated.
12. We found and protected time for teachers to meet, learn, and reflect together about the all-important work of improving behavior and achievement across the school.

During the last few days of the first school year of my tenure, the effects of these directions became clearly apparent. Every teacher in the building had to move classrooms. For some, this meant packing up years of accumulated resources and materials. This was certainly a stressful time, but also an exciting time, as the new teams continued to meet, build relationships, and plan for the new school year. Passion and purpose were unleashed. In my first September at Cloverdale, the parking lot, with the exception of the school secretaries and me, was typically empty by 3:45 P.M. By the second September of my tenure, there were still many cars there at 6:00 P.M.—a clear sign of renewed commitment. By the end of year 2, we had reduced the recorded discipline incidents by some 80% and began to see a very positive trend in student achievement.

CASE STUDY: LANCEWOOD PUBLIC SCHOOL REVISITED— CHANGING STRUCTURES, PURPOSE, AND PEDAGOGY

Changing structures, purpose, and pedagogy brings about more caring and responsible relationships at Lancewood Public School and leads to improved learning of all.

As introduced in Chapter 3, Lancewood Public School was a suburban, 700-plus-student, junior-kindergarten-to-grade-8 school receiving additional students at grades 7 and 8 from other elementary schools. Lancewood was my fourth principalship. My introductory visit to a number of classrooms on the third floor, which housed over 200 grade 7 and 8 students, was unforgettable. It was the end of the school day. Students ran, pushed, and shoved, frequently jostling me as I made my way down the corridor. I was troubled by the students' lack of engagement in their learning in some of the classrooms and surprised to learn that the brighter pupils were tracked into classes for the gifted, even though the district already had classes in place for students formally designated as "gifted."

Within the first few months of my appointment to this large elementary school, it became apparent, especially within the intermediate division (grades 7 and 8), that there was huge variance in the students' behavior, learning experience, and achievement. A lack of engagement, participation, and success characterized the classes of students assessed to have lesser abilities. Even more worrisome was the involvement of some students in violent activities and others in just plain silly or mean-spirited behavior. For instance, we had experienced a number of fights involving both boys and girls and outbursts in classrooms where removing the student (in one case forcibly) appeared to be required, as well as many, many cases in which students provoked others with cruel words. The quality of work from these classes, the attitude that the students had toward learning, and their overall facility to do well in school seemed to be in serious jeopardy. I thought one of the main issues was the quality of teaching.

Now, somewhere in my dark history I was known as a good classroom teacher. Perhaps if I took over some of these classes, I thought, I could demonstrate how the students could become more engaged in their learning. Much to my dismay, even my most energetic lessons, designed to facilitate maximum participation, failed to penetrate the students' experience. There seemed to be five or six classes with students who were very tuned out, and these were where the bulk of our discipline problems arose. Constantly inundating the school office were students who disrupted their classes.

Changing Structures, Purpose, and Pedagogy

What to do? My colleagues on the school design team and I embarked on a series of conversations with the teachers who were responsible for the young adolescents in our school. We examined the behavior and achievement of the students. As explained in Chapter 3, we gathered information from across the school and studied reports and papers on topics relating to the intellectual, social and emotional needs of adolescent learners. Consensus emerged indicating that one structural issue—tracking—was contributing to the poor levels of engagement in the lower ability classes. It was the teachers of the two top-track classes who were most vocal and wondering about the experiences of the less able students. However, to me, there was more to this than simple de-tracking. Students needed to have more ownership and responsibility, more substantive and interesting things to do, and more opportunities to succeed and to provide leadership for others. Instructional pedagogy demanded attention across all classes.

After about 5 months of data collection, analysis, and discussion, my design team and I published the paper presented in Figure 6.3 for discussion among the staff. The assumptions we identified to guide our work pointed to the necessary strategic directions for the future of the school and led to concrete action.

Figure 6.3. A Proposal for Lancewood Public School

A MODEST PROPOSAL FOR THE ORGANIZATION AND PROGRAM FOR LEVELS SIX, SEVEN, AND EIGHT

A paper prepared by the school design team for staff discussion

Curriculum

The three curricula to be considered in the education of our pupils and are

- The Personal Curriculum
- The Developmental Curriculum
- The Paper (School or District) Curriculum[13]

The demands of three curriculums need not be in conflict. However, school organization can either help or hinder the facilitation of these differing kinds of curriculum demands.

THE PERSONAL AND DEVELOPMENTAL CURRICULA

Needs of the young adolescent are known and must be accounted for in any plans that we have for the future. Emotional/social factors are significant during this somewhat unstable time of rapid change and growth development.

Research suggests emotionally secure classrooms that are stable, consistent, and caring over time are more likely to assist the pupil in developing a confident personality with a positive view towards learning. Such classrooms are characterized by: a feeling of general warmth; encouraging moderate expressions of emotion and feeling; democratic group decision-making leading to stimulating activity; the use of non-punitive control techniques high in clarity and firmness

Figure 6.3. A Proposal for Lancewood Public School (continued)

and shifting states of order (much talking, active learning followed by quiet, etc.). This need for variety has often wrongly been used as a basis for establishing rotating classes and subjects.

Assumption 1

Stable, emotionally secure, consistent and caring environments can best be established by teachers who know their pupils well and who have a close personal relationship with each pupil. Such relationships are best achieved and enhanced when the teacher and the pupil have a significant relationship that extends beyond the usual single academic year.

The pupil's sense of security and level of self-esteem are very much determined by the adequacy of his or her performance. It is no accident that the thirty or more pupils identified by staff at Lancewood as being "at risk" almost without exception are pupils who are achieving poorly, who have low self-esteem and are viewed as having behavioural or attitude problems. The implications here are clear and formulate a number of assumptions upon which we will need to act.

Assumption 2

Abilities varied widely within each of our classes. For instance, the reading levels may range from as low as grade three to as high as high-school graduation. The curriculum and expectations need to be structured to ensure that each pupil will experience success. If we have but one level of expectation for a grade 7 pupil then by definition a significant group of pupils must fail; there is no alternative for them. For these pupils the cycle of failure must be broken. To achieve this it will be necessary for all pupils to be known well by their teacher.

This position is grounded in the Ontario Secondary School Guidelines. It is a basic policy in the curriculum of Ontario that individual differences are accommodated to the greatest extent.

Early adolescence requires special attention to the following: developing a knowledge and understanding of the self, developing the skills needed to get along with others, and opportunities for counselling with relation to these and other personal problems. (Ontario School Guidelines, pp. 5 and 6)

Physical (including sexual) changes that occur during this period (as recognized in the health curriculum) require special attention.

Assumption 3

Teachers who have a close, caring and sustained relationship with each pupil best meet their very special needs. This in no way diminishes the role of the guidance counsellor, whose particular skill can be made available to all classroom teachers in planning and to the class for specific purposes.

Encouraging self-understanding and self-acceptance as well as acceptance of others will require time and a deliberate attempt to both teach and support pupils to develop these understandings.

Figure 6.3. A Proposal for Lancewood Public School (continued)

THE PAPER CURRICULUM

There is tremendous pressure at the intermediate (grades 6–8) level to "cover the extensive curriculum" so that the pupil will be ready for the "reality of high school." Historically, middle schools have often gone to the extreme of becoming more like a high school than the high school itself. The curriculum has been fragmented as subject specialists have sought to cover all the knowledge that is required.

With respect to this view, Ontario Secondary School Guidelines are quite clear: The focus in the intermediate division must be on the integration of learning experiences designed for the pupil.

Assumption 4

Most human activity is a purposeful search for pattern. Learning experiences gain power if they are part of organized and meaningful wholes.

The image of the learner promotes the image of "a self-motivated self-directed problem solver, aware of both the processes and uses of learning and deriving a sense of self-worth and confidence from a variety of accomplishments." Exploratory learning takes place when a pupil takes the initiative to seek experiences in which he/she is interested because of personal needs, talents or purposes. The purposeful search for pattern is advantaged through project work and interdisciplinary teaching and learning.

Assumption 5

The major goal of the curriculum is "intellectual independence" which comes about when the pupil comes to exert a significant control over his/her own learning. Activities involving choice help the pupil move away from the reliance on external approval and control and allow the development of intrinsic values that are consistent with personal purposes as well as those of society.

Individual differences as discussed above need to be addressed not only in terms of the choice of materials, teacher expectations, mutual goal setting and program requirements, but also in terms of assessment evaluation.

There seems to be some conflict between the notion of assessment as it relates to process versus product. Various guides from the ministry however deal with this issue. For instance English at the secondary level is evaluated as follows; writing as process: 20 to 30%; small group or interactive learning: 20 to 30%; word and study habits: 20 to 30%; summative evaluation (i.e. tests and products etc.): 20 to 30%.

Assumption 6

Assessment and evaluation are to focus on the pupil's day-to-day participation and the quality of the strategies that he/she uses in the resolution of the many activities with which the pupil is challenged. Thus observation skills, pupil interviews, demonstrations, self evaluation, portfolios and the teaching of others become key strategies to be utilized in assessment for learning.

Although most of my teacher colleagues anticipated the contents of the discussion paper, having contributed to at least parts of it, the document served its purpose well in extending the debate toward the practical and the actionable. In addition, I strategically released the paper when the union contract enabled teachers to opt out of continuing at Lancewood the following school year. Valuable attrition began the next morning, when I found three letters on my desk from teachers of intermediate grades declaring that they would not return in the fall. This, along with a couple of well-earned promotions, enabled me to hire teachers who would bring skills attuned to enabling pupils to have more choice, ownership, and responsibility in their learning and contributions to school life. Not surprisingly, most of those hired had no experience with the grade 6 through 8 age group, but brought a strong, student-centered approach they had developed in working with younger students.

Strategic Actions During the First 15 Months

Particularly for grades 6, 7, and 8 teachers and students, the following actions were taken in order to address both social and academic needs.

1. We established a Continuous After-Learning Review process where we gathered information about the students' learning and behavior in order to inform our judgments and practices. (See Chapter 5).
2. We established clusters of classes and teachers who would sustain a relationship by working together for a period of 2 to 3 years. Each cluster or team included teachers who taught multi-age classes and teachers who took their class on to a 2nd or 3rd year.
3. Student clusters spanning the three levels also included, where possible, ongoing relationships with such support staff as special education, French, music, teaching assistants, and lunchroom supervisors.
4. Each cluster was allocated a suitable space where the three or four classes involved could meet together to share, celebrate, plan, and discuss current issues and develop common expectations with regard to behavior.
5. Each cluster was physically located on a different floor and asked to build supportive relationships and roles in working with younger students on those floors.
6. Each cluster of teachers had a range of strengths, including math/science, the arts, and perhaps physical education, thus diminishing the need to have pupils on unnecessary rotations of teachers and rooms.

7. We assigned students to each cluster heterogeneously and by family (i.e., siblings were assigned to the same cluster).

8. We designed minimal formal timetabling for each cluster (i.e., only when teachers outside the cluster were involved).

9. We planned and implemented a more integrated curriculum. In designing common themes, we were able to cut across grade levels and permit the patterns that exist in our world to become more obvious. Furthermore, the integration of the curriculum was seen as a major tool in reducing the pressure inherent in subject fragmentation and in the real or imagined pressure to "cover the curriculum."

10. We developed a schoolwide assessment and evaluation policy with a strong emphasis on students' explorations, investigations, demonstrations, and presentations. We met in groups of four or five with cross-grade and cross-subject representation to share and learn about effective practices in assessment and evaluation.

11. Homeroom teachers assumed the major responsibility for the health and guidance curriculum.

12. We recognized the individuality of our pupils to the degree that we developed differing but realistic expectations that ensured that all pupils experienced daily success. As Eliot Eisner says, we moved toward increasing the variety in pupil performance while raising the mean.[14]

13. We implemented a pupil-led, goal-setting strategy involving parents and teachers (see Chapter 3 for details). The goal-setting process placed parent and pupil initially in the role of expert and enabled parent, pupil, and teacher to share in goal-setting that was reviewed and revised at least at three times during the school year.

14. We ensured that all students had time for class meetings where they had the opportunity to problem-solve together with regard to school and class expectations and with respect to developing a healthy self-concept and an acceptance of and respect for others.

15. We explored collegially the implications for student choice within the context of the day-to-day curriculum. By this, I mean we wanted to see how and to what extent we could enable pupils in grades 6, 7, and 8 to have more choice, control, ownership, and responsibility for their own learning.

By the end of the first 15 months, discipline issues had greatly diminished, older students had developed specific leadership roles in working with younger students, and the entire school was working in teams. The quantity and quality of student reading and writing had noticeably improved across the whole school.

CASE STUDY: SUTTON HEIGHTS SECONDARY SCHOOL

At a secondary school where student and parent expectations and viewpoints differed significantly from those of teachers, a dynamic, newly appointed principal challenges the existing culture in order to improve teaching and learning and foster a more responsive and coherent experience for students.

Sutton Heights Secondary School in suburban Ontario was reputed to have the highest number of student suspensions in the district and chronic issues of racial tension and misbehavior.[15] Recent surveys of their community, teachers, and students resulted in a considerable discrepancy between how the various stakeholders viewed their school. Teachers were significantly more positive about the students' and parents' experience than the students and parents themselves. Simultaneously, looming on the immediate horizon was the promise of mandated secondary school reform, coupled with significant budget cuts. Sutton Heights had undergone rapid changes in student population, from being a small, predominantly White Anglo-Saxon village to a now large multicultural, new-immigrant community where many parents commuted long distances to work.

Developing Strategic Directions

Within this context, the representative school improvement team, including teachers and the principal, had established a number of action teams, perhaps none more important and visible than the 10-member school climate team. This team had met many times, carried out focus-group discussions with teacher colleagues, and was anxious to get to action. Each member of the climate team conducted student focus groups in 4 of their own classes, meaning that some 40 classes across the school had the opportunity to brainstorm their response to this important focus question: Describe the conditions under which you and your fellow classmates learn best. In their own words, the students literally produced a classic text on adolescent learning.

The main themes of the students' work were compelling. Students asked for more voice, choice, and options in their learning. They were keenly aware that choice leads to ownership and commitment. Opportunities to follow their passions and interests were, for the most part, lacking. They recognized that different students learn in a variety of ways and have differing strengths to be capitalized on. They strongly identified the need to be able to record, express, and share their learning with others by using a variety of media, according to the nature of the topic and their personal strengths. Lectures and note-taking were described as boring and a waste of their time.

The school climate team met regularly and forged seven strategic directions. Their work was informed by the focus groups with students, by discussions with colleagues, by data from the parent/student/teacher surveys, and by schoolwide assessment data. These directions were developed using the consensus-building workshop approach developed by the Institute for Cultural Affairs.[16] The school climate team participants were ten educators representing various stakeholders across the school, including the union representative. My role as facilitator was to structure the process to ensure maximum participation and the clarification of ideas. Each participant brainstormed answers to the focus question, What is the ideal school climate for Sutton Heights Secondary School that will improve student learning? They recorded on index cards a brief phrase or thought to capture each idea. The cards were then discussed to invite clarification, clustered, and categorized by similar intention. Finally, the school climate team named the categories, the outcome being the seven strategic directions. In Figure 6.4, the seven strategic directions are shown in bold type at the top of the columns, and listed below are the brainstormed concepts that were recorded on index cards and classified together.

The power of this kind of consensus-building activity is as follows:

- Each participant contributes approximately the same number of cards, and their contributions are included (none are discarded) and honored by all.
- The process works best when there is a variety of views (i.e., it thrives on diversity).
- Naming the categories, although challenging and time-consuming, brings conceptual clarity to the group's thinking and paves the way to action.
- The process leads to strategic directions that, when quickly followed up on, can engender very effective action.

The strength of the directions the team developed was their integrated nature, in which an activity in one area contributed to the development of other areas. The team shared its directions with colleagues (98 teachers) at the next staff meeting and facilitated a process whereby teachers could meet in groups and brainstorm specific actions for each direction. Sustained professional learning and development continued from this point on.

Figure 6.4. Brainstormed Ideas for Improved Student Learning, Categorized by Strategic Direction

Focus Question:

What is the ideal school climate for Sutton Heights Secondary School that will improve student learning?

Demonstrate Respect for Self and Others	Foster a Secure Learning Environment	Value Diversity	Demonstrate and Share a Purposeful Program	Engage in Active learning	Encourage Optimism	Celebrate
A sense of belonging (esp. students)	Everyone takes responsibility for their actions	Cross-curricular consultation	Being able to demonstrate everyday value in what is being taught	Students are in charge of many aspects of the day	Students look forward to coming every day	Students are delighted by their own and others' successes
Mutual respect	Safe and secure learning environment	Define roles to support warm climate	More opportunity for one-to-one tutoring	Active pupil involvement in the learning process	Students and teachers love to be here and want to do their best	Success is frequently celebrated, thereby encouraging everyone to strive for it
Respect for differences	Clear code of behavior with support from district, administration, and community	Teachers are allowed to employ their own strengths to the advantage of pupils	Relevant programming	Students become more responsible for their own learning	Cheerful atmosphere	Recognize success in all its forms
Show respect for self and others (elders included)	Respect for school property	Encourage creativity and initiative	Learning, sharing	Have patience in learning (and teaching)	Be optimistic	Encourage self-confidence
Accommodate individuals	Safe	Support for the arts as well as business and computers	An open, inquiring learning atmosphere	Pupil-centered		Become unified in some ways (e.g., school sweater)
Students and teachers have a friendly, caring rapport						

Positive relationships	Students are involved emotionally and actively in keeping standards of behavior high	Foster extra-curricular and co-curricular activities to support courses	Consistent practices	All students using time effectively
Courtesy in language and behavior	Everyone gets along, everyone knows and adheres to the rules	Broad program stressing traditional academic forms, mental and physical fitness		
Honesty and integrity are highly valued and encouraged; honesty is a trait valued by all	Safe and caring	Mandatory involvement in at least *one* extracurricular per semester for all junior students		

Strategic Actions Taken During the First 15 Months

The representative school improvement team (SIT), which included representation from the school climate group and the various academic departments, worked with their principal to facilitate the following actions:

1. The Principal established a representative school success and school climate team to study the results of the survey, gather further data, and initiate appropriate actions.
2. The SIT orchestrated the completion of a comparative parent, student, and teacher survey and used the analyses to stimulate a dialogue about the school's responsiveness to student needs.
3. The SIT worked with the principal to create a sense of urgency around this new improvement work of the school.
4. The principal actively supported the school climate team's effort to focus much of their efforts on improving teaching and learning.
5. The principal personally reassigned the course selections for some 80-odd pupils during the first 2 to 3 weeks of school after the guidance department said it was too late to alter pupil selection of courses.
6. The principal had the front entrance to the school cleaned, redesigned, landscaped, and beautified within the first 4 weeks of school.
7. The team established landscaping projects in order for pupils to create quiet and reflective areas within the school grounds.
8. The school climate group arranged information sessions for teachers where knowledge and responsive classroom practices about the diversity of the community were shared and discussed.
9. The principal and the SIT instituted shared decision-making procedures for establishing goals, priorities, and focused professional development opportunities.
10. The SIT began to implement a more active and engaging professional learning and development program that included guest speakers, brown paper bag lunch discussion groups, classroom inquiry discussions, and the regular sharing of student progress data.
11. The SIT implemented a renewed emphasis on student leadership, with a student leadership council that was able to create and participate in many worthwhile schoolwide projects.
12. The principal actively supported the establishment and continuation of multidisciplinary teaching and learning programs.
13. Time for team planning and reflection was found and protected.

14. The SIT initiated and supported an effective peer counseling and conflict resolution program.
15. The SIT aligned budget expenditures with school purposes and program goals.

LESSONS LEARNED ACROSS THE SCHOOLS

In the four cases, through the planning of strategic directions and related actions, the schools have been recultured. It is as Michael Fullan states, "Reculturing is the name of the game."[17] But a particular kind of culture must be created. Practice is constantly examined and reviewed. Enquiry underpins the work of the school. The teacher collective continuously discusses learning experiences, ideas, practices, and possibilities, and this ongoing collaboration deepens the understanding of and commitment to moral purpose and understanding the learning needs of the individual pupil. Moving the act of teaching into the collective realm of improving ideas, shared practice, and reflection is very much about creating a new and exciting workplace culture. Context, in each case, identifies those factors that make the school, the purposes, the priorities, and the strategy unique. Clearly, each context presents different needs and requires a different approach. A one-size-fits-all approach to schooling and improvement is obviously not appropriate.

David Hopkins recently put forward a systemic approach to educational reform that has three key features:

- adopting a pedagogy designed to enable every young person to reach his potential
- an approach to teaching that sees teachers as designers of increasingly powerful learning experiences
- the redesign of the landscape of schooling, with independence, innovation, networking, and lateral responding as its central characteristics[18]

What I like about this systemic portrait is the focus on the classroom and appreciation of the simple fact that school improvement is very much about the learner and how teachers teach. Further into his book is a chapter on what Hopkins calls personalized learning. Personalized learning means high-quality teaching that is responsive to the different ways students achieve their best.[19] Learning is customized! Again, it is refreshing to see the attention now being devoted to the learner, to students having a voice in formulating their own educational goals, to the flexibility in time and support in helping diverse learners achieve those goals, and to the responsiveness in shaping teaching around the way different youngsters learn.

School improvement research has demonstrated the vital importance of teacher development in school-level change.[20] Teacher learning and development are very much about building not only personal professional capacity but also the capacity of the organization to learn and continually improve.

Finally, and not surprisingly, school improvement research has reinforced the importance of leadership in securing school-level change. It has shown that leaders within improving schools have vision and drive change forward. They *take charge!* It has also demonstrated that within improving schools leadership is shared and distributed.[21] However, it's more than just the fact that it is shared and distributed that counts. It is very much about *how* leadership is shared and for *what* purposes. There are schools where leadership, with respect to extracurricular activities, special events, sports, assemblies, parent meetings, fundraising, and so on, is shared and distributed, but these purposes hardly impact on the learning and life chances of all pupils. The sharing of leadership necessary for improvement attends systemically and coherently to the learning experience of each and every learner and the professional learning and development of all teachers.

Conestoga, Cloverdale, Lancewood, and Sutton Heights presented differing contexts and unique challenges requiring systemic thinking and action. In each case the work was characterized by the following:

- bringing a sense of urgency to the work
- documenting and reviewing the learning experience of the students
- clarifying and building common and compelling purposes
- restructuring to enable fulfillment of those purposes
- examining exemplary and improving classroom practice
- forging relationship-based teams where teachers working and learning together is common
- rekindling the passion for teaching
- extending teacher-student relationships beyond a single school year
- creating a culture of inquiry and informed, collegial action (a professional learning community)

Identifying strategic directions can be a project in itself. But the powerful thing taking place within these cases is the alignment of the actions (or small projects), creating a synergy as each action adds value to others occurring simultaneously. In our cases, the strategies were unique and reflected the informed needs of the students and idiosyncratic context of each school and community. Working with a design team and carefully planning the strategies brought coherence to the work of the school and, in particular, to the experience each student had with the curriculum.

What I think worked well in these examples was the emphasis on execution—getting things done—quickly moving to action. Bossidy et al. claim that *execution* is the gap nobody knows.[22] They claim many organizations find the setting of strategic goals compelling but fail to follow through on the nitty-gritty of executing the many aligned actions necessary to implement them. In these cases, effectively implementing the key strategic directions required an ongoing, robust dialogue among all players, and the principals involved certainly fostered and enabled this on a continuous basis. Dialogue became the core of the newly created workplace culture and the basis for action. Many schools I visit have compelling and often lofty goals but seem almost paralyzed when it comes to execution. Freedman argues that implementation is the hands-on work of leaders and identifies the nine blocks to successful execution shown in Figure 6.5.[23] Alongside these obstacles, I have outlined examples of how they manifest themselves in schools.

Figure 6.5. Blocks to Successful Execution

Obstacles or Blocks	The Problem in Schools
Strategic Inertia	Not knowing how to start; teacher isolation, professional privacy, or teacher resistance
Lack of Stakeholder Commitment	Not having everyone on board from the beginning—it is about participation (see Chapter 7)
Strategic Drift	Not focusing on the big picture and losing your way; being overcome by external pressures
Strategic Dilution	Lack of intensity of actions, particularly capacity-building; or too many unrelated directions leading to watered-down, weak approaches
Strategic Isolation	Weak communication caused by poor staff relations (Staff members don't get to see or hear about the growth and actions of others, resulting in a loss of direction, coherence, and energy.)
Failure to Understand Progress	No means of assessing progress (Without key indicators to demonstrate progress, the destination proves elusive.)
Initiative Fatigue	Too much happening but not enough of the important stuff getting done; no cyclic energizing
Impatience	Leaders demonstrating unrealistic expectations
Not Celebrating Success	Failure to enjoy, acknowledge, and celebrate the journey

Thinking and acting strategically, and ensuring robust implementation, is the work of school leaders! In secondary schools, this is not something to delegate to department heads, nor in elementary schools to team leaders. These designated school leaders have significant roles to play, but the principal should be actively involved with them and others supporting, encouraging, and participating in this most vital work.

In applying these lessons to your own context, *take charge* of the improvement agenda by executing strategic directions and subsequent actions. As you do so, keep in mind the following guidelines:

- *Focus the Work of the School on Teaching and Learning.* Teaching and learning are what improvement is all about—not single factors—but THE thing. Focus on high-quality teaching across the school that is responsive to the diverse needs, interests, and passions of the learner and the ways in which they achieve their best.
- *Develop Compelling Moral Purposes.* They drive the work of the school and engage teachers in this work. Whether it was taking off classroom doors, reorganizing a large school into four smaller ones, or de-streaming grades 6, 7, and 8, the purposes were clear and compelling to all concerned.
- *Identify and Address Blocks or Obstacles.* Key to moving forward strategically is identifying and removing or improving obstacles or blocks to the school's purposes. This is about addressing the gap between our collective intentions and the current reality. It is that which intervenes between what we want to do and getting it done.
- *Know the Student Extraordinarily Well.* Research and writing about new pedagogies, learning styles, multiple intelligences, the implications of brain research, cooperative learning, pupil-centered learning, and so on tell us much about improving student learning and development. The key to all of these approaches is knowing the student(s) well. Thinking and acting strategically is about building the capacity of teachers; structuring time, classes, roles, and subjects; and continuously gathering information in order to know the student well.
- *Document the Experience of Students Across Classes, Subjects, and the School.* Decisions about purposes, programs, and actions to be taken in each case were based on carefully gathered information that reflected students' learning needs and, in particular, their experience with the curriculum and with one another. In other words, the work of the school is broadly informed and inquiry led.
- *Realize that Structure Matters.* Many schools take on new initiatives and layer them over old structures. Structures are essentially concerned with time, space, roles, and responsibilities. Structures are the

arrangements through which people are distributed in relation to one another within an organization. Structures are what bring people together or keep them apart, through space, time, and the hierarchies of position and power. Structures similarly represent and reinforce power hierarchies through *chains* of command, *levels* of decision-making, and so forth. Structures also help or hinder the purposes that people pursue within their organizations, making those purposes easier or harder to attain. When thinking of structure, the guiding principle is form follows function. If you want to improve teacher–student relations and have more caring responses to student needs, then you have to structure the schedule so that teachers and students have substantial time together to build lasting relationships. I should add that changing structure by itself achieves little. If the structure fails to accommodate purpose or function, then the change becomes difficult to achieve.

- *Invest in Social as well as Academic Capital.* Schools, perhaps more than any other organization, are about building and sustaining constructive, knowledge-rich, caring, community-building, and growth-provoking relationships. Often, in our drive to improve student learning and development, to implement the latest innovation or curriculum mandate, we forget that effective schools emerge from huge investments in social as well as academic capital.

- *Build Relationships.* Successful leadership is about building relationships. Successful schools are about relationships, not only teacher–student relationships, but also relationships among teachers, between the principal and his or her colleagues, and between the school and parents. Where the district plays a supportive role, clearly the relationships between school-based and district-based educators also require cultivation.

- *Align Purposes, Directions, and Actions.* Effective change is systemic and coherent; it involves all players at all levels within the organization. Perhaps the single most important lesson in the above cases is that purposes, strategic directions, and specific actions are aligned. There may be many specific tasks and actions, but it is the coherence brought about through distributed and shared leadership that adds value and creates synergy across the actions.

- *Quickly Move to Action.* It is by no means an accident that across the four schools described here, there was a great sense of urgency generated around the new work of the school. Effective principals understand that improving teaching and learning doesn't have to take forever. It is strategically smart, they realize, to develop early action, momentum, and excitement around compelling purposes.

- *Attend to the Details of Implementation.* This is the work of the school leader. Execution is about following up, communicating the strategy, supporting colleagues, sitting in on meetings, removing obstacles, finding the time, building the capacity to move forward, and aligning the actions of self and others.
- *Don't Delegate. Capacitate!* Involving your colleagues in the work of the school is much more than delegating tasks to groups and committees. It is about ensuring that the responsible team has the capacity—in particular, the skill to design the work, ongoing support, and training when the skill set is not available within the group. That is what enables the team to develop their capacity to complete this task and ones like it in the future.
- *Invest Your Time in Capacity-Building.* School principals are typically capable people, anxious to improve the chances of their pupils and to get things done. Our career paths often take us from small schools where, due to limited human resources, we take on superhuman roles, trying to be everything to everyone. This approach will not suffice in larger organizations, where successful principals spend little time doing the work of the school and most of their time investing in the capacity-building of others.
- *Recognize that Context Matters.* It would appear that the strategic directions developed in these cases worked well. But it is essential to realize that they worked *in a particular context during a particular time period.* They were, by and large, built from the ground up. They may transfer to your context—but only when you and your colleagues work together to create similar actions and directions that are responsive to your school's reality.

REFLECT ON THESE QUESTIONS

1. How do strategic directions get created and acted on in your school/district?
2. Strategic directions flow from agreed-upon, morally compelling purposes. What processes will enable you and your colleagues to gather the necessary engagement and commitment to move from purpose to action quickly?
3. What are the opportunities and blocks/obstacles to enacting constructive and aligned strategic directions to be implemented effectively in the context of your school/district?
4. How and to what degree are strategic directions aligned with one another and with school purposes? How would you know?

5.   The four cases described above are characterized by a sense of urgency and excitement, in which the confluence of aligned directions seems to create a momentum of its own. How might you bring this same sense of urgency, energy, and synergy to the work of your school/district?

6.   Developing strategic directions emerges out of informed dialogue with colleagues. What kinds of information might you and your colleagues gather in order to ensure that the emerging strategic directions are truly responsive to the needs of your student population?

7.   Execution is everything! What are the many things you can do to get to action fast and to sustain those actions and gains?

8.   Most school improvement planning neglects to build in ways of knowing whether agreed-upon strategic directions are making a difference to the learning lives of students and the work of teachers. How might you design ways of knowing the efficacy of your strategic directions into the process of implementing them?

9.   Successful schools differ from ordinary schools by their profound preoccupation with teaching and learning. How would you go about causing such a strategic shift in your workplace context?

10. In each of these cases, there were specific directions requiring the restructuring of time, timetable, teaching teams, and planning teams. Typically, principals are appointed at the beginning of the academic year, which often means it is hard to restructure until the beginning of the following year. Given this reality, how will you move quickly to action?

11. In schools faced with diversity, poor achievement, and/or behavioral difficulties, one strategic direction has to be to deepen the knowledge teachers have of the individual student. This is about improving and sustaining relationships between teacher and student. How might you implement such a direction in your context? What specific actions might you take?

FOR FURTHER READING

Harris, A. (2002). *School improvement: What's in it for school?* London: Routledge Falmer.

This is an excellent, nicely written synopsis of the school improvement literature, which I find most helpful in reflecting on improvement work.

Hopkins, D. (2007). *Every school a great school—Realizing the potential of system leadership.* Berkshire, UK: Open University Press.

Possibly the most current and informed view on school and system improvement, bringing together lessons from the United Kingdom and other parts of the world.

CHAPTER 7

Orchestrating the Concert: Learning to Work Together

Everything in this book requires all teachers in school—and the principal—to work together. In this chapter you will learn about

- building a culture of participation;
- the issues and practicalities of working collaboratively in schools;
- three schools whose cases illustrate challenges in working together; and
- valuing diverse worldviews, building commitment and trust, finding consensus, and moving quickly to action.

On the surface, it seems as though nothing could be easier than for teachers to work collegially, yet wherever I travel and work, truly collaborative workplace cultures can be very hard to find. This is the real challenge for school leadership: Courageous leaders need to *take charge* and act fearlessly, with tenacity and confidence, in order to facilitate participation across their organization. This chapter explores challenges I have observed and confronted and approaches I have found useful in learning to work together.

RECOGNIZING A CULTURE OF PARTICIPATION

In schools where teachers engage in capacity-building, professional learning, and important decision-making, participation is valued, deliberate, purposeful, supported, and central to the work of the organization. Experienced members model and demonstrate their practical knowledge for the less experienced; questions are constantly asked; practice is continuously shared and reviewed; common values are developed; and, most important, teachers talk, talk, and talk some more. The currency of participation is dialogue about practice and learning, constructive stories of students' accomplishments and learning experience, new ideas and innovations, professional readings, and reflection. In forging relationships through participation, the community becomes stronger.

Participatory school cultures look and sound like the following:[1]

- Adults in the school *talk* about practice. The conversations and questions about teaching and learning are frequent, continuous, concrete, and precise.
- Adults *engage* together in work on curriculum by planning, designing, researching, and evaluating the experience of learners and the curriculum.
- Adults in the schools *initiate* innovative ideas, *documenting, sharing, and evaluating* the progress of students and program implementation
- Adults in the schools *teach* one another, *modeling and demonstrating what they know* about teaching, learning, and leading. Craft knowledge and the experience of the learner are revealed, articulated, and shared.
- Adults *constructively contribute* to shared and informed decision-making about the important aspects of the work of the school.
- Adults *examine and reflect* on their own learning and participation as they work toward enacting shared purpose.
- Adults *build common purpose* and *make explicit the values* that underpin relationships and the work of the school.

Practices of participation, as described here, occur first of all in the more formal, facilitated work of the school but, over time, come to permeate the professional conversation of the staffroom, hallways, parking lot, and social events.

THREE STORIES OF EDUCATORS PARTICIPATING IN CHANGE INITIATIVES

I want to share three stories from my experience as provincial coordinator of the Creating a Culture of Change Initiative.[2] Schools applied to the teachers' union in order to have a pair of trained facilitators who were practicing educators visit and support the collaborative work of the school. Along with the facilitators, I visited the schools.

Rob: So Much Talent, So Little Participation

We were sitting in the staffroom of a rural school in northern Ontario where we were initiating a new improvement project. While waiting to meet with the principal, we got talking to Rob, an enthusiastic geography teacher. I quickly discovered that he had spent time in my home country, New Zealand. While there, he walked and photographed the spectacularly rugged Milford and Routeburn hiking trails. In Africa, he had spent time in the Kalahari and the Serengeti and had his photographs published by *National Geographic*, *Canadian Geographic*, and other magazines. His love of and passion for the outdoors and photography were infectious. We could have listened to him all day. Our discussion ended all too soon, and as we moved down the hall for our meeting, I remarked to my facilitator colleague, "What a treasure to have someone like this teach in your school." At the end of our meeting with the school's principal, Margaret, I casually mentioned my delight in meeting Rob and commented on how fortunate it must be for the students to have such a passionate, worldly teacher to work with. Imagine my surprise when Margaret responded with a tirade of quite offensive descriptors about Rob's lack of commitment, claiming he came to school late and left early, hardly ever attended staff meetings, and, when he did, always had a contrary point of view and generally was uninvolved in the workings of the school. So much talent, but so little participation!

Traveling to many countries where I visit many schools, I have met numerous teachers like Rob. On a later visit to the school, I was able to chat further with Rob and his principal. Rob was clearly a well-informed, articulate, and opinionated teacher. He explained that he felt that his colleagues were not very interested in his views and that overtime he found it easier for everyone if he kept his opinions to himself and focused his energies and interests on the classroom and his life outside of school. He no longer dared to be different!

Gary: Commitment by Coercion

My second visit took me to a school south of my base in Toronto. Gary, the principal, had applied to the CCC initiative to have project facilitators work in his school. During the preliminary discussions, he explained that he wanted his colleagues to start using more innovative approaches to their teaching, such as learning to link assessment more closely to instruction and use cooperative learning techniques. Gary recognized that improved teaching and learning are the answer to student success.

An expectation of the CCC project is that participating teachers and principals must come to an agreement about the nature of their project and, in particular, demonstrate a commitment to work together. Gary agreed to engage his colleagues in forging a common purpose, thus eliciting commitment. I never heard from him until the very last day of the academic year. At four o'clock in the afternoon, as I was struggling to leave my office, the phone rang and it was Gary. He sounded breathless. "I have the commitment, Paul. We are ready to go." "Send me the application and I'll get something organized in the new school year," I said, and quickly escaped for my long-awaited holiday.

When I returned in September, the application from Gary's school was on my desk. I called him again to clarify how his colleagues had come to express their commitment to the goals of the project. He assured me that on the last day of school they had clearly indicated their willingness to work together toward the goals described in the application. On that basis, I assigned two facilitators to visit with the staff at the school to collaboratively develop an approach to implementing school goals.

Within minutes of their leaving Gary's school after this initial visit, I received an exasperated call from my facilitator colleagues. It had gone poorly. Some teachers were obviously uncomfortable with the visit, others seemed unclear as to why facilitators were in the school, and one teacher was openly hostile. The principal was apologetic. But where was the commitment? Where were we to go with this project?

I called Gary the next morning. Dismayed that he had invited my colleagues into his school without the commitment of his teachers to a common purpose, I felt that an explanation was due. "Tell me more about this commitment you assured me that teachers have given," I said. With some encouragement, he told me the story. It was the last day of the school year. In the morning, a district consultant presented a workshop on differentiated instruction, showing how assessment is linked to accommodating varied abilities and learning styles of pupils. This apparently went well. After a sumptuous lunch, Gary asked for a commitment of all teachers to work toward these more responsive teaching practices. A mixed reception greeted his request, ranging from enthusiasm to a complete lack of interest. The more teachers resisted, the harder Gary pushed for agreement.

Finally, as the afternoon wore on and everyone began thinking about their vacation, Gary presented an ultimatum: His meeting would not adjourn until he received commitment from all to work together on implementing these practices and procedures in their classrooms. Upon hearing this, I imagined him holding fiercely onto the door handle of the staffroom and saying, "No one leaves for vacation until we have a commitment!" Gary dreamed the great dream but failed to uncover the morally compelling purpose. Thus, there I was at his school, trying to figure how to right an almost impossible situation.

Ken: The Power of a Morally Compelling Question

My third visit took me to a large suburban school. Ken was the principal of the 80-teacher Cranberry Secondary School. He had attended a presentation on leadership that I facilitated in his district and afterward was interested in having me work with teachers in his school. He said the problem at his school was that his colleagues were not interested in improving or talking about their work. Often, only half his teachers attended staff meetings. The average age of his teaching staff was 49 years. In explaining what he wanted for his school Ken said, "I just want my colleagues to get excited about something, anything, that would enable the students to do better at school. "He wanted to rid the staff of lingering lethargy he believed inhibited student engagement and success.

Not one to duck a challenge, I volunteered to work with his colleagues. In about a month, the school was having a Professional Activity Day. As it was to be a Friday, I suggested we include Thursday evening, choose a magical retreat location, and appoint a truly representative stakeholder team to plan with me. I provided dinner (I have no research to support the concept, but I am convinced that all great teams are fueled by sharing great food) for the planning team and asked them what it would take to get all teachers to attend and participate in the upcoming retreat. They answered, as I knew they would, "Teachers would have to know this time together will make a difference for kids."

There is a wonderful facilitative strategy called "Open Space Technology" that I find extremely effective in unleashing the passion and energy of participants in shared learning activities. Open Space Technology is a unique process whereby participants identify the issues, set the agenda, allocate the time, find a space, and structure the conversation according to their needs. Open Space works on four principles and one basic law. Here are the four principles:

- Whoever comes is the right person.
- Whatever happens is the only thing that could happen.
- When it starts, it is the right time.
- When it is over, it is over.[3]

The Law of Two Feet states, "Whenever you feel you can no longer contribute or benefit by your presence, you know that your colleagues will value your using your two feet to take you someplace where you can." Incidentally, this remarkable law can transform meetings. It is guaranteed to rejuvenate and improve dull and irrelevant faculty meetings. School principals who have convinced their district administrator to adopt this rule have been delighted with how purposeful their district meetings have become.

Open Space requires the development of a focus question, capturing the imagination of participants as they grasp core values and issues and unleash their passion for action. In this case, the planning team and I framed the following morally compelling question: What are the issues and opportunities with respect to improving the life chances of all pupils at Cranberry High School, for which I have a passion and am prepared to accept responsibility (at least for the period of this retreat)?

The strategy initially requires each participant to identify at least one issue, write it in large print on a 36 x 18–inch sheet of paper, stand up and read out their issue for all to hear, and then paste their issue paper on a large blank wall.

Ken shared his fears with me. He felt that when it came to the point of identifying an issue, his colleagues would be silent; some would probably leave, and the whole process would break down. His prediction was not very reassuring for me as facilitator, but I have learned to trust in the process. Ken was as astounded as I was relieved when it came time for teachers at Cranberry High to identify an issue and every participant stood up and boldly called out their issue. There is nothing like a good, morally compelling question and a planned, participative process to unleash the passion of teachers.

Thinking About These Stories

Each of the examples raises important questions about building a participatory culture in schools, particularly those with a growth-inhibiting existing culture. In the first case, Rob represents a unique, informed, diverse, and articulate worldview, particularly with respect to education. Margaret has not thought about how to make the most of his diverse views. What I have learned about schools over the years is that we who work there are not very tolerant of diversity. We have not learned to work with, capitalize on, and value diversity in our teacher colleagues. But diversity is a resource!

Principals tend to hire in their own image, as do superintendents. As a result, there is a "sameness" in schools' staffs, and therefore the workplace culture tends to promote and value conformity. Furthermore, teachers, obviously involved in the lives of their students and being the sensitive individuals they are, do not enjoy confrontation and tend to do everything they can to avoid it. But participatory schools have learned to value and advantage richness and diversity, in which a variety of perspectives contributes to the learning and work of all. Diversity is viewed as a valuable resource. In particular, these schools have searched out and regularly use participatory processes that thrive on diversity. Teachers in these participatory schools have had the opportunity to reflect on, learn to value, and respect nonconforming views. Divergent views can coexist!

In the second example, Gary, who had a good idea, struggled to build ownership in the work of the school. By resorting to a desperate trick, he embarked on a change initiative without the necessary commitment of his colleagues. Gary had decided ahead of time what the initiative would be and did not enable his colleagues to shape it. Gary was what I call a "program implementer." He knew, perhaps intuitively, that something "needed to be done" about teaching and learning. He seized upon a strategy, in this case linking assessment to classroom practice in order to diversify classroom practices and procedures, and sought to have his colleagues adopt it. The problem Gary faced, as with most mandated policy and ideas, was that his colleagues were rightly suspicious of his motives. His confrontational strategy in obtaining his colleagues' cooperation was fraught with danger.

Researchers such as Michael Huberman, who studied the life cycles of teachers, tell us that early in their careers, teachers often buy heavily into an innovation by making considerable sacrifice in terms of time, emotional labor, and personal resources.[4] More often than not, the effort leads to disillusionment and grief as the innovation is either superseded by another or a new or thoughtless principal suddenly abandons the innovation.

For example, in one of the schools where I was principal, in order to address issues of reading and writing, we had built up a literacy program emphasizing personal reading and writing. But my successor quickly moved to ban personal writing, limit personal reading, and then implement a commercial textbook and skills-based literacy program. My former colleagues spoke of their sense of powerlessness, frustration, and loss of what they felt was their professional voice and integrity. Some continued the more personal approach, maintaining pupil reading and writing folders by keeping them hidden in a locked closet and only bringing them out when the new principal was least likely to be visiting their classrooms. My point here is not so much about which principal had the right idea. Rather, it is about what the experience meant to teachers and their attitude toward change. Such a change can also be damaging to students when something they have committed intensely to is superseded by another, very different approach that devalues their past efforts. At the end of the day, such pedagogical shifts provide little hope for building sustainable practice.

Gary also could learn some lessons about uncovering moral purpose rather than trying to impose it (see Chapter 1). There are ways of designing participation that will hugely increase the engagement of colleagues in new and exciting approaches. One example occurred at Ken's school, where the development of a morally compelling question and use of a strong facilitative process focusing on engagement unleashed and honored participants' voices. It became the key to unlocking the passion of his colleagues.

Ken, Margaret, Gary, and principals like them need to build into their organizations the capability to facilitate the participation of colleagues, including

- a robust process of inquiry,
- values and norms of participation,
- designed interactive processes implemented by skilled facilitators,
- and an infrastructure to support the learning of all teachers.

They need to understand that talking at teachers, merely providing colleagues with information without the opportunity to examine, question, and move to consensus and action, is an ineffective strategy, no matter how appropriate the information or innovation is. Information only becomes knowledge through interaction. Knowledge only leads to action when it is morally compelling.

ATTENDING TO WORKPLACE CULTURE

Whether or not a school is participatory is reflected in and manifested by its workplace culture. A workplace culture is about relationships and how participating teachers perceive their world and the world of their colleagues. Furthermore, more than any other factor, a school's workplace culture determines its potential to adapt, grow, learn, and respond to the needs of its students, community, and an ever-changing curriculum. In the case of Rob, described above, we see one segment of the school's culture in action. A potentially talented teacher with an informed worldview is isolated because of his knowledge and somewhat differing views. Cultures of professional privacy and teacher isolation are commonplace in schools worldwide. However, culture, and in this case workplace culture, is a social invention that exists to give meaning to human endeavor. Culture provides

> stability, certainty and predictability. People fear ambiguity and want assurance that they are in control of their surroundings. Culture imbues life with meaning and through symbols creates a sense of efficiency and control. Change creates existential havoc because it introduces disequilibrium, uncertainty, and makes day-to-day life chaotic and unpredictable.[5]

It is because of this potential disequilibrium that many teaching cultures appear resistant or nonadaptive to change, seeking to maintain stability, certainty, and predictability. Therefore, the most important work of school leaders is to design and orchestrate the development of a new, more participative, and adaptive workplace culture.

Historically, and more often than not today, schools as workplaces are characterized by pervasive individualism. As Kevin, a young high school teacher, explained in one of our secondary school reform project schools, "I am responsible to cover the content of my subjects and to help my students do well . . . I don't see why we need to have meetings to share practices . . . and as for decision-making, why can't the administration just do the right thing?"[6] Like many of his colleagues, Kevin teaches alone, in a separate room behind closed doors. In his four short years of practice, he has neither observed a colleague teach nor had one observed him; he has rarely, if ever, discussed his practice with others or shared responsibility for implementing new curriculum or assessment and evaluation procedures. His is a professionally private world where he, like many of his young colleagues, has quickly learned the culture of his workplace and embraced it with certainty and gusto. Workplace culture, as Kevin perceives it, may be described as "Whatever it is one has to know or believe in order to operate in a manner acceptable to its members."[7] Kevin has figured out the culture of his workplace; he has a model based on his surrounds through which he interprets events and relates to others.

Because many hold this counterproductive view of culture, its pervasiveness and importance in either provoking and supporting or blocking and hindering growth and improvement, we need to understand and attend to workplace culture. Educators in schools need not only to have a knowledge of productive work cultures, but also to apply these perspectives to important deliberations on the purposes and work design of the school.

Gareth Morgan provides another helpful view of culture:

> In talking about culture we are really talking about a process of reality construction that allows people to see and understand particular events, actions, objects, utterances or situations in distinctive ways . . . cohesive groups are those that arise around shared understandings, while fragmented groups tend to be those characterized by multiple realities.[8]

I like this view of culture because it makes apparent that the most successful schools are those where teachers share a coherent view of the future and school purposes and take deliberate and collective action with them in mind. As a result, students share a consistent, cohesive learning experience where what counts as progress in one class is the same as in any other. This collectively constructed view translates into coherence across the learning experiences of students within the school. In comparison, less successful schools lack coherence and are much more individualistic, private, and eclectic in their approaches to teaching and learning.

My colleague Andy Hargreaves makes an important distinction between individualism and individuality. In examining this distinction, which Figure 7.1 clarifies,[9] think about Kevin, my former colleagues at Southern Cross Public School, and other stories you have read in this chapter.

In concluding his comments on individuality, Hargreaves says, "Individuality, as the power to exercise independent, discretionary judgment, is therefore closely linked to senses of competence. Indeed, threats to individuality, mandated requirements to carry out less than fully understood judgments of others are closely linked to senses of incompetence." As leaders in education, we have to think about how our actions support individuality and how we can deal with policy and curriculum mandates in ways that ensure the confidence and the power for colleagues to exercise professional judgment. Well-designed participatory cultures hold out the promise of empowering individuals regardless of worldview while finding ground for collective and effective action.

STRATEGIC PROCESSES FOR BUILDING PARTICIPATION

Many of my principal colleagues struggle with the workplace cultures they inherit, as Ken, Margaret, and Gary did. Struggling with an existing culture

Figure 7.1. Individualism Versus Individuality

Individualism	Individuality
Isolation	Personal independence
Professional privacy	Self-actualization
Defensive	Exercise of personal discretion
Help-giving is infrequent	Demonstrates initiative and creativity in one's work
Little planning and problem-solving with colleagues	Often supported by trusting leadership
Avoids participatory cultures	Can contribute significantly to participatory cultures
Perhaps unrealistic in making assertions	Tentativeness and realism in making assertions

is counterproductive. As Buckminster Fuller once said, "You never change things by fighting the existing reality. To change something, build a new model that makes the existing model obsolete."[10] The case of Southern Cross Public School described in Chapter 5 is an example of how this idea looks in practice.[11] There, rather than worry about the existing culture, I moved quickly to create a new one. Southern Cross was like most primary schools. When teachers did share and plan together, this work only occurred by grade level. In contrast, I organized the work of the school around cross-grade and, whenever possible, cross-subject teams for the purposes of planning, learning, and deciding together.

Teachers can learn from one another. The broader the range of interactions and the more diverse the experiences and views, the richer the learning and increase in capacity of the organization. The challenge in designing the work of the school in this way is to ensure that one has strong facilitative processes that thrive on diversity and value individuality while creating more collective approaches to developing purpose and improving classroom practice.

Forming Representative Stakeholder Planning Teams

The importance of stakeholder representation in planning and carrying out the work of participative schools, particularly larger ones, cannot be underestimated! However, the notion of representation and the role representatives play are rarely appreciated. Consider the example from North Ridge Secondary School, discussed in Chapter 5.[12] North Ridge had over 1,600 pupils and a staff of approximately 85. Early in the CCC process, participating schools were asked to form a faculty stakeholder representative planning team. I arrived at North Ridge on a Friday afternoon to have an initial meeting with the principal and the newly formed team. My research colleague and I were quite surprised when we walked into the principal's office and met with a team composed of one male principal and nine sharply dressed, smart younger women—this in a staff where the average age was 50 years and more than half the teachers were male.

I decided to work through with the team the notion of stakeholder representation. I asked them the following questions:

- Who are the stakeholders?
- How might representatives be chosen?
- What do representatives do?
- Who do they represent?

The group was dynamic and easily identified various stakeholders, including subject departments and age and experience representation, and were quick to move toward balancing the question of gender. I asked them to think about stakeholders outside the usual framework of departments, age, and gender, and an interesting observation emerged. A long-running tradition at North Ridge was for about 20 to 25 teachers, mainly male, to meet for a beer at the local pub on Friday afternoons. This important stakeholder group was not represented on the planning team.

This example from North Ridge raises some interesting dilemmas. Imagine the planning team proceeding when 50% of the staff were not represented. When 25% (the Friday-afternoon pub group) of the unrepresented staff met every week to talk over events, imagine how the older staff members would feel or react at a staff meeting at which new plans were introduced. With some negotiation, North Ridge was able to put together a more representative team.

A first step in selecting a planning team includes identifying who the stakeholders are. The second is to figure out how the selection process will work and how colleagues will perceive it. Representation by self-selection or nomination is preferred. From a principal's perspective, this may be unnerving, perhaps raising fears that a less than strong group will plan the all-important work of the school. However, my approach has been to ask for nominees who are well qualified for the role. In this case, I typically ask for nominees who are known for their "excellence and knowledge in teaching and learning," who will be "open and honest in their communication" and who will "respect and value diversity."

Representation also requires the chosen to communicate on behalf of their particular group. Selecting representatives without some kind of infrastructure means that there is no way for them to purposely bring their group together in order to gather colleagues' ideas and to brief them on the thinking of the planning team. The purpose of having stakeholder input is to ensure that the varied needs of participants are understood by the planning team in order for the team to make wise and informed decisions. The rationale for having representatives is to ensure that participants feel their views are known and accounted for and to build a sense of ownership of the directions and work of the school.

Using Time Productively

Schools are busy places. Bound by traditional structures of time, they make it very difficult to free up the all-important time for collaboration, shared learning, and joint work. However, it is imperative in the participative school to create shared time to actively address the vital work of improving teaching and learning. Staff meetings present significant opportunities for learning, capacity-building, and shared decision-making. These do not have to be the passive, information-laden, and frequently boring sessions they customarily have been. To transform staff meetings in the varied contexts where I have worked, I have usually structured the traditional 90-minute staff meeting as shown in Figure 7.2.

When it comes to the "business" of running the school, providing information, planning events, decisions, and problem-solving can be left to teams, stand-up meetings (where participants meet for 5 minutes at break time to discuss issues or make decisions), and key organizers who are charged with getting things done. Leaders need to protect "prime time" for the prime event—building capacity around teaching and learning.

Let us look at some of the kinds of decisions that get made in schools. In Figure 7.3 we see examples of the many decisions that are made in schools, arranged by the degree to which they impact student learning.[13]

Participatory processes are effective means of knowledge-building and decision-making. However, they are time-consuming and require some members of your team to have facilitation skills. Reserve these approaches for the learning and the decisions that matter. Figure 7.3 is an attempt to identify when it is and isn't fruitful to use participatory approaches. Clearly, the items in the right-hand columns are those that have the most impact on the life chances of pupils and thus require the participation of all.

Valuing Facilitation Skills

Facilitation in schools is founded upon a number of fundamental assumptions, not the least of which is the deep belief in the profound wisdom and creativity of teachers who, given a supportive context, a compelling purpose, participatory processes, and norms that value diversity, are collectively capable of astounding accomplishments. Facilitated group work empowers participants, embraces diversity, fosters creativity and alternative solutions, builds shared vision, and ensures a commitment to the agreed-upon outcomes.

Facilitation skills can be learned! They are an essential part of the educational leader's repertoire of growth-provoking skills.[14] They may not be your strong suit when it comes to leadership, but that's no cause for worry. They are an important capacity to have deeply entrenched throughout your organization, but it is not necessary for the principal to be the person with trained facilitator abilities. Participation builds values and creates effective behavioral norms. Participation can be greatly enhanced through the use of effective facilitation skills. In Figure 7.4 we see the difference between facilitated participatory groups and conventional groups.[15] The norms for participatory groups suggested in this chart lead to the creation of a collaborative workplace culture.

Figure 7.2. Transforming the Structure of Staff Meetings

Time	Activity	Process
First 70 Minutes	*Learning and Capacity-Building* This might include the examination of data gathered from classrooms across the school, such as the "Taking a Slice Activity" described in Chapter 3; an examination of writing or reading samples or of student/teacher/parent surveys, etc. It might include actively viewing and responding to a video of relevant exemplary practice or occasionally to a pertinent responsive workshop. Whatever the activity, it must address the agreed-upon purposes of the school and build on and/or extend previous learning. It would be rare for the activity to be isolated, and unacceptable for it to be irrelevant.	Strategies include inquiry, data-sharing, storytelling, informed focused dialogue, reflection, knowledge-building, facilitated activity, active engagement, talk, talk, and talk some more.
Next 15 Minutes	*Shared Decision-Making (when required)* There are occasions when decisions are significantly important and relevant to the purposes of the school and a consensus is required to move forward. Obviously, major consensus tasks such as developing the purposes of the school require far more time than can ever be found during a regular staff meeting.	Equal participation is fostered, leading to consensus-building; decisions are informed.
Final 5 Minutes	*Announcements and Information* Information is distributed prior to the meeting and this time is merely to answer questions of clarification. Or better still: Time is given to reflect on the process.	Key questions of clarification are asked. Each individual is given a chance to question, comment, or pass.

Figure 7.3. Educational Impact Determines Participatory Decision-Making and Learning

LEAST PARTICIPATION ◄────────────► MOST PARTICIPATION

Zero Impact Decisions	Minimal Impact Decisions	Core Impact Decisions	Comprehensive Impact Decisions
Parking spaces Lunchroom supervision Staff lounge Social fund Bus duties Refreshments Fund-raising Smoking policy Timetable construction	Textbook selection Parent programs Sports programs Discipline policy	School budget Curriculum Deployment of personnel Discipline practice Timetabling principles	Uncovering the morally compelling purposes of the school Strategic action planning Professional and organizational learning Classroom and cross-school inquiry Improving teaching and learning Hiring of personnel Personnel evaluation

Developing Relational Trust

Participatory cultures emerge around the sharing of common purposes, constructive relationships, and an infrastructure for supporting inquiry and learning. Relationships demand participation and are dependent on the development of trust among participants. They require unconditional support and form a climate enabling participants to risk sharing part of their innermost selves.

When we ask our colleagues to place their classroom practice on public view in a climate of trust, we are not asking them to risk criticism or ridicule, but to experience encouragement, helpful support, and understanding. Consider the story of James. During the first few months of my tenure as principal of Southern Cross Public School, we had been meeting regularly in our 2-hour professional growth sessions. At the end of each session, each participant had an opportunity to comment or to ask a question about either the process or the content of the session. Each time we went around the table, participants were given the choice of posing a question, commenting, or passing. As participants became more comfortable with the process, they had more to contribute. However, James was interesting because when his turn to respond came, he always paused and then passed. During this

Figure 7.4. Behavioral Norms of Facilitated Participatory Groups Compared with Conventional Groups

Participatory Groups	Conventional Groups
Everyone participates, not just the vocal few.	The fastest thinkers and most articulate or loudest speakers get more airtime.
People give one another room to think and get their thoughts all the way out.	People interrupt one another on a regular basis.
Opposing viewpoints are allowed to coexist in the room.	Differences of opinion are treated as *conflict* that must be solved.
People draw each other out with supportive questions, e.g., Is *this* what you mean?	Questions are often perceived as challenges, as if the person being questioned has done something wrong.
Each member makes an effort to pay attention to the person speaking.	Unless the speaker *captivates* their attention, people space out, mark papers, or watch the clock.
People are able to listen to one another's ideas because they know their own ideas will be heard.	People have difficulty listening to one another's ideas because they are busy rehearsing what *they* want to say.
Each member speaks up on matters of controversy. Everyone knows where everyone stands.	Some members remain quiet on controversial matters. No one really knows where everyone stands.
Members can accurately represent one another's point of view—even when they don't agree with them.	People rarely give accurate representations of the opinions and reasoning of those whose opinions are at odds with their own.
People refrain from talking behind other peoples' backs.	Because they don't feel permission to be direct *during* the meeting, people talk behind one another's backs *outside* the meeting.
Even in the face of opposition from the person in charge, people are encouraged to stand up for their beliefs.	People with discordant, minority perspectives are commonly discouraged from speaking out.
A problem is not considered solved until everyone who will be affected by the solution understands and contributes to the reasoning.	A problem is considered solved as soon as the fastest thinkers have reached an answer. Everyone else is then expected to "get on board" regardless of whether s/he understands the logic of the decision.
When people make an agreement, it is assumed that the decision still reflects a wide range of perspectives.	When people make an agreement, it is assumed that they are all thinking the same thing.

4-month period, our dialogue was focused on literacy learning, and our data collection and discussion examined the teaching of writing.

It was early in December, our last session prior to Christmas break. At the end, James, who was the only teacher not to have contributed during the previous 4 months, finally spoke. He said, "I have a question. I'm doing what you [his colleagues] are doing. Each day in my grade 2 class, I ask my pupils to write on topics of their own choice. They write and write and write, and at the end of each day, I collect the writing and put their papers in my briefcase and take them home. My question is this: What do I do with all this writing?" There was silence. His colleagues were surprised, first because he had spoken at all and second because he had such an important, fundamental question. Then they responded. One teacher said, "James, I had that same problem when I started, and here's what I did. . . ."Another said, "It's important to realize that you can't respond to all the writing and that you need to attend to some more than others. . . ."And so it went on. This was a pivotal moment in the development of trust within the group.

Just as it is important to help children respond constructively to one another's writing or reading, it is equally vital in collaborative groups to learn to respond constructively to the diverse realities of our colleagues. Each question or comment by a colleague represents his or her position at that particular time. Building trust is about recognizing that we all have different positions and that to have a position different from that of a peer is okay. It would have been easy to respond to James's question with criticism. It would be effortless to say, "Why would you drag all that writing home each night?" But we know, as adult learners, that we don't respond well to harsh criticism. I think that if James had been criticized that first time he spoke, he may not have spoken again. From that time on, we all looked forward to James's comment or question at the end of each session. Over the following months and years, we came to understand that James had given our discussion and work some really deep thought, and we would look forward to his questions, knowing that they would really challenge us. Without trust, none of this would have been possible. No trust—no constructive talk!

Robinson very clearly makes the link between increased levels of trust in schools and benefits to students. She states that "in schools where trust levels increased over a three-year period, teachers reported a greater willingness to try new things, a greater sense of responsibility for their students, more outreach to parents, and stronger professional community involving more shared work, more conversations about teaching and learning and a stronger collective focus on student learning."[16]

Leading Courageously and Quickly Moving to Action: Roles for Leaders

Participation can create a dynamic and motivating atmosphere in your school. This is an atmosphere where there are

- feelings of openness and optimism;
- a sense of achievement, accomplishment, and personal satisfaction;
- individuality and multiple viewpoints are welcomed and valued;
- there is great ownership of and commitment to the decisions of the group; and
- participants work collegially to build a community focused on improving the life chances of all students.

It takes courage, a mindful strategy, and fearless action to *take charge* by investing in and trusting your colleagues. Facilitating the learned processes of constructive participation enables all to contribute to the important work of the school. School leaders can focus on pedagogy and community-building by using their time and abilities to improve participation when they

- *Invest in quality training in facilitating participative processes for themselves and many or all colleagues.* It is important for your school to have the capacity to work constructively in teams. Teamwork requires design, purpose, and the development of norms, values, and attitudes that can, with training, be developed to high levels of effectiveness. This requires much more than putting a group of people together in a room.
- *Develop a school design team representing stakeholders.* The design team's role is to orchestrate the work of the school, that is, the inquiry, learning, and participation of colleagues; decision-making; and consensus-building. Design team members must have their ear to the ground, speak on behalf of their constituents, and, equally importantly, keep them informed about the planned work of the school.
- *Ensure that participative processes are used for the most compelling aspects of the work of the school.* This is essential to improving the life chances of all pupils. Everyone does not need to participate in everything. But for the important core decisions of the school,

particularly those related to developing moral purpose and related professional learning, it is most important for all voices to be heard and consensus found.

- *Model participation, curiosity, tentativeness, and adult learning principles.* Actions speak louder than words. Teachers are very mindful about what it is their leaders attend to and value. Invest your time in modeling and demonstrating those behaviors of inquiry and valuing alternate perspectives. Show, above all, that you are a learner, too: If the design team calls for teachers to gather data, then leaders should also go into the classrooms and gather data.

- *Build in time to reflect on participation.* Reflection is not only important for the content of teamwork but equally so in early years for building a culture of inquiry and examination. It is consequential to continuously and collectively reviewing how the team is learning to work together in order to build norms of participation and collegiality.

- *Respect and value a diversity of informed opinions.* Encourage colleagues to support their positions with real evidence. Value and respect the opinions of others. Use powerful facilitation techniques that thrive on diversity to welcome and encompass varied perspectives.

- *Employ external facilitation.* When colleagues are skeptical about participation or your organization lacks experience or capacity to constructively lead participative processes or events, consider using outside facilitative expertise. Outside facilitators can bring skill and objectivity to the process while at the same time contributing to capacity-building of the organization.

- *Work with the design team to ensure that decisions lead to concrete, specific, and fast action.* Often, teachers and/or their leaders reach decisions but seem to have no means of enacting them. Participatory, strategic design needs to include plans for how and when things are going to be done and who is going to do them (see Chapter 6).

- *Document the progress of participants toward fulfilling the goals and work of the school* (see Chapter 3). Documentation, which many think of as an art form inasmuch as it usually is a multidimensional, multimedia presentation, is the basis for reflection and learning. It enables the organization to maintain memory over time. It is a powerful tool of accountability. It tells us when innovation is improving the life chances of all.

THE POWER OF PARTICIPATION

It was early in the spring. We started our work at 4:00 P.M. Forty-five participating teachers, the principal, and the vice principal from Churchill Public School, a K–8 school in western Ontario, had already put in a full day's work and yet were eager to tackle the challenging labor before them. Simply put, the task was to find a way to use the new, voluminous, and sterile curriculum to truly improve the lives of their pupils. The government's plan was strong on mandate and pressure but seriously short on support and resources. The purpose of the evening was to develop a strategic plan leading to specific and fast action. At 8:00 P.M., 90 minutes after supper break, as facilitator I had to ask the following question: "We have reached the planned completion time, yet our work is not finished—what do you want to do?" The teachers were adamant. They wanted to complete the task.

By 9:30 P.M., we had agreed on the final changes to five strategic directions from which specific actions would flow. Five action teams, enabling all participants to join one of their own choosing, were formed to plan out actions as early as the next week. Exhausted, glasses of wine in hands, we stood around reflecting on the evening's events. I was curious and asked, "Why is it you are here at this time of the evening? How is it you have been prepared to give of your own time to this work?" The teachers were clear about their motivations. "We're tired of being done to," they said. "We are tired of being criticized. Tonight is important to us because it enables us to begin to *take charge* . . . to take some control over our work and our destiny . . . to turn this curriculum into something that works for our pupils. When you feel so publicly threatened, it feels great to be part of a group that stands for something worthwhile." The passionate teachers at Churchill were finding empowerment, energy, purpose, and security by participating confidently and assertively in constructively dealing with what appeared to them to be an unreasonable externally imposed innovation. *Taking charge* has its rewards!

REFLECT ON THESE QUESTIONS

1. Describe the nature of your school community! How and to what extent do you and your colleagues respect and value diversity within your community? What would people of diversity (race, color, gender, culture, belief, etc.) tell you? Give some specific examples.
2. Describe the collaboration skills colleagues across your school/district demonstrate. How and to what extent are they present during teamwork?

How might you and your colleagues go about improving them?

3. How and to what extent are teachers with contrary opinions welcomed and included in decision-making across the school? If diverse opinions are not welcome, how might you change that?

4. Which decisions in your workplace require consensus across the entire teaching staff? What do you and your colleagues understand consensus to be? How would you know when consensus has been reached?

5. If you were able to follow a typical student through her entire career at your school, in what ways would her learning experience be similar or aligned from class to class and from year to year? If it is the case that their experience is eclectic, varying greatly from teacher to teacher, what is the imperative to try and align expectations about teaching and learning experiences? How would you go about building greater coherence across the learning experiences of all pupils?

6. Describe the workplace culture in your school/district. How does it compare with Judith Warren Little's description of participatory cultures summarized early in the chapter? If the culture is not participatory, how might you go about changing that?

7. Describe the part of the work of the school that may be described as "joint work." What is the relationship between this joint work and student learning experiences and learning?

8. When you have a *good idea* with respect to teaching and learning, how might you go about successfully implementing it schoolwide?

9. How might you turn a *top-down* mandate into a *bottom-up* commitment?

10. What is the nature of the shared or distributed leadership in your school? How and in what ways might these opportunities build reserve capacity into your school organization? How would you know if this is the case?

FOR FURTHER READING

Bennett, B., & Rolheiser, C. (2001). *Beyond Monet*. Toronto: Bookation.

This hands-on book focuses on how to integrate a variety of instructional skills and strategies based on knowledge of how pupils learn. Check out the website at www.beyondmonet.ca.

Garmston, R. (1999). *The adaptive school: A sourcebook for developing collaborative groups*. Norwood, MA: Christopher-Gordon.

Garmston provides excellent practical strategies to develop collaborative groups and teams in your school.

Hargreaves, A. (1994). *Changing teachers, changing times*. London: Cassell.

This book, particularly chapters 8 to 11, provides a well-articulated, insightful look into school cultures.

International Association of Facilitators. (2000). Facilitator competencies. *Group Facilitation: A Research and Applications Journal, 2*(2), 24–31.

The International Association of Facilitators has identified six core competencies.

CHAPTER 8

Participation for Growth and Improvement

This book is predicated on two key foundations of school change: a morally compelling purpose and a participatory workplace culture. Upon these stand four pillars of continuous improvement:

- Knowing the student well through evidence-gathering; fostering student voice; and developing deep, lasting relationships.
- Developing intellectual capital through the intensification of continuous personal and collective professional inquiry, learning, and development.
- Forming strong professional relationships to value and support one's colleagues. Most school and district personnel claim to have good relationships with one another and with their students. However, an effective school needs to move beyond mere congeniality to professional intimacy.
- Powerful and cohesive pedagogical responsiveness in teaching across all classrooms, for example, personalized teaching and learning.

In Figure 8.1 you can see how these four pillars are supported by the two key foundation stones: morally compelling purpose and a participatory culture. Purpose and culture underpin the pillars of improvement.

EXAMINING THE FOUR PILLARS OF IMPROVEMENT

Working with these four pillars of improvement is hard to do in many school settings, as often the purposes, culture, structure (particularly the use of time and what counts as work), traditions, external pressures, community expectations, and leadership conspire to support the status quo. Most schools, of course, contain elements of the pillars, but few genuinely embody all of these traits. Images throughout the course of the book portray an intensification (increased time, commitment, pervasiveness, and connectedness) of the work devoted to them. Specifically, the four pillars are detailed in the pages ahead.

Figure 8.1. Rethinking and Intensifying the Focus and Work of the School

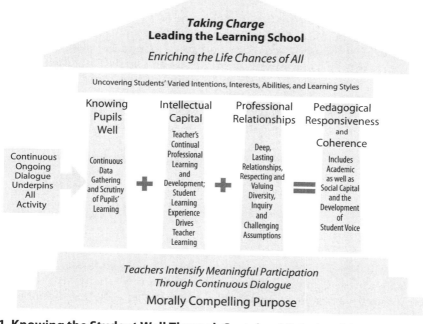

1. Knowing the Student Well Through Sustained Relationships and Evidence-Gathering

Responsive and adaptive pedagogical practice is only possible when teachers know their students extraordinarily well. Knowing each student well means having a lasting, personal relationship with each but also gathering frequent evidence of student accomplishments and learning experiences in the classroom and examining that with others. Extending the personal and learning relationship beyond a single year to 2 or 3 years enables the knowing and caring to deepen and sustain. Organizing schools in ways that truly prevent such knowing and intimacy of relationships (for example, rotating students for short periods of time with 8 different teachers) does a great injustice to the life chances of the many. Students in close relationships with their teachers can play an extraordinarily important role as information-gatherers who document and share their reflections on their own learning and that of others. Here, assessment becomes learning! Teachers' commitment to knowing each student well means that they are constantly gathering and reflecting on the students' learning experience to inform practice. In this way, assessment serves learning.

2. Developing Intellectual Capital Through Continuous Personal and Collective Professional Learning and Development

Continuous and intensified personal and collective professional learning and development is the key pillar in building capacity within schools to enable the responsive pedagogy necessary to improve the life chances of all students. This continuous learning, when deeply embedded in the day-to-day work of teachers and the learning of their pupils, is a highly intellectual activity. Sergiovanni describes this intellectual capital as the sum of what everyone in the school knows and shares that can help the school be more effective in enhancing the learning and development of students.[1]

The word *collective* refers to individuals who act together with common purpose. It suggests the aggregate of the group—a holistic approach. So even though actions take place in individual classrooms across the school, the actions are interrelated. Focusing on the way this interrelating is done reveals collective and mental processes that are highly developed.[2] A collective mind is distinct from an individual mind because it inheres in the pattern of interrelated activities among many players. Weick and Roberts describe the concept of mind as a disposition to act with heed. Heed, they quote Ryle in explaining, is when people act more or less carefully, critically, consistently, purposefully, attentively, studiously, vigilantly, conscientiously, and pertinaciously—all descriptors of teachers who are responding mindfully (see Chapter 2) to the intentions and needs of their learners.[3]

3. Forming Strong Professional Relationships

Relationships matter! Most school and district personnel claim to have good relationships with one another and with their students. However, to really form effective professional relationships is to move beyond mere congeniality. Robust professional relationships are not so much about liking one another as they are about

- encouraging and respecting a diversity of experiences and perspectives;
- valuing the transparency and nuances of colleagues' professional practice;
- honoring the professional obligation of colleagues to challenge the status quo;
- reveling in and arguing from a multitude of perspectives; and
- supporting one's colleagues as risk-takers, student advocates, learners, and knowledge-builders.

The implications for school and district leaders are significant! Diverse views are to be solicited and valued with equality, regardless of the experience or role of the advocate. In order to work and learn together, principals need to employ the thoughtfulness and strategic action of a leader or leaders. Professional relations are important, for without them the opportunities to learn together and collectively work together toward common purpose are seriously constrained.

4. Pedagogical Coherence and Responsiveness

Pedagogical coherence and responsiveness ensure that each student constantly receives appropriate instructional experiences in each and every classroom. Students must receive consistent messages about what it is to be a reader, an author, a problem-solver, a lifelong learner, an inquirer, or a scientist. These messages and understandings are created over time, when opportunities to reflect and collectively explore the meta-cognitive aspects of various tasks and disciplines are integral to daily learning and teaching.

Coherence is about ensuring that regardless of the classroom, what counts and is valued in one learning context is valued and assessed in others. Building pedagogical coherence means that high expectations, when permeating all classrooms, are transparent and responsive to the interests, intentions, abilities, learning style, and cultural and linguistic nuances of each learner.

CONNECTING COLLECTIVE INTELLECTUAL CAPACITY-BUILDING AND PROFESSIONAL RELATIONSHIPS

The stories and experiences related in this book portray schools intensifying the intellectual learning and development of teachers and their professional relationships with one another and their pupils. This intensification (perhaps best illustrated in Southern Cross Public School in Chapter 5 and Lancewood Public School in chapters 3 and 6), where teachers and principal engage in 100 hours per year of continuous after-learning review, requires schools to rethink how teachers use their time, how they think of teachers' work, and how the workday, work week, and work year are designed and structured. Attempting to create the depth and quality of learning and the professional intimacy and trust in relationships necessary to build the required capacity by overlaying these practices onto existing traditional structures of schooling is likely to be a futile and frustrating experience for all concerned.

Intensification is about increasing time and energy, and strengthening commitment and engagement in personal and professional development and learning. It is about fostering the deep professional relationships required to learn and work effectively together. Lest the reader think that this intense work will burn everyone up in a cloud of smoke, it is important to distinguish between work that is morally compelling and intellectually and emotionally rewarding and work that is purposeless rather than purposeful, routine rather than dynamic, predictable rather than surprising, and unrewarding rather than gratifying. At the end of the previous chapter, we read the story of Churchill Public School, where, because of the confluence of purpose and relationships and an excitement about intellectual challenge, the entire staff worked into the night in order to *take charge* of the learning agenda. Fullan argues for a full exploitation of this positive energy that is related to longevity and, hence, greater sustainability.[4]

Note that in the cases of Southern Cross, Lancewood, Conestoga, and Cloverdale public schools, time for professional learning, team planning, and classroom inquiry was carefully planned for, highly valued, and protected. Furthermore, at Southern Cross and Lancewood, I moved to implement quiet times, where teachers knew they would have certain weeks put aside where there would be no meetings, visitors, or interruptions in order for them to focus entirely on their classrooms, students, and teaching. Fullan refers to this as cyclical energizing, in which periods of energy and engagement, coupled with periodic breaks for recovery, provide stewardship for lasting organizational energy.[5]

There is a dynamic and important connection between the development of collective intellectual capacity and forming deep professional relationships. This interrelationship is illustrated in Figure 8.2. The figure shows that only when professional relationships and the intellectual capacity run deep do we attain the collective wisdom leading to the informed action necessary to improve the life chances of all. The engine of this development is described in detail in Chapter 5, in the case of Southern Cross Public School, where dialogue fueled by the continual collection of classroom evidence led to collective and informed action. Ongoing dialogue informed by the transparent experience of the learner, exemplary classroom practice, and current research leads to informed, collective practice. The dialogue is focused and ongoing and seeks to examine critical incidents gathered across classrooms in order to uncover fundamental assumptions underpinning current and future practice.

Figure 8.2 has two dimensions. From bottom to top we increase time, sophistication, and efforts to fully develop intellectual capacity. Moving across the chart, we go from undeveloped toward deeply developed professional relationships. Starting with quadrant 1, we move diagonally from

Figure 8.2. Connection Between Intellectual Capacity and Professional Relationships

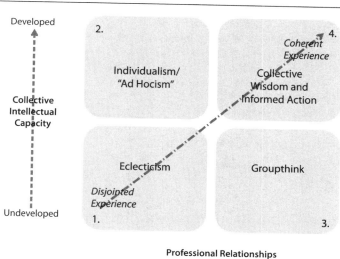

eclectic practice providing disjointed, possibly conflicting experiences for learners to quadrant 4, which intensifies the work and relations and provides for the development of collective wisdom and deeply informed action, resulting in a rich, coherent learning experience for the student.

One frequent criticism of collaborative ventures is the potential for them to lead to uninformed groupthink. In quadrant 4, the intensity of data-gathering, dialogue, and access to current research and to exemplary practice explored in the context of deep professional relationships ensures the quality and coherence in actions that follow.

The stories shared within this book point the way forward and provide examples of how school can be rethought in light of the implications of these four pillars. To capture the shifts expressed or implied in the text, I have summarized them in Figure 8.3. What you see there are continuums that schools have to move along from each perspective that is necessary to implement the four pillars.

RECOGNIZING EFFECTIVE LEADERSHIP

Images of leadership portrayed in this book seek to elucidate leadership in which the source of authority is grounded in authentic evidence gathered

Figure 8.3. Rethinking School: What Will Be Different?

Perspective	From	To
Student	Extrinsically motivated; little ownership or choice in their learning	Intrinsically motivated; deep, lasting relationships with teachers; having significant voice in their own learning; gatherers of learning information and reflective decision-makers
Purposes	Fixed, rooted in external policy and mandates, and solely focused on compliance	Morally compelling; emerging from the authentic identified needs of young people in our community; rooted in student experience and emerging from the interrogation of relevant evidence
Strategic Directions	Often imposed from the outside; generic in nature, with little ownership or commitment	Collaboratively developed, with a high degree of ownership; leaders integrally involved in implementation and focused on the life chances of pupils
Curriculum	Fixed, mandated, one size fits all, time-dependent, rushed for the sake of covering the material	Negotiable; responsive to student intentions, abilities, learning styles, and linguistic and cultural idiosyncrasies; time-flexible
Learning Experience of Pupils	Eclectic teaching and disjointed learning experience; teacher-directed	Sustainable, pedagogically-responsive teaching and coherent learning experience
Assessment	Assessment of learning, preoccupied with external evaluations	Assessment for and as learning, preoccupied with knowing the pupil well; focused on documenting and learning from authentic classroom experiences
Teacher Learning	Externally driven and dependent on outside expertise; insufficient, ad hoc, and intermittent	Continuous and strategically designed to advance purposes and future of the organization; intensified; linked and embedded into the everyday routine and work of all teachers

Team Learning	Focused on task accomplishment with little attention to process; focused on individuals rather than teams	Inclusive; focused on growth development, building collaborative skills, and extending leadership opportunities
Organizational and Professional Learning	Superficial and unconnected to previous skills	Intensified; extends and improves accomplishments and builds reserve capacity; organization is continually learning and improving over time
Relationships	Congenial, superficial, short-term, and lacking the depth required for building relational trust	Deep, trustworthy, lasting, purposeful, and professional; preoccupied with the purposes of the organization and knowing pupils and colleagues well
Community	Lacking awareness of the impact of policies and practices; tunnel vision; attempts are made to control community influence	Deeply involved in the development of purposes and in embracing accountability measures; acknowledging of interdependence; educators strive to involve community meaningfully
Leadership	Possessing a management orientation; belief in the inevitability of the curriculum and context; feeling powerless to change the future so they manage the present safely	Leadership-oriented; choice and innovation are always possible; responsive, pervasive, coherent, and improved pedagogy is the priority with continuous learning as the overarching strategy

from classrooms and beyond. These images are therefore professionally and morally defensible. By this I mean that the purposes emerge from the collective examination of the student's life and learning experiences. Thus, the school community is defined by shared purposes, values, beliefs, commitments, and behavior in order to improve the life chances of all. It is a shared reality! It is morally compelling!

The focus of the leader's attention is improved pedagogical responsiveness developed through the collective intellectual inquiry and capacity of teachers.[6] The leaders portrayed here devote at least 50% of their time to this all-important work and complement it by spending another 10% of their time developing and improving their own knowledge, capabilities, self-reflection, and skills. Leadership described throughout the book illustrates the value and incredible importance of modeling, demonstrating, and valuing the virtues and behaviors necessary to facilitate the continuously learning and improving organization. Leaders of leaders foster and engage in inquiry, reading, risk-taking, informed dialogue, and reflection. They demonstrate vulnerability and curiosity and ask many questions of substance (some examples of these appear in the reflection questions at the end of each chapter) in order to deepen their own and their colleagues' understanding of the work and actions to be taken. They are learners extraordinaire and make this practice transparent to all.

Informed dialogue is the currency of continuous improvement! Nurturing, facilitating, and thoughtfully participating in the sustained dialogue that permeates staff meetings, professional inquiry, evidence-gathering and reflection, planning, and executing actions is what the leaders portrayed here do. They are curious, wondrous, reflective, and ask important and sometimes difficult questions as they demonstrate that they are learners, too. In fostering this dialogue at every opportunity, they contribute substantially to the intensification of professional relationships.

Leaders portrayed here move to action fast! Life is short, the stakes high, and student needs and aspirations immediate and important. So whether it is the principal at Sutton Heights personally reordering the class schedules of 80 students within the first weeks of school; my restructuring Cloverdale into four smaller schools in order to ensure that our pupils were well known and teachers developed deep, sustainable professional relationships and had the opportunity to lead; or the actions my staff and I took to implement a high-performing learning community at Southern Cross Public School, the leadership portrayed here is given to action. We know how to *take charge* and to execute!

Some school leaders believe in being constantly visible in hallways and classrooms in their schools. They lead by walking around. We can use this precious time to ensure that

- actions take place as planned;
- colleagues have the support and encouragement they need;
- opportunities (such as learning from the teacher down the hall) are advantaged;
- obstacles (such as finding time) are removed or navigated around; and
- the important details of implementation are not overlooked.

The leaders here know that the future of the school and their students is not inevitable! They act in ways that enable colleagues to develop sophisticated and complex approaches to pedagogy that are coherent yet responsive. The curriculum must be negotiable. To achieve this, effective leaders are highly committed and fully participative in the rich and rigorous intellectual life of their colleagues. They seek ways to adapt or change the traditional structures of schooling to facilitate and intensify relationships and the professional learning and development necessary to create a high-performing learning community.

CONCLUSION

In today's climate, educational leaders can easily become overwhelmed in a veritable tsunami of agendas and pressures and fall back on a "management" stance that will safely see them through the day but, in doing so, diminish the opportunity of improving the learning experiences and life chances of students and teachers in the future. As I pointed out in Chapter 1, working in quadrant 1 and playing the compliance game by focusing on the operational at the expense of improving teaching and learning beckons in times of relentless pressure and complexity. The pressures of overload and fragmentation and for schools to improve on standardized testing and the sometimes conflicting agendas of governments, parents, and teachers' unions can starkly contrast with the compelling needs of our students.

Finding a constructive way forward requires courage in leadership and, at times, practicing relentlessness, fearlessness, tenacity, appreciation, risk-taking, faith, trust, and passion as you *take charge* of the learning agenda. You will need to be *relentless* in focusing the energy, passion, and time of your teacher colleagues and particularly yourself on the compelling moral purposes that drive the work of the school. Practice *fearlessness* in attending to the variety of intellect, learning styles, cultural and linguistic diversity, and student interests and passions in the face of standardization. Be *tenacious* in holding onto the big picture, understanding that meaningful change that will make a difference to your students takes time and that half measures do your students a disservice.

Demonstrate *appreciation* for your pupils, fostering student voice in all aspects of the learning endeavor by enabling their roles as information-gatherers, decision-makers, teachers, and leaders. Practice *risk-taking* by modeling and demonstrating to your colleagues that you are willing to embrace new ideas, new approaches, and novel solutions to the challenging issues of teaching and learning. Have *faith* in the long term by intensifying the capacity and capabilities of your colleagues in order that they may experience leadership, responsibility, and success. Know that your colleagues are well trained, continuously improving and growing, appropriately informed, prepared, and supported: *Trust* them to do the job well. What they can do today with support they will tomorrow accomplish independently. Finally, understand that effective schools are about deep professional relationships and that part of your role is to unleash the *passion* of your colleagues and pupils as they discover the excitement and fulfillment in successfully working together as they continually improve their craft.

All this requires the development of an infrastructure (including time, space, and new roles and responsibilities) that is adaptive and responsive to the needs of all learners as they pursue goals in which they clearly have a stake. It is only by *taking charge* of the teaching and learning agenda that school leaders can positively impact the life chances of all their pupils.

Afterword:
The Last Word

When I was a boy, my Granddad often complained that I would insist on having the "last word" in any argument with him. As a veteran of the First World War, a victim of mustard gassing in the trenches, and a survivor of the great flu pandemic (he named my mother after the nurse who risked her own life to tend to him), this arch-Victorian, Albert-watched martinet was outlasted by few in any argument or debate. So I should warn my colleague and good friend, Paul Shaw, that when he invites me to write the afterword, or last word, he is asking someone who has had a lot of practice in the art!

For me, the point of having the last word used to be to defeat your opponent, be victorious, trump their ace, and prove you were right all along. There is still a bit of that about me sometimes, I have to confess—and it has its place—but mainly, like Paul Shaw and his approaches to leadership, I have appreciated over an almost equally long career that there is another, better, higher purpose in being granted the last word. This is to see the last word not as a closing argument, as a final point in a debate, or as a withering remark expressed in a final parting shot that asserts one's own supremacy. The last word in a book, rather, is more like a toast at an awards ceremony or a vote of thanks at the end of a fine performance delivered by someone else. This kind of last word is a tribute to and reflection on others' accomplishments, not a triumphal assertion of one's own—and it is in this spirit that I am delighted to be able to have the last word in Paul Shaw's remarkable leadership book.

Paul Shaw may not be the absolute "last word" in leadership. I am not sure that anyone has that distinction or that anyone ever will. But his words, as I hope you have found, are definitely worth reading. He is a leader among leaders who writes from within the leader's own perspective without being hidebound by it.

I first met Paul when I was establishing the International Centre for Educational Change in Toronto. He was directing a large project funded by the Ontario Teachers' Federation called Creating a Culture of Change. This project provided coaching support to large numbers of schools that were trying to bring about positive change and networked the schools with one another. Paul was already experiencing and advocating for the power of professional learning communities on a large scale.

After this, he took up what was then an unusual appointment coordinating a strategic professional development and change partnership between one of Canada's largest school districts and two universities. Until this point, most partnerships had been located in single universities with several school districts. This turned the tables—making the district the center of gravity. Paul approached me to ask if I was interested in working with the partnership. It was a very busy time and the honest answer was that I wasn't. But like all good leaders, he believed in what he was supporting, persisted in persuading me to get involved, and found ways to support the effort.

The result was that together we secured funds to support six secondary schools in their efforts to develop school-directed improvement related to their own priorities, using six frames of analysis to help them open out their questions and develop strategic solutions—moral, emotional, structural, cultural, political, and leadership-related. We began with large and inclusive workshops for interested schools in which we insisted that the participating teams should include staff members not always in the first wave of change in their schools. This made for interesting and challenging workshops initially, but once convinced, critical masses of the schools' staffs then supported the work.

Together with our colleagues Dean Fink and Corrie Giles, and supported by Shawn Moore, we met monthly with all the principals and vice principals of the participating schools to share recent successes, discuss openly the impact of the new government's reform agenda, and examine an item of research on a topic chosen by them. The leaders said and still say to this day that it was one of the most important professional learning experiences of their careers.

When the government changed in the midst of our project and implemented a neoliberal agenda that reduced teachers' preparation time, implemented a mandatory curriculum at breakneck speed, and did all this in a climate of criticism of the teaching profession and a resulting teachers' strike, our leaders' meetings became a safe space for principals and their deputies to discuss openly the negative impact on extracurricular activities, on their staffs' health and well-being, on the ability of teachers to even return their students' work on time, and on their own sheer capacity to go on when everything seemed to be falling apart around them. An improvement project turned into a survival and support project and became an act of leadership in itself as we collected data documenting the impact of the government's policies on the schools, which then enabled us, from a research basis, to critique and challenge the strategies in public, on television, and in the press. It was a kind of leadership that we could offer to the leaders and teachers who in turn we were serving.

In all this, Paul was a resolute defender of the truth, a witness to the suffering that educators were enduring, and yet a moral and ethical spur to leaders' efforts to remember that amid all the disturbance, there were still children to serve, improvements to be made, and things to be done to the highest standard possible, in spite of the obstacles. He was ever and always a good colleague, too—always pulling his weight (as we all were) on the unfashionable grunt work of case report writing and data analysis, as well the more glamorous pirouetting in meetings and professional development sessions. For Paul, distributed leadership never degenerated into abrogation of his own responsibilities. All the time, he led with and through others. And whenever I needed someone to confide in regarding my own leadership challenges—in my own institution or with the wider political agenda—Paul was always available to help.

I can testify that Paul Shaw epitomizes his four pillars of leadership consistently in his own practice. He has an unswerving moral commitment to all students and to the idea and ideal of teaching as a profession requiring long training and hard reflection rather than something that draws in a bunch of idealistic or opportunistic fly-by-nights with little training and preparation who are left to make it up themselves as they go along. These moral purposes are evident in his own challenging principalships and in his improvement efforts on the northern frontiers of Pakistan and among the re-emerging nations of the former Soviet Bloc.

Paul has powerfully committed himself to supporting professional learning around compelling common questions as a lever for change. To watch him operate open-space technology with a group of educators to generate their own powerful questions and search for answers to them together is a marvel to behold. When Paul talks about *taking charge*, you might fear you are in for a bit of a bossy ride, but in the end, Paul's power is in his capacity to energize others—and that is what he wants other leaders to do, too.

Community is the glue that binds everything together and emboldens people's efforts to take greater risks in making changes that will help all students. Paul's commitment to professional learning communities, to networks of change, to strategic partnerships, and to creating learning communities for principals as well as for teachers is compelling evidence of this.

Last, Paul understands as a leader, that one outstanding teacher or one outstanding school or leader is not sufficient to bring about the kinds of improvements that are needed for all our children. In building networks and partnerships, and now in reflecting on his decades in leadership, Paul understands the importance of systemic coherence being built not so much through structures and alignment but through trust, learning, and improved relationships.

None of what Paul Shaw has written about in this book is particularly radical or revolutionary. It is supported by the findings of solid research, as he shows at the outset and throughout his text. You can see close affinities, for example, with my own book with Dennis Shirley on *The Fourth Way* of educational change[1] exemplified in some of the world's highest-performing systems, where we point to six pillars of purpose, three principles of professionalism, and seven catalysts of coherence that are the essential and interrelated ingredients of high-performing systems.

But what many leaders must surely have appreciated about Paul is that he analyzes and illustrates all these pillars of leadership and improvement from the taut gut and true grit of his own leadership practice. For too long, educational leaders have been at the receiving end of pious sermons and perorations from academics who have little experience of school leadership themselves, and sometimes no experience of working in schools at all. Paul Shaw shows that the answer to this is a not a set of disconnected anecdotes or pithy homilies, nor even an effort to play academics at their own game by supporting every statement by endless references.

Paul is sensitive to research but not a slave to it. He makes practice into a powerful platform, not a defensive enclave. Paul Shaw gives dignity to leadership practice as a form of knowledge—craft knowledge, as he calls it—that has power and value in its own right. Paul Shaw is a leader's leader, and this book is rightfully for them. It is a worthy legacy of a leadership life lived with honesty and integrity. This book may not be the last word on leadership, but the words within it and the messages they convey are ones that will surely last.

—Andy Hargreaves

Notes

Introduction

1. Quoted in Stansfield, B. (2000). *The courage to lead: Transform self, transform society.* Gabriola Island, Canada: New Society Publishers, p. 235.

2. Leithwood, K., Seashore Louis, K., Anderson, S., & Wahlstrom, M. (2004). *How leadership influences student learning.* Toronto: Ontario Institute for Studies in Education, University of Toronto

3. Robinson, V., & Hargreaves, A. (2011). *Student-centered leadership.* San Francisco: Jossey-Bass, p. 9. Effect size is a way of measuring differences between two groups, for example, between a group that has been exposed to a particular leadership dimension and one that has not.

Chapter 1

1. Fullan, M. (1993). *Change forces: Probing the depths of educational reform.* London: Falmer.

2. See Wheatley, M. (1994). *Leadership and the new science.* San Francisco: Berrett-Koehler.

3. Fullan, M. (1999). *Change forces: The sequel.* London: Falmer.

4. Sirotnik, K. A. (1990). Society, schooling and teaching, and preparing to teach. In J. I. Goodlad, R. Soder, & K. A. Sirotnik (Eds.), *The moral dimension of teaching* (pp. 296–327). San Francisco: Jossey-Bass.

5. Shaw, P. (2003). Leadership in the diverse school. In S. Schecter & J. Cummins (Eds.), *Multilingual education in practice: Using diversity as resource* (pp. 97–112). Portsmouth, NH: Heinemann.

6. Adapted from (1996). Malaguzzi, L (Ed.). *The hundred languages of children—The rights of children* (Catalogue of the exhibition). Reggio Emilia, Italy: Reggio Children, p. 214.

7. McMullen, K. (2003). *Measuring success: Progress report on the quality of public education in Canada.* Toronto: The Learning Partnership.

8. Duigan, P., & MacPherson, R. (Eds.). (1992). *Educative leadership: A practical theory for new managers and administrators.* London: Falmer Press, pp. 19–20.

9. Evers, C. W. (1992). Ethics and ethical theory in educative leadership: A pragmatic and holistic approach. In P. Duigan & R. Macpherson (Eds.), *Educative leadership: A practical theory for new administrators and managers* (p. 21–41). London: Falmer Press.

10. Ruddick, J., & Demetriou, H. (2003). Student perspectives on teaching practices: The transformative potential. *McGill Journal of Education*, 38(2), 274–288.

11. See Chapter 8, Figure 8.3, for a chart summarizing the rethinking of schools as proposed in this book.

12. Retrieved from www.conferenceboard.ca/topics/education/learning-tools/employability-skills.aspx

13. Wheatley, M. (1994). *Leadership and the new science*: San Francisco: Berrett-Koehler.

14. Sergiovanni, T. (2000). *The lifeworld of leadership: Creating culture, community and personal meaning in our schools.* San Francisco: Jossey-Bass, p. 4.

15. Sergiovanni, T. (1992). *Moral leadership: Getting to the heart of school improvement*. San Francisco: Jossey-Bass.

16. Shaw, P. (1988). *Teacher's assumptions, interactions and the development of writing: An exploration into emergent literacy*. Toronto: University of Toronto.

17. Ontario Ministry of Education. (1980). *Issues and directions*. Toronto: Author.

18. Eisner, E. (2001). What does it mean to say a school is doing well? *Phi Delta Kappan*, *82*(5), 367–372.

19. Postman, N. (1995). *The end of education*. San Francisco: Jossey-Bass, pp. 61–62.

20. For an excellent and classic treatise on this idea, read Parker Palmer's (1998) book on teaching, *The courage to teach: Exploring the inner landscape of a teacher's life* (San Francisco: Jossey-Bass).

21. Barth, R. (1991). *Improving schools from within*. San Francisco: Jossey-Bass.

22. This work on perspective has been informed by the work of the Bailey Alliance in Vacaville, California.

23. Sirotnik, *Society, school and teaching*.

Chapter 2

1. For a good discussion of this issue, see Chapter 7 of Fullan, M. (2007). *The new meaning of educational change* (4th ed.). New York: Teachers College Press, pp. 129–154.

2. See Chapter 4 in Fullan, M. (2001). *The new meaning of educational change* (3rd ed.). New York: Teachers College Press, pp. 49–67.

3. Allington, R. (1977). If they don't read much, how they ever gonna get good? *Journal of Reading, 21*(1), 57-61; Stanovich, K. (1986). Matthew effects in reading: Some consequences of individual differences in the acquisition of literacy. *Reading Research Quarterly, 21*(4), 360–407.

4. Irwin, J., & Doyle, M. (Eds.). (1992). *Reading/writing connections—Learning from research*. Newark, DE: International Reading Association.

5. Miller, J., & Sellers, W. (1990). *Curriculum perspectives and practice*. Toronto: Copp Clark Pitman.

6. Zaleznick, A. (1977, May). Managers and leaders: Are they different? *Harvard Business Review*, pp. 126–135.

7. Bennis, W., & Nanus, B. (2003). *Leaders: The strategies for taking charge*. New York: Harper Collins.

8. Pondy, L. R. (1989). Leadership is a language game. In H. J. Leavitt, L. R. Pondy, & D. M. Boje (Eds.), *Readings in managerial psychology* (pp. 224–233).Chicago: University of Chicago Press.

9. An excellent book on the subject of framing is Fairhurst, G., & Sarr, R. (1996). *The art of framing*. San Francisco: Jossey-Bass.

10. Leithwood, K. (2001). 5 reasons why most accountability measures don't work. *Orbit Magazine for Schools, 32*(1), 1–5.

11. Pittman, T. S. (1998). Motivation. In D. Gilbert, S. Fiske, & G. Lindsay (Eds.), *The handbook of social psychology* (Vol. 1, 4th ed., pp. 549–590). Boston: McGraw-Hill.

12. Covington, M. V. (2000). Goal theory, motivation and school achievement: An integrative review. *Annual Review of Psychology, 51*, 171–200, p. 175.

13. Ibid., p. 175.

14. Langer, E. J. *The power of mindful learning*. Cambridge, MA: Perseus Books.

15. Ibid., p. 49.

16. Ibid., p. 4.

17. Ibid., p. 4.

18. Ibid., p. 110.

19. Folger, T. (2003, October). Nailing down gravity: New ideas about the most mysterious power in the universe. *Discover*, 34–40.

20. Eisner, E. (2001). What does it mean to say a school is doing well? *Phi Delta Kappan*, *82*(5), 367–372.

21. Ibid.

22. Marshall, R. (2004, October). Creative juices: True innovation flows from a freethinking, rule flouting, convention-busting mindset. *MacLean's*, p. 8.

23. Olson, D. (2003). *Psychological theory and education reform: How school remakes mind and society.* Cambridge, UK: Cambridge University Press, p. 139.

24. Sergiovanni, T. (1998). Leadership as pedagogy, capital development and school effectiveness. *International Journal of Leadership in Education, 1*(1), 44.

25. Daly, H. E., & Farley, J. (1971). *Ecological economics: Principles and applications.* Washington, DC: Island Press.

26. Hansford, D. (2008, March 1). Growing pains: Is economic expansion worthwhile if it lowers our quality of life? *New Zealand Listener*, p. 9.

27. Hargreaves, A.,& Fink, D.(2005). *Sustainable leadership.* San Francisco: Jossey-Bass.

28. Fullan, M. (2005). *Leadership & sustainability: System thinkers in action.* Thousand Oaks, CA: Sage.

29. Adapted from Boomer, G. (1992). Negotiating the curriculum. In G. Boomer, C. Onore, N. Lester, & J. Cook (Eds.), *Negotiating the curriculum: Educating for the 21st century* (pp. 4–14). New York: Routledge, p. 10, Figure 2.

30. Ibid.

31. Hopkins, D. (2007). *Every school a great school.* London: Open University Press.

Chapter 3

1. Bennett, B., & Rolheiser, C. (2001). *Beyond Monet.* Toronto: Bookation, p. 94.

2. Collins, J. (2001). *Good to be great.* New York: Harper Collins, p. 12.

3. Young, D. (1992). *Adult learning principles* (Unpublished doctoral dissertation). University of Toronto, Toronto.

4. Chapter 2 in Glickman, C. (1993). *Renewing America's schools: A guide for school-based action.* San Francisco: Jossey-Bass.

5. Barrs, M., Ellis, S., Hester, H., & Thomas, A. (1989). *The primary language record.* London: Centre for Literacy in Primary Education (CLPE). Also, a second book by the same authors: (1990). *Patterns of learning.* London: CLPE.

6. Barrs et al., *Primary language.*

7. Depree, H., & Iverson, S. (1994). *Early literacy in the classroom. A new standard for young readers.* Lower Hutt, New Zealand: Lands End Publishing, pp. 55–64.

8. Brown, J., & Duguid, P. (2000). *The social life of information.* Boston: Harvard Business School Press.

9. Elmore, R. (1996). Getting to scale with good educational practice. *Harvard Educational Review, 66*(1), 1–26.

10. Cochrane-Smith, M., & Lytle, S. (1992). Communities for teacher research: Fringe or forefront? *American Journal of Education, 100*(3), 298–323.

11. Anderson, G., Herr, K., & Nihlen, A. S. (2007). *Studying your own school: An educator's guide to qualitative practitioner research.* Thousand Oaks, CA: Sage.

12. Kemmis, S., & McTaggert, R. (1988). *The action research planner* (3rd edition). Victoria, Australia: Deakin University, p. 6.

13. Earl, L. (2003). *Assessment as learning*. Thousand Oaks, CA: Corwin Press.

14. Anderson, G., Herr, K., & Nihlen, A. (2007). *Studying your own school: An educator's guide to practitioner research*. Thousand Oaks, CA: Corwin Press.

15. Hargreaves, A., Shaw, P., Fink, D., Giles, C., & Moore, S. (2002). *Secondary school reform: The experience and interpretations of teachers and administrators in six Ontario secondary schools* (Final report). Toronto: Ontario Institute for Studies in Education, University of Toronto.

16. Paul Shaw, project leader with the International Centre for Educational Change (ICEC). (2001 to 2003). *Estonian Canadian Partnership on Leadership and School Improvement*. Toronto: Ontario Institute for Studies in Education, University of Toronto.

17. Wilson, K., & Daviss, B. (1996). *Redesigning education*. New York: Teachers College Press.

18. Malaguzzi, L. (Ed.). (1996). *The hundred languages of children* (Catalogue of the exhibition). Reggio Emilia, Italy: Reggio Children.

19. Many thanks to Carol Anne Wien for her description of the panels and their use.

20. Graves, D. (1983). *Writing: Teachers and children at work*. Portsmouth, NH: Heinemann.

21. Sirotnik, K. A. (2002). Promoting responsible accountability in schools and education. *Phi Delta Kappan, 83*(9), 662–673.

22. Shepherd, L. (1991). Psychometricians' beliefs about learning. *Education Researcher, 20*(7), 6–12.

23. Earl, L., & LeMahieu, P. (1997). Rethinking assessment and accountability. In A. Hargreaves (Ed.), *Rethinking educational change with heart and mind: 1997 ASCD yearbook* (p. 162). Alexandria, VA: Association for Supervision and Curriculum Development.

24. Ibid.

Chapter 4

1. Newman, J. (1987). Learning to teach by uncovering our assumptions. *Language Arts, 64*(7), 727–737.

2. Argyris, C. (1976). Increasing leadership effectiveness. New York: Wiley.

3. MacGilchrist, B. (2007). *Leading the intelligent school*. Nottingham, UK: National College for School Leadership.

4. Glasser, W. (1986). *Choice theory in the classroom* (rev. ed.). New York: Harper Collins, p. 9.

5. Ibid.

6. Boomer, G. (1982). *Negotiating the curriculum*. Sydney, Australia: Ashton Scholastic.

7. Corson, D. (1998). *Changing education for diversity*. Buckingham, UK: Open University Press. This book provides excellent examples of viewing diversity as a resource.

8. Cooperrider, D., & Whitney, D. (n. d.). *A positive revolution in change: Appreciative inquiry*. Retrieved from http://appreciativeinquiry.case.edu/uploads/whatisai.pdf

9. Robertson, J. (2005). *Coaching leadership*. Wellington, New Zealand: NZCER Press. This is an excellent resource on coaching.

10. Daphne McNaughton, principal of Saanich Elementary School on Vancouver Island, British Columbia, clarified for me the roles that outsiders can play in working with insiders.

11. The four projects—part of the Peel University Partnership—are the Classroom Inquiry Project at Nahanni Way Elementary School in Mississauga with Patrick Solomon from York University and Paul Shaw; the Change Frames Project on secondary school reform with Andy Hargreaves and Paul Shaw; the Early Childhood Inquiry Group with Carol Ann Wien and Barbara Clegg from York University; and the Knowledge Forum project with Mary Lamon from OISE/UT and Ron Owston from York University.

Chapter 5

1. Mitchell, C., & Sackney, L. (2000). *Profound improvement: Building capacity for a learning community.* Lisse, The Netherlands: Swets and Zeitlinger.

2. Timperley, H., Wilson, A., Barrar, H., & Fung, I. (2007). *Teacher professional learning and development: Best evidence synthesis iteration.* Wellington, New Zealand: Ministry of Education.

3. Ibid., p. xxvi.

4. Ibid., p. xxxi.

5. Ibid., p. xxxv.

6. Ibid., p. xi.

7. Shaw, P. (1997). *Creating a community of practice: A case study.* Draft paper presented at the 6th National Conference in Educational Research in collaboration with the International Network, PACT, Faculty of Education, University of Oslo, Norway. An abridged version of this case was published as a chapter (Shaw, P. [1999]. Purpose and process in effective learning communities. In J. Retallick, B. Cocklin, & K. Coombe [Eds.], *Learning communities in education.* London: Routledge). This version shows more of the actual practice than previous attempts.

8. Upius, R., & Smithrim, K. (2003). *Learning through the arts: A final report to the Royal Conservatory of Music.* Toronto: Royal Conservatory of Music.

9. Wells, G. (1981). *Learning through interaction: The study of language development.* Cambridge, UK: Cambridge University Press.

10. Berliner, D. C., Resnick, L. B., Cuban, L., Cole, N., Popham, W. J., & Goodlad, J. I. (1997). "The Vision Thing": Educational research and AERA in the 21st Century. Part 2: Competing visions for enhancing the impact of educational research. *Educational Researcher, 26*(5), 13–27.

11. Bruer, J. (1993). *Schools for thought: A science of learning in the classroom.* Cambridge, MA: MIT Press.

12. Nelson, J. (2001). *The art of focused conversations for schools.* Toronto: Canadian Institute of Cultural Affairs.

13. Ibid., p. 13.

14. See Chapter 2 in Fullan, M. (2001). *Leading in a culture of change.* San Francisco: Wiley.

15. The notion of "critical incidents" is explained by Judith Newman in her 1987 article: Learning to teach by uncovering our assumptions. *Language Arts, 64*(7), 727–737.

16. Ibid.

17. Yankelovich, D. (1999). *The magic of dialogue: Transforming conflict into cooperation.* New York: Simon and Schuster.

18. Fullan, M. (2008). *Culture of change.*

19. Booth, D. (1994). *Classroom voices: Language-based learning in the elementary school.* Toronto: Harcourt Brace Canada. Also see Paul, L. (1988). *Growing with books: Children's literature in the formative years and beyond.* Toronto: Ontario Ministry of Education. See as well the video (1989) *Growing with Books* from the Ontario Ministry of Education.

20. Hargreaves, A. (1994). *Changing teachers and changing times.* New York: Teachers College Press.

21. Royal Commission on Learning. (1994). *For the love of learning* (Vol. 3). Toronto: Queen's Printer for Ontario, p. 3.

22. Fullan, M. (2007). *The new meaning of educational change* (4th ed.). New York: Teachers College Press.

23. Sergiovanni, T. (1998). Pedagogical leadership. *International Journal of Educational Leadership, 1*(1), 37–46.

Chapter 6

1. Freedman, M., & Tregoe, B. (2003). *The art and discipline of strategic leadership.* New York: McGraw-Hill.

2. Stanfield, R. B. (1999, Fall). Transparent strategy. *Edges Magazine,* pp. 2–4.

3. Adapted from Spencer, L. J. (1989). *Winning through participation.* Dubuque, IA: Kendall Hunt.

4. I found my first job as a school principal through an ad in the Toronto *Globe and Mail* classifieds.

5. Schlechty, P. (1990). *Schools for the 21st century.* San Francisco: Jossey-Bass, p. 134.

6. Fullan, M. (2007). *The new meaning of educational change* (4th ed.). New York: Teachers College Press.

7. Gerstner, L. (2002). *Who says elephants can't dance?* New York: Harper Business, p. 233.

8. Senge, P. (1990). *The fifth discipline.* New York: Doubleday, p. 22.

9. See Alfie Kohn's writing, in particular: Kohn, A. (1996). *Beyond discipline: From compliance to community.* Alexandria, VA: Association for Supervision and Curriculum Development.

10. See Chapter 7 on individualism.

11. Leithwood, K., & Montgomery, D. (1986). *The principal profile.* Toronto: Ontario Institute for Studies in Education, University of Toronto, pp. 18–19.

12. See Schecter, S., & Cummins, J. (Eds.). (2003). *Multilingual education in practice: Using diversity as a resource.* Portsmouth, NH: Heinemann.

13. This view of the curriculum is borrowed from the work of David Elkind.

14. See Eisner, E. (2001). What does it mean to say a school is doing well? *Phi Delta Kappan, 82*(5), 367–372.

15. See Hargreaves, A., Shaw, P., Fink, D., Retallick, J., Giles, C., Moore, S., Schmidt, M., & James-Wilson, S. (2000). *Change frames: Supporting secondary school teachers in interpreting and integrating secondary school reform* (Final report). Toronto: Ontario Institute for Studies in Education, University of Toronto.

16. Stanfield, B. R. (2002). *The workshop book: From individual creativity to group action.* Gabriola Island, Canada: New Society Publishers.

17. Fullan, M. (2001). *Leading in a culture of change.* San Francisco: Jossey-Bass, pp. 43–44.

18. Hopkins, D. (2007). *Every school a great school.* London: Open University Press, pp. 14–15.

19. Ibid., pp. 51–72.

20. Timperley, H., Wilson, A., Barrar, H., & Fung, I. (2007). *Teacher professional learning and development: Best evidence synthesis iteration.* Wellington, New Zealand: New Zealand Ministry of Education.

21. Harris, A., Day, C., & Hadfield, M. (2001) Headteachers' views of effective school leadership. *International Studies in Educational Administration, 29*(1), 29–39.

22. Bossidy, L., Charan, R., & Burck, C. (2003). The gap nobody knows. In J. V. Gallos (Ed.), *Business leadership: A Jossey-Bass reader* (pp. 475–495). San Francisco: Jossey-Bass.

23. Freedman, M. (2003). The genius is in the implementation. *Journal of Business Strategy, 24*(2), 26–31.

Chapter 7

1. Adapted from Little, J. W. (1987). Teachers as colleagues. In V. Richardson-Koehler (Ed.), *Educators' handbook: A research perspective* (pp. 491—510). White Plains, NY: Longman.

2. Bascia, N., & Shaw, P. L. (1994). Creating a culture of change: A work in progress. *Orbit Magazine, 25*(2), 19–23.

3. Owen, H. (2008). *Open space technology: A user's guide* (3rd edition). London: Berrett-Koehler.

4. Huberman, M. (1988). Teacher careers and school improvement. *Journal of Curriculum Studies, 20*(2), 119–132.

5. Deal, T. (1987). The culture of schools. In L. Shieve & M. Schoenheit (Ed.), *Leadership: Examining the elusive.* Alexandria, VA: ASCD, p. 24.

6. Kevin was interviewed as part of the "Change Frames" project, an inquiry into secondary school reform in Ontario.

7. Goodenough, W. (1957). Cultural anthropology and linguistics. In P. Garvin (Ed.), *Report of the seventh annual round table meeting on linguistics and language study* (pp. 167–73). Washington, DC: Georgetown University Press

8. Morgan, G. (1996). *Images of the organization* (2nd ed.). Newbury Park, CA: Sage, p. 137.

9. Hargreaves, A. (1994). *Changing teachers, changing times.* London: Cassell.

10. A well-known oral aphorism of Buckminster Fuller. Exact source unknown.

11. The stories told about Southern Cross Public School are based on my time there as principal and in no way reflect on or refer to those who currently lead the school.

12. Hargreaves, A., & Shaw, P. (1996–2002). *Networks of change.* Toronto: Ontario Ministry of Education. North Ridge Secondary School is one of six schools studied.

13. Adapted from Glickman, C. (1998). *Renewing America's schools: A guide for school-based action.* San Francisco: Jossey-Bass, p. 33.

14. International Association of Facilitators (IAF). (2000). Facilitator competencies. *Group Facilitation: A Research and Applications Journal, 2*(2), 24–31. The International Association of Facilitators has identified six core competencies.

15. Adapted from Kaner, S., Lind, L., Toldi, C., Fisk, S., & Berger, D. (2007). *Facilitators guide to participatory decision-making* (2nd ed.). San Francisco: Jossey-Bass, p. xviii.

16. Robinson, V. (2007). *School leadership and student outcomes: Identifying what works and why* (ACEL monograph series). Winmalee, Australia: Australian Council for Educational Leaders, pp. 7–8.

Chapter 8

1. Sergiovanni, T. (1998). Leadership as pedagogy, capital development and school effectiveness. *International Journal of Leadership in Education, 1*(1), 37–46.

2. Weick, K., & Roberts, K.(1993). Collective minds in organizations. *Administrative Science Quarterly, 38,* 334.

3. Ryle, G. (1949). *The concept of mind.* Chicago: University of Chicago Press.

4. Fullan, M. (2005). *Leadership and sustainability.* Thousand Oaks, CA: Corwin.

5. Ibid.

6. Robinson, V. (2007). *School leadership and student outcomes: Identifying what works and why* (ACEL monograph series). Winmalee, Australia: Australian Council for Educational Leaders. This monograph identifies this leadership factor as having a 0.84 (highly significant) effect on student learning.

Afterword

1. Hargreaves, A. & Shirley, D. (2009). *The fourth way: The inspiring future for educational change.* Thousand Oaks, CA: Corwin Press.

Index

An *f* or *t* after a page number indicates a figure or table, respectively.

About the Author

Dr. Paul L. Shaw is president of Southern Cross Educational (Canada) Inc., an educational consulting company. He works with principal groups, school districts, and governments to design and develop programs for the professional learning of participants. He is also a research and teaching associate with the Faculty of Education at the University of Victoria in Greater Victoria, British Columbia, where he teaches graduate courses in school improvement, educational change, professional learning communities, and educational leadership in contexts of diversity. Dr. Shaw has consulted with and lectured in many school districts across North America and around the world, including in Estonia, Pakistan, Australia, the United Kingdom, and Egypt. He has been an acclaimed principal in four schools and continues to facilitate numerous school and district improvement teams. He has spoken at many educational conferences, bringing the experience of a successful practitioner as well as the rigor of an academic to bear on the world of the school and the student. To learn more about Dr. Shaw and keep up with his latest projects, please visit www.paulshaw.ca.